THE HARLEM RENAISSANCE REVISITED

THE
HARLEM RENAISSANCE
REVISITED: Politics, Arts, and Letters

Edited by
Jeffrey O. G. Ogbar

The Johns Hopkins University Press
Baltimore

© 2010 The Johns Hopkins University Press
All rights reserved. Published 2010
Printed in the United States of America on acid-free paper
9 8 7 6 5 4 3 2 1

The Johns Hopkins University Press
2715 North Charles Street
Baltimore, Maryland 21218-4363
www.press.jhu.edu

Library of Congress Cataloging-in-Publication Data

The Harlem Renaissance revisited : politics, arts, and letters / edited by
Jeffrey O.G. Ogbar.
        p. cm.
    Includes bibliographical references and index.
    ISBN-13: 978-0-8018-9460-2 (hardcover : alk. paper)
    ISBN-10: 0-8018-9460-3 (hardcover : alk. paper)
    ISBN-13: 978-0-8018-9461-9 (pbk. : alk. paper)
    ISBN-10: 0-8018-9461-1 (pbk. : alk. paper)
    1. Harlem Renaissance.   2. African Americans—New York (State)—New
York—Intellectual life—20th century.   3. African American arts—New
York (State)—New York—20th century.   4. African Americans—New York
(State)—New York—Politics and government—20th century.   5. Harlem
(New York, N.Y.)—Intellectual life—20th century.   6. New York
(N.Y.)—Intellectual life—20th century.   7. Harlem (New York,
N.Y.)—Politics and government—20th century.   8. New York (N.Y.)—Politics
and government—20th century.   9. African Americans—Intellectual life—
20th century.   10. African Americans—Politics and government—20th
century.   I. Ogbar, Jeffrey Ogbonna Green.
    E185.89.I56H37 2010
    974.7'1043—dc22   2009035578

A catalog record for this book is available from the British Library.

*Special discounts are available for bulk purchases of this book. For more information,
please contact Special Sales at 410-516-6936 or specialsales@press.jhu.edu.*

The Johns Hopkins University Press uses environmentally friendly book
materials, including recycled text paper that is composed of at least 30 percent
post-consumer waste, whenever possible. All of our book papers are acid-free,
and our jackets and covers are printed on paper with recycled content.

CONTENTS

PART III: LITERARY ICONS RECONSIDERED

PART IV: GENDER CONSTRUCTIONS

PART V: POLITICS AND THE NEW NEGRO

THE HARLEM RENAISSANCE REVISITED

Introduction

Jeffrey O. G. Ogbar

In the aftermath of World War I the social, intellectual, and political land-scape of the United States transformed itself. A sanguine sense of modernity followed a global war that had resulted in unprecedented death and suffering. New technologies, the expansion of democracy to (white) women, and a modern music—jazz—came to mark the beginning of a new era. Yet at the same time a per-vasive moral torpor and fear of change led to the reemergence of the country's oldest and most powerful terrorist organization, the Ku Klux Klan. The Klan and other white-supremacist groups engaged in horrifying acts of violence against black people and mounted firm resistance to extending the basic principles of civil and human rights to people of color. In the 1920s, as some opportunities expanded for African Americans, ubiquitous limitations on them provided a fas-cinating moment when they struggled to restore hope.

Competing impulses—a sense of promise, anger, and cynicism—provided the framework in which, however strangely, black intellectuals and artists produced a special historical moment in America. It was a period of artistic explosion that found black people exploring the challenges of being black in a virulently anti-black society. Simultaneously, other black artists relegated whites to the margins and therefore illuminated a world where blacks stood at the center of analysis and synthesis, not necessarily as a suffering lot of mournful victims. Still others, motivated by anger and hope, nourished a stubborn faith in the ability of America to live up to its ideals—even if one could locate little supporting evidence. These people, whom philosopher Alain Locke called "the New Negroes," created rich discursive expressions that were both resistive and strikingly hopeful.

The convergence of various factors, including African American migration, progress, resistance, and creative expression fomented the Harlem Renaissance. From literati such as Zora Neale Hurston, Langston Hughes, and Jessie Redmon Fauset to visual artists such as Augusta Savage and Aaron Douglas to the wildly popular sounds of jazz or the black nationalism of Marcus Garvey, Harlem in the 1920s supplied a bold statement. As the term *renaissance* suggests, Harlem became headquarters of what James Weldon Johnson predicted would be "the intellectual [and] cultural center for Negroes in the United States."[1] He referred less to a rebirth of artistic expression than to a coincidence that gave black artists unprecedented access to publishers, museums, patrons, playhouses, concert halls, and benefactors. All this happened while the country as a whole underwent economic expansion and greeted signs of modernity: automobiles, electricity, running water, skyscrapers, and the heralded yet elusive practice of democracy. Indeed, the New Negro (as well as the "New Woman") was inextricably bound to the postwar "New Era" and its uneven move toward new opportunities and freedoms. Hundreds of thousands of African Americans moved from the South into cities in the North and West, altering the cultural and social landscape of the country in the process. The specter of hate, violence, and intolerance still proved common enough to force the New Negro to adopt constant vigilance, organization, and protest. Black people had to be realistic about the hopefulness of the moment.

The horrors of antiblack race riots in more than twenty cities in 1919 helped mark the unofficial beginning of the Harlem Renaissance. The Great Depression and the Harlem riot of 1935 brought an end to it. Between 1919 and the stifling heat of New York in the summer of 1935 a wide range of figures challenged both white and black Americans to imagine race from a new vantage point. More often than not, the leading figures in these endeavors used art as their vehicle of expression. Their art was not always explicitly resistive to prevailing stereotypes of black people. The hugely successful Broadway play *Shuffle Along* created a space for black creativity and love onstage while employing black stock figures that were at times crude, unscrupulous, and bombastic. Jean Toomer's *Cane* and Nella Larsen's *Passing* embraced themes and styles that were anathema to the conventional representations of blackness in fiction. In the realm of politics the NAACP cofounder and *Crisis* editor W. E. B. Du Bois remained optimistic that the mass of white Americans could be convinced that democracy, freedom, and civil rights were good for all, not just for whites. Marcus Garvey, the founder of the Universal Negro Improvement Association (UNIA), did not believe whites could be collectively reformed. Garvey was a staunch supporter of black nationalism—the belief that black people must establish a black nation-state for their survival and freedom. He built his mass movement on this cynicism about whites but placed faith in blacks.

This volume brings together fresh perspectives from recent scholarship on the Harlem Renaissance. Although it covers only part of the story, it asks again what the Harlem Renaissance was all about, especially in terms of its major figures and its arts, letters, and political landscape. It reimagines the temporal and spatial boundaries of what historians have considered the Harlem Renaissance: 1920s Harlem, New York City, with connections in other American cities, most notably Chicago. The volume also explores iconic figures of the era and spotlights important figures that are not as widely known. This revisiting makes use of social history and literary criticism. It delves into the demography of Harlem, providing insightful examinations of the common people who collectively provided a foil to the lives of the artists and their segment of the community. The native voice expands here to include southern and international elements with connections to Harlem—making it a veritable metropol of the Anglophone black world. Across the globe people found in Harlem inspiration and hope, as well as a cause for protest.

In what respects was the Harlem Renaissance an extension of a longer tradition of black artistic and political expression? How was it a stylistic departure from what came before? What about the lived experience of the people of Harlem and other major black communities in the country? To what degree did class and gender complicate the discussions and interrogations of race in this period? Moreover, how can the spatial and temporal parameters of the Harlem Renaissance be expanded? The five sections of this book explore these questions and much more. They delve into the major figures of the Harlem Renaissance and reveal fresh perspectives of them and their contributions to the historical moment that highlighted the best examples of both hope and frustration in America. Indeed, as revealed here, these two notions—hope and frustration—are not mutually exclusive but often are inextricably bound, the latter inspiring the former into action. This action may be the resistive work of novelists, playwrights, activists, and jazz artists who rejected the hostile stereotypes of the misanthropic minstrel, obsequious servant, or docile Negro of old.

Ultimately, these essays explore the hope and resistance that informed the cultural work of the period. But what does it mean to create art that refutes stereotypes of black people? From the creativity of Duke Ellington to the conspicuously bourgeois wedding of Yolande Du Bois and Claude McKay, refutation of hostile stereotypes abound. Are these refutations always conscious efforts? Are they explicitly resistive? In what ways are the black nationalist politics of the era hopeful? In what ways do the internationalist dimensions of discourse provide a new perspective to counterhegemonic cultural production in the era? Indeed, resistance takes many forms, as does hope. Yet resistance implies some degree of hope that the activities it undertakes will not be in vain. Therefore, resistance is dependent on hope. These concepts were constantly engaged with each other while shaping the big picture of this historical moment.

The first part, "Aesthetics and the New Negro," provides a foundation for the study of the Harlem Renaissance by exploring how the cultural production of the period was in some respects sui generis but in other ways part of a longer literary and cultural tradition. A scholarly consideration of the rich topography of Harlem, beyond the clichés of well-dressed literati and smoke-filled nightclubs, is the central focus of the second part, "Class and Place in Harlem." The third part, "Literary Icons Reconsidered," helps expand the parameters of discussion and scholarly inquiry on several major figures of the Harlem Renaissance. The fourth part, "Gender Constructions," adds to a growing corpus of works on the sexual identities of major figures from the era. The final part, "Politics and the New Negro," broadens the framework around which the Harlem Renaissance is conceptualized. It demonstrates that the activities of the period were not confined to the arts, or to the city of New York, but were part of a larger resistive framework that found purpose outside the United States and in various political spaces.

Together these essays provide new perspectives on the discursive world and historical era of Harlem's most celebrated period. Broad in scope and creative in attention, they pull together disparate events, people, and ideas united by the desire to push back against oppression and by the belief that freedom will not always be elusive.

NOTE

1. James Weldon Johnson, "Harlem: The Culture Capital," in *The New Negro*, ed. Alain Locke (New York: Albert and Charles Boni, 1925), 311.

PART I: Aesthetics and the New Negro

ONE

African American Representations on the Stage

Minstrel Performances and Hurston's Dream of a "Real" Negro Theater

Mónica González Caldeiro

After the publication in 1937 of her novel *Their Eyes Were Watching God,* Zora Neale Hurston received a barrage of critiques that mainly expressed a misunderstanding of her work. Some of them related the plot of her book and her style with the language of minstrelsy. Otis Ferguson of the *Republic* disapproved of the use of "the speech difference" since, for him, "[to] let the really important words stand in Webster and then consistently misspell all the eternal particles that are no more an aspiration in any tongue, is to set up a mood of Eddie Cantor in blackface" (quoted in West, 110–11). Richard Wright, in an unfortunately ironic remark, considered that Hurston "exploit[ed] that phase of Negro life which is 'quaint,' the phase which evokes a piteous smile on the lips of the 'superior' race" (ibid., 115).

The tragedy of this irony resides in the writer's accusation that Hurston was indeed furthering a series of stereotypes about African American life, the very thing that Hurston had been fighting throughout her career as a dramatist. By 1937 she was already an experienced playwright and producer who had been pursuing the dream of a "real Negro theater," hoping to eradicate the image of African Americans perpetuated by minstrelsy. Wright was probably not aware of Hurston's position.

His assessment may have angered her, since her plays and concerts were usually a response to other shows that Hurston knew and disliked, precisely because of the ridicule she found in their portraits of African American life.

Throughout her theatrical work Hurston tried to reverse the image of the African American people that had been represented on the stage since the nineteenth century. Furthermore, her intent to sow the seeds of a "real" Negro theater was a response to the shows of the period, which were written by white playwrights but dealt with African American issues.

The Theater of the Harlem Renaissance: Images of Blackness and Minstrel Traditions

Hurston's career as a dramatist began before she moved to New York in 1925. In those years African American artists struggled to dignify the role of the black performer, derided by nineteenth-century minstrelsy and popular culture. Black theater during the Harlem Renaissance was characterized by the coexistence of a serious black drama and the popular entertainment that had made Harlem fashionable for white audiences. Black life became a subject of interest for the general public, who went to the theaters in search of images of "the primitive life" of "black" performances, since blackness had been constructed as a stereotype by the minstrel show. The places to go for downtown audiences to see black musical revues were either the Harlem nightclubs or the Broadway theaters, where some of the shows incorporated comedy based on the minstrel pattern and gave it a new shape, embellishing it with a black female chorus. According to Jean Lee Cole and Charles Mitchell, the plays that dealt with African American themes were "limited to (1) a handful of musical revues that often indulged in exoticism or caricature or (2) well-meaning but demeaning pieces by white playwrights" (xvi). Henry Louis Gates Jr. added that "the roots of black theatre in the twenties were buried in the soil of minstrelsy and vaudeville" (17), something that made the efforts to construct a serious African American drama more difficult.

Among black musical revues we can include *Shuffle Along*. Although theater historians like James Weldon Johnson and Allen Woll have argued that this show broke the barriers of segregation in Broadway and even legitimized the black musical—because it proved that whites would pay to see the plays created and performed by blacks—"it did not end segregation entirely." As Woll puts it, "two thirds of the orchestra was reserved for whites, and blacks were seated in the remaining third. Once again, the box office controlled the seating patterns" (72).

The balcony was called "Nigger Heaven" because it was usually the only place where blacks could sit inside the theater. The comic team was formed by F. E. Miller and Aubrey Lyles in blackface, whose "burlesque of two ignorant Negroes going into 'big business' and opening a grocery-store was a never-failing producer of side-shaking laughter" (Johnson, 188). Reading these lines and taking into account that, according to Johnson, "all New York" went to see the show, and that *Shuffle Along* regularly played to mixed audiences, makes us wonder whether, in spite of the fascination that the show awoke in intellectuals like W. E. B. Du Bois and Langston Hughes, it spread the deriding stereotypes about blackness—for both white and black audiences—that had been popularized so widely in minstrelsy. In general, white critics wanted black musical theater to follow the comic minstrel pattern, and when it did not, they complained and accused the artists of trying to be "too white." The play remained in New York for a year and then went on the road for two years, further nurturing the public interest in African American productions. According to James Hatch the influence of *Shuffle Along* " 'kicked off' a series of imitations and set the style for the 1920s" (Hill and Hatch, 244).

There were several attempts to construct a serious African American drama during the 1920s. Harlem saw not only the rise of an experimental theater but also the birth of what has been called the Little Theater Movement (also the Art Theater Movement). Although it promoted African American folklore, it was endorsed by northern intellectuals such as W. E. B. Du Bois, Alain Locke, Jessie Redmon Fauset, and James Weldon Johnson. The plays were meant not only to break with minstrel stereotypes but to go further than the mere use of black characters to show "the soul of a people." They were usually folk dramas that showed social injustice, like Willis Richardson's *The Deacon's Awakening* (1920) and *The Chip Woman's Fortune* (1923).

Alain Locke and W. E. B. Du Bois (with the KRIGWA players) were the main forces that promoted this movement, although they did so from different approaches. Locke insisted that an art theater would be more remarkable in the struggle for the advancement of the race, while Du Bois only accepted art for the sake of propaganda, preferring plays that presented racial issues on the stage.

In the second group of plays, "the demeaning pieces by white playwrights," we can highlight Eugene O'Neill's *The Emperor Jones* and *All God's Chillun Got Wings*, as well as Marc Connelly's *The Green Pastures*, as they were the most popular and acclaimed shows before 1930. O'Neill's one-act play *The Moon of the Caribbees* played in 1918 at the Provincetown Playhouse (New York) with white performers, and the one-act tragedy *The Dreamy Kid* was produced at the same theater in 1919 with a black cast, but these plays received only favorable comments. It was not until *The Emperor Jones,* produced at the Provincetown Playhouse in 1920, with Charles Gilpin playing the role of the Emperor, that O'Neill's work began to receive more critical attention.[1] *The Emperor Jones* tells the story of Brutus Jones, an African American who, after killing a man and going to prison, escapes to an island in the Caribbean, where he declares himself emperor. After a rebellion he runs through the jungle until he is killed.

O'Neill's play was acclaimed by the critics, Charles Gilpin was highly praised for his performance, and the production even provided jobs for blacks in New York City. The play, however, did not have a good reception among many African Americans, especially the black press: "A writer of the *New York Negro World* calls attention to the fact that Charles Gilpin's play, *The Emperor Jones,* is very harmful to our people and says that it leaves an impression that the prejudiced South is prompting in various other ways. It is in the order of *Birth of a Nation* so far as the impression referred is concerned. This is certainly to be regretted, if true" (quoted in Hill and Hatch, 227).

Gilpin defended his participation in the play, arguing that it legitimated the performance of an African American actor in a serious role—totally different from the minstrel-like performances that black artists were usually forced to play. Even so, "Eugene O'Neill's image of the emperor fleeing through the jungle until he is reduced to a savage by his fears displeased many Blacks" (Hill and Hatch, 227), in spite of the fact that the author's intention had been to make a psychological study of the main character. Even in the last decades of the twentieth century O'Neill's play was criticized. Houston Baker Jr. has pointed out that he would have praised the play "if only O'Neill had bracketed the psycho-surreal final trappings of his Emperor's world and given us the stunning account of colonialism that remains implicit in his quip at the close of his list of dramatis personae" (88).

On May 15, 1924, O'Neill returned with the play *All God's Chillun Got Wings,* produced at the Provincetown Playhouse with a mixed cast (Paul Robeson in the leading role, with Mary Blair, a white actress, as his female counterpart). The expectation about the play began several months before the opening, when it was known that a black actor and a white actress were going to play the role of a black man that falls in love with a white girl and marries her, and she kisses his hand. A great controversy began in the New York press, with articles and editorials spreading racial hatred in order to stop the production. Publications like Hearst's wrote in its editorials:

We refer to the play in which a white woman marries a black man and at the end of the play, after going crazy, stoops and kisses the Negro's hand.

It is hard to imagine a more nauseating and inflammable situation, and in many communities the failure of the audience to scrap the play and mutilate the players would be regarded as a token of public anemia. (quoted in Johnson, 194)

Finally, there were no riots during the opening of the production, which indicated to James Weldon Johnson that "the rabid newspapers were not expressing public sentiment, but were striving to stir up a public sentiment" (195), something that is worth taking into account if we consider the lousy work conditions of African American artists of the period or even the social problems that affected African Americans in their everyday lives. In spite of the expectation, *All God's Chillun Got Wings* was not as successful as *The Emperor Jones*, probably because "it was not so good a play" (ibid.).

Until 1926 several white playwrights had tried to experiment with the topic of African American life in the South, but these attempts had usually either failed completely or received little praise. The first play to succeed dealing with this issue was *In Abraham's Bosom*, by Paul Green, produced at the Provincetown Playhouse. It was a drama and "was closer and truer to actual Negro life and probed deeper into it than any drama of the kind that had yet been produced" (Johnson, 207). The play was a success, and Paul Green was awarded a Pulitzer Prize in 1927.

Marc Connelly's *The Green Pastures*, one of the most acclaimed shows of the period, depicted African Americans as "stereotypically simple and childlike" in a play that offered a white vision of Afro-American religion and the black vernacular (West, 155). For someone like Hurston, who was very sensitive about her own culture, this cultural "robbery" was damaging. *The Green Pastures* was acclaimed, however, even by African American intellectuals like James Weldon Johnson, who affirmed that

[if i]n *Porgy* the Negro removed any lingering doubts as to his ability to do intelligent acting, [i]n *The Green Pastures* he established conclusively his capacity to get the utmost subtleties across the footlights, to convey the most delicate nuances of emotion, to create the atmosphere in which the seemingly unreal becomes for the audience the most real thing in life. *The Green Pastures* is a play so simple and yet so profound, so close to the earth and yet so spiritual, that it is as high a test for those powers in the actor as any play the American stage has seen—a higher test than many of the immortalized classics. It is a play in

which the line between the sublime and the ridiculous is so tenuous that the slightest strain upon it would bring the whole play tumbling down. (Johnson, 218)

Zora Neale Hurston and the Dream of a "Real Negro Theater"
Mule Bone: *Constructing a Blues Aesthetic*

In the drama *Color Struck* Hurston had included a cakewalk, a dance that had been a usual recurrence in the last part of the minstrel show. Her insistence on using manifestations of African American culture that had been damaged by the dominant culture's "robbery" seems to prove that, even in the early stages of her dramatic career, Hurston had been thinking about rewriting the tradition used by minstrelsy to offer a different portrait of African American life. The use of the cakewalk in black theatrical representations encountered some opposition. According to Hill and Hatch "some felt the cakewalk was a degrading reminder of slavery and should not be staged; others defended its performance as a unique high-stepping dance created by African Americans" (152). The cakewalk had negative connotations owing to its inclusion in the finale of the white minstrel shows. We know now, however, that the dance had been created for subversive purposes, such as mocking the "superior race." As Karen Sotiropoulos has pointed out, "the cakewalk had also evolved out of the experiences of Africans enslaved in America. It grew from the ring shout, a style of worship and dance that survived the Middle Passage. The dance developed when enslaved blacks were forced to perform for their owners, and in response, mocked their white audience by exaggerating European dance styles. Such black double-entendre underlay much of black expressive culture and played a central role in the lives and work of black minstrels" (22). As a result of this kind of conflict Hurston's intention might easily have been misunderstood.[2]

The rewriting of tradition was only a part of Hurston's vision of creating a "real Negro theater." She mentioned her idea for the first time in a letter to Langston Hughes in 1928: "Did I tell you before I left about the new, the *real* Negro art theatre I plan? Well, I shall, or rather *we* shall act out the folk tales, however short, with the abrupt angularity and naivete of the primitive 'bama nigger. Just that with naive settings."[3] Since 1926 they had been planning together the creation of a "black jazz and blues opera" (Gates, 8). Derived from her vision and the coauthorship with Hughes, the play *Mule Bone* was born. The plot was taken from the folktale, collected by Hurston, "The Bone of Contention," but Hughes made several changes to the play.

Leaving aside Hughes's and Hurston's differences over *Mule Bone*, the fact is that the play differs from the story in a central motif: the substitution of a girl for a turkey, creating a folk scene for two best friends who are quarreling over Daisy. This replacement "alarmed" Hurston, since she "had not intended her tale to be that of two men fighting over their sexual prowess, but rather that they would prove who was the better hunter and man" (Cole and Mitchell, xxviii). By introducing the sexual interest in a comic character, the play was nearing a popular form of minstrelsy in which two friends usually fought for a girl.

Mule Bone presented another fundamental problem: characterization. By using black broad comic types, the danger of falling into the trap of generalization and stereotyping was considerable. As Lynda Marion Hill puts it, "Because the comedic quality of the play can be viewed as broadly pertaining to black folklife, its style is similar to broad portrayals in vaudeville, burlesque, and (more damning) the minstrel show—where characters tend to be types rather than fully developed people" (182).

The play, however, introduced several interesting elements that were aesthetically new, like the use of black vernacular as a sort of black people's creative expression different from the one that was usually presented on the stage, as well as the insertion of blues as a part of African American life and culture. By portraying the characters in a way that was widely developed in the minstrel tradition, Hurston and Hughes wanted to introduce a reversal of the stereotypes too anchored in minstrelsy. According to George Houston Bass, "the authors of *Mule Bone* envisioned their play as an 'authentic' portrayal of black comic characters and the rich uses of language and laughter southern black folk had invented as a way of creatively coping with the harshness of being black in America" (2). Hurston always tried to show in her work an independent image of her race, far away from the burden of racism, and autonomous from the oppression of white supremacy.

The Great Day: *Reversing Black Musical Revues*

During a continuous period of three years Hurston became obsessed with the production of the revue *The Great Day*, which finally opened in 1932 at the John Golden Theatre on Broadway; it was also performed in other locations in New York, like the New School. With *The Great Day* (and the concerts that followed it) Hurston may have achieved the dream of performing onstage the "authentic" Negro theater that she had tried to write two years before with Langston Hughes in *Mule Bone*.

In *The Great Day* Hurston had included her research materials, collected both in the South and in her expedition to the Bahamas. As she reports in her autobiography, "I did the concert because I knew that nowhere had the general public ever heard Negro music as done by Negroes" (*Dust Tracks on a Road,* 279). In fact, *The Great Day* "was an artistic success but the 1920s vogue for black musicals was considered over and no offer materialized" (Cole and Mitchell, xiv).

After the show closed, she revised it and added the one-act *The Fiery Chariot,* and renamed the show *From Sun to Sun.* According to Cole and Mitchell (xiv), in 1933 she got a group of actors, dancers, and singers and assembled two concert-like shows, *From Sun to Sun* and *All de Live Long Day,* and these ran throughout Florida in Eatonville, the Rollins College, the Municipal Auditorium in Orlando, and Bethune-Cookman College in Daytona Beach. *Singing Steel,* a different version of the revue, was performed at the Chicago Women's Club Theater and the University of Chicago in 1934. In 1939 *The Fire Dance* (the Bahamian dance included in *The Great Day*) was performed in Orlando as part of the Works Progress Administration's "National Exhibition of Skills."

Hurston's intention with *The Great Day* went further than showing "real Negro" music and dances to the Broadway audiences. She had chosen dark-skinned performers on purpose, to counter the race prejudice that dancers in musical revues should have a light skin color. With the female chorus in black musical revues, white-oriented Harlem nightclubs and Broadway shows imposed their version of black beauty that responded to the demands of the white gaze in the audience. At the Cotton Club "these Ziegfeld-esque spectacles promoted a strictly regulated version of beauty that would be acceptable to white audiences—the homogenous sepia chorus line was composed uniformly of 'high yaller' female dancers who were under twenty-one years of age and over five foot six in height" (Watson, 126).

Polk County: *Creating a Black Folk Opera*

On October 10, 1935, *Porgy and Bess* opened, produced by the Theatre Guild. Although Gershwin's production is considered a classic of its time, it represented the end of the black musical tradition that had been in vogue throughout the first decades of the twentieth century. Furthermore, some critics consider that "this musical version of the 1927 DuBose and Dorothy Heyward Broadway play revealed the height of white usurpation of what had initially been a black cultural form" (Woll, 154).

Since the time of the early minstrel shows there had been an assurance of "authenticity" when dealing with black issues. One of the first troupes, the Virginia

Minstrels, announced that the material of the shows was the "real southern Negro" (Hill and Hatch, 94). After the Civil War, and with the incorporation of black performers into stage culture, the troupes of African American minstrels were "billed as 'real and original'" while they helped to perpetuate the stereotypes imposed on them (Woll, 1). They had no alternative to wearing blackface, however; it was their only chance to perform onstage. By the time Zora Neale Hurston was living in New York, the minstrel show was almost a cliché, but musical revues had made Harlem fashionable. When Gershwin's *Porgy and Bess* was produced, George Gershwin insisted that it was a "folk opera," in spite of the fact that the "spirituals" were his creation and not the collective voice of a people.

Zora Neale Hurston was a prolific dramatist who worked intensely on her theatrical career—in spite of not having seen her major plays produced—and she was aware of what was happening on the Broadway scene. According to Cole and Mitchell she openly hated those plays by white playwrights that pivoted on exotic images, and her goal was to "show what can be done with our magnificent imagery instead of fooling around with bastard drama that can't be white and is too lacking in self respect to be gorgeously Negro" (16). Her last play, *Polk County*, was her final word about this cultural appropriation. Coauthored in 1944 with Dorothy Waring, *Polk County* was written to counter Gershwin's "folk opera," which she did by creating a black musical rooted in the blues culture and the "jook."

The play tells the story of Leafy Lee, a "slim mulatto girl" who arrives at the quarters of the Lofton Lumber Company in South Central Florida. There she begins a close friendship with Big Sweet and everyone else who welcomes her warmly into the community. Dicey, another girl from the quarters, becomes jealous of Leafy because of her light skin color, while showing the same concern as Emma in the play *Color Struck*. Leafy arrives with the desire of learning how to sing the blues, the perfect excuse for the development of songs and performances that give substance to the musical. In this happy context Dicey tries to distract Big Sweet through different strategies with the intention of killing Leafy, Big Sweet's protégée. At the end of the play, in the middle of My Honey's and Leafy's wedding, Dicey tries to kill them by immobilizing the other people with a voodoo spell, which does not work, and the couple gets happily married.

Polk County has some biographical connections with *Mules and Men*: Leafy Lee as an alter ego of Hurston at her arrival to Polk County to collect folklore and "lies," her relationship with Big Sweet, and the encounter with Dicey, since Hurston found herself in the middle of a quarrel in a "jook."[4] The relevance of the relationship between the play and the author's life is not as important as the question of the interconnection between the author's work and the theatrical creation. It is very clear that Hurston used the materials collected in her expeditions for her literary work, but in the case of *Polk County* it becomes especially remarkable because she planned this play before writing *Mule Bone* with Langston Hughes: "Do you want to look over what I have on our show? Lets call it 'JOOK' that is the word for baudy [sic] house in its general sense. It is the club house on these saw-mills and terpentine stills. Then we can bring in all of the songs and gags I have."[5]

From 1929 she had wanted to write a play in which the "jook" was one of the places to be represented. To Hurston it was there where blues and African American culture were born. As she puts it in "Characteristics of Negro Expression," "musically speaking, the Jook is the most important place in America. For in its smelly, shoddy confines has been born the secular music known as blues, and on blues has been founded jazz. The singing and playing in the true Negro style is called 'jooking'" (40). Going further, she adds, "The Negro theatre, as built up by the Negro, is based on Jook situations, with women, gambling, fighting, drinking" (41). It means that the idea of *Polk County* may have pursued her for at least fourteen years—the most prolific time of Hurston's literary career. This statement implies that *Polk County* is the result of years of collecting folklore and ideas about African American culture and its performative representation.

The play *Polk County* has several similarities with *Mule Bone:* from the search of an aesthetic of the blues to the inclusion of folktales and songs—some of them even repeated in the two plays—*Polk County* sometimes seems a rewriting of the play she coauthored with Hughes. One of the main differences is the treatment of the female characters: the portrait of female comradeship and self-determination, the criticism of the image that the male characters project on the black woman, and the relation that Hurston creates between the woman and the blues by making her a pillar in the culture of her community differ significantly from the almost flat character of Daisy in *Mule Bone*. Even though the characters in *Polk County* are still related to the world of "gambling, fighting, drinking," and voodoo practices that might embarrass many African Americans, we should take into account that Hurston wrote this play as a counterattack on the stereotypes of blackness so prominent on the Broadway stage, so *Polk County* still maintains a subversive intention of change.

We could wonder whether Zora Neale Hurston achieved her dream. Although it is clear that she did not realize her purpose, since none of her major plays was produced during the course of her life, with *The Great Day* she was "satisfied in knowing that [she] established a trend and pointed Negro expression back towards the saner ground of our own unbelievable originality" (*Dust Tracks on a Road*, 285). Several critics consider the fact that *Mule Bone* was not staged a tragedy for the African American theater of the era, as this play could have helped to change the course of black theatrical tradition while presenting a unique freshness of language that debunked the minstrel stereotype. *Polk County* had the same objective, and it even represents a more intensive conception of the blues as a vibrant part of African American culture. The play, however, was written long after the heyday of the black musical theater of the 1920s and 1930s, and its production would have been too late for the trends in musical performances.

From our point of view today we might think that the characters in Hurston's plays are flat or broad, but in her time she responded to a dominant conception that dehumanized the people of her community and made them seem void of any human depth, apart from the performance of the minstrel role and the stereotypical representation of the "happy slave." As is well known, the fact that her fiction did not show directly social injustice toward African Americans was greatly criticized by her contemporaries. Nevertheless, the musical comedies of Zora Neale Hurston wanted to subvert the status quo and went even further than the theater of protest and the lynching dramas by showing autonomous human beings whose lives were not determined by racism or slavery.

Several critics have pointed out that Hurston only mentioned briefly her relation with the Harlem Renaissance in her autobiography *Dust Tracks on a Road*, although the importance of her literary participation during that period is indisputable. Hurston scholars know that her most acclaimed work, *Their Eyes Were Watching God*, was written in 1937, long after the renaissance. In the years preceding the publication of her novels in the mid-1930s, however, she was intensely dedicated to her dramatic career and worked together with other writers and intellectuals, collaborating in new aesthetic projects like the magazine *Fire!!*

As happened with the works of other female playwrights of the Harlem Renaissance, Zora Neale Hurston's dramatic work fell into oblivion. Recent studies, however, have proved her prolific theatrical creation, highlighting her role in the African American artistic renaissance of the 1920s. Her intense effort to define the culture of her community linked her strongly with the Harlem literati, and her attempt to vindicate southern roots in drama related her to the authors of the Little Theater Movement that rose in Harlem during this period. In spite of the fact that some scholars have been digging out Hurston's dramatic work during the last decade, its legacy of blues, humor, and African American folklore still remains a treasure waiting to be rediscovered, studied, and produced.

NOTES

1. From www.eoneill.com/artifacts/EJ1.htm: *The Emperor Jones* opened at the Playwrights' Theatre on Monday, Nov. 1, 1920. The play was an original New York production produced by the Provincetown Players and directed by George Cram Cook. It moved to Selwyn Theatre on Dec. 27, 1920; to the Princess Theatre on Jan. 29, 1921; and to the Walnut Street Theatre in Philadelphia on Nov. 21, 1921. Brutus Jones, Emperor, was played by Charles S. Gilpin; Harry Smithers, a cockney trader, by Jasper Deeter; an Old Native Woman by Christine Ell; Lem, a native chief, by Charles Ellis; Jeff by S. I. Thompson; the Prison Guard by James Martín; the Auctioneer by Frederick Ward Roege; and the Congo Witch Doctor by Michio Itow.

2. Although she placed second in the *Opportunity* literary contest for *Color Struck*, the play was never produced.

3. Hurston to Hughes, April 12, 1928 (in Kaplan, 116).

4. See chapter 9 in Hurston, *Mules and Men*.

5. Hurston to Hughes, spring-summer 1929 (in Kaplan, 143).

BIBLIOGRAPHY

Baker, Houston A., Jr. "Modernism and the Harlem Renaissance." *American Quarterly* 39, no. 1 (spring 1987): 84–97.

Bass, George Houston. "Another Bone of Contention: Reclaiming Our Gift of Laughter." In *Mule Bone: A Comedy of Negro Life*, 1–4. New York: HarperPerennial, 1991.

Cole, Jean Lee, and Charles Mitchell, eds. *From Luababa to Polk County: Zora Neale Hurston Plays at the Library of Congress*. Baltimore: Apprentice House, 2006.

Gates, Henry Louis, Jr. "A Tragedy of Negro Life." In *Mule Bone: A Comedy of Negro Life*, 5–24. New York: HarperPerennial, 1991.

Hill, Errol G., and James Hatch. *A History of African American Theatre*. Cambridge, UK: Cambridge University Press, 2004.

Hill, Lynda Marion. *Social Rituals and the Verbal Art of Zora Neale Hurston*. Washington, DC: Howard University Press, 1996.

Hurston, Zora Neale. "Characteristics of Negro Expression." In *African American Literary Theory: A Reader*, edited by Winston Napier, 31–44. New York: New York University Press, 2000.

———. *Dust Tracks on a Road*. New York: HarperPerennial, 2006.

———. *Mules and Men*. New York: HarperCollins, 1990.

Hurston, Zora Neale, and Langston Hughes. *Mule Bone: A Comedy of Negro Life.* New York: HarperPerennial, 1991.

Johnson, James Weldon. *Black Manhattan.* New York: Da Capo Press, 1991.

Kaplan, Carla, ed. *Zora Neale Hurston: A Life in Letters.* New York: Doubleday, 2002.

Sotiropoulos, Karen. *Staging Race: Black Performers in Turn of the Century America.* Cambridge, MA: Harvard University Press, 2008.

Watson, Steven. *The Harlem Renaissance: Hub of African American Culture, 1920–1930.* New York: Pantheon, 1995.

West, M. Genevieve. *Zora Neale Hurston & American Literary Culture.* Gainesville: University Press of Florida, 2005.

Woll, Allen. *Black Musical Theatre: From "Coontown" to "Dreamgirls."* Baton Rouge: Louisiana State University Press, 1989.

TWO

No Negro Renaissance

Hubert H. Harrison and the Role of the New Negro Literary Critic

Ousmane Kirumu Power-Greene

On March 12, 1927, a provocative article ran in the *Pittsburgh Courier* entitled "'No Negro Literary Renaissance,' Says Well Known Writer." The "well known writer" identified in the title was none other than Hubert H. Harrison, the Caribbean-born Afro-American orator, intellectual, and organizer who had lived and worked in Harlem for more than two decades. Harrison denied the existence of a literary renaissance in Harlem, chastised the "noxious . . . Greenwich Village neurotics who invented it," and rebuked those blacks who, for their own benefit, perpetuated the idea during the 1920s. "If anyone, in public, should care to pick any decade between 1850 and 1910," Harrison demanded,

> I will undertake to present from among the Negroes of that decade as many writers and (with Schomburg to back me) as many lines of literary and artistic endeavor as he can show for this decade. And I go further! I will also undertake to show (with perhaps three exceptions) more able Negro writers for any decade in that period than can be found today. The challenge is open to anyone—but I do suggest that they read some of the things referred to before they take up the challenge.[1]

Eager to encourage a debate among leading intellectuals, the editors of the *Pittsburgh Courier* included a note beneath the title claiming that "equal space" would be provided for "any literary critic qualified to reply" to Harrison's charge. Sure enough, black attorney John P. Davis wrote in, rejecting Harrison's critique and arguing that the outpouring of essays, poetry, music, and art during the 1920s did indeed represent a "renaissance."[2] But, as Harrison's biographer, Jeffrey Perry, points out, even Alain Locke, one of the architects of the "New Negro Renaissance," would admit by 1928 that only the "interest of whites" had kept alive the notion of an artistic renaissance in Harlem.[3]

By the time Harrison published his controversial rejection of the Harlem Renaissance in 1927, Harrison was respected by blacks and whites alike, revered by scholars, who often took to calling him "Dr. Harrison," and practically worshiped by radicals on the left—especially Cyril Briggs and A. Phillip Randolph. Although some middle-class reformers may have despised him, they most certainly read his editorials or heard his lectures. Harrison's tireless attempt to educate the masses through public lectures even enticed the common person to pause and listen to his arresting soapbox discourses on numerous topics—from science to history.

Although Harrison's popularity led thousands to attend his funeral after his untimely death in December of 1927, his influence has only recently been noted by scholars. Perry argues, in fact, that "Harrison's willingness to directly challenge prominent leaders in leftist and African American circles stung many of the people most likely to keep his memory alive." Furthermore, Harrison's uncompromising posture caused "organizations that might have publicly preserved his memory [to make] little effort to do so."[4]

Born in St. Croix, Virgin Islands, in 1883, Hubert H. Harrison immigrated to the United States in 1900. By 1910 he had not only published in the *New York Times* but had also made an enemy of Booker T. Washington by challenging his leadership in the pages of the *New York Sun*. Washington responded by having an associate see to it that Harrison was fired from his job at the post office. Between 1911 and 1914 Harrison organized, wrote, and lectured for the Socialist Party, establishing the Colored Socialist Club in 1912. His growing frustration with racism within the Socialist Party bubbled to the surface, and when he wrote an article criticizing fellow socialists who clung to racist beliefs, he was suspended from the party. In 1916 he shifted gears, coining the phrase "Race First" and establishing the Liberty League.

With the publication of *The Voice* in 1917, Harrison became a pioneering journalist of the New Negro movement. When Marcus Garvey arrived in Harlem, it was Hubert Harrison who introduced Garvey to crowds in New York and provided him with the groundwork to build the UNIA (Universal Negro Improvement Association) into a mass movement.

By 1920 Harrison had endured one failed newspaper, a failed magazine (the *New Negro*), and a failed organization (the Liberty League). With much of the membership of the Liberty League defecting to Garvey's UNIA in 1920, Harrison became the managing editor of the *Negro World*, which he maintained until 1922. When he broke from Garvey in 1922 for, as Harrison put it, Garvey's "bombastic, conceited, and arrogant" nature, he became a freelance editor for the New York Board of Education and published articles and essays in numerous magazines and newspapers. In 1924 he established his last organization, the International Colored Unity League, and traveled from the Northeast to the Midwest lecturing on various topics and recruiting people into his new organization until illness forced him to cease giving lectures. When he died, on December 17, 1927, Hubert H. Harrison left an intellectual legacy that rivaled many of the nation's leading public intellectuals.

Perhaps one of Harrison's most important roles was championing the notion of the New Negro movement. Harrison was the quintessential "New Negro"—uncompromising, eager to challenge whites who sought to denigrate black culture and black life, and unwilling to follow established leaders who called for patience or compromise. Harrison promoted black artistic, dramatic, and literary achievement, establishing a "Poems for the People" section in his *New Negro* magazine. Although he challenged the notion of a "Harlem Renaissance" during the 1920s, he still believed art, drama, and fiction were important to the New Negro movement.

Rather than championing art and literature that served as propaganda, Harrison believed the artist and writer should present creative works that were authentic expressions of the black experience in America and the world.[5] Works that exaggerated the plight of black people, or misrepresented the black experience, needed to be challenged by New Negro intellectuals, who had an obligation to uncover the inadequacies of such works for the general public. Consequently, Harrison relished his role as a critic, and he encouraged readers to approach works of art, literature, and drama with an equally critical eye. In his view the role of the professional critic or the book reviewer is to "explain the purpose of the author, [and] tell whether he attains it . . . so the casual reader may know whether it is worth his while to read it." Ultimately, Harrison argued, "criticism may be regarded either as a science or as an art. In either case it has its laws and methods which must be followed if any good results are to be obtained."[6]

While Harrison challenged black critics, he was particularly caustic toward whites who took to the task of literary criticism without serious consideration of the quality of black works and, instead, offered sophomoric analysis. The problem with these white literary critics, Harrison argued, was that they approached black works of creative expression without any foundation, and this led to impressionistic criticism that failed to offer any incisive view of the work and was akin to the opinion of the "man in the street."[7] Without any familiarity with a previous generation of black writers and artists, how could white critics speak authoritatively about the black works in the 1920s or declare that they represented the pinnacle of black creative expression?[8]

Excited by this seemingly untapped well of black talent, white patrons and publishers arrived in Harlem eager to recruit black talent. But white art patrons and publishers were not the only ones interested in Harlem. Novelists, playwrights, and artists also found inspiration in "Negro life" uptown, provoking Harrison to criticize black editors, writers, and socialites who encouraged what he viewed as a parasitic relationship between these artists and black people, culture, and lifestyle. Harrison's rejection of the notion of a Harlem Renaissance reflects an intellectual posture and sensibility that expressed in no unclear terms that "New Negro" intellectuals would not allow the white establishment, or black American "guardians of the gate," to exploit the base aspects of black life in Harlem for profit or pleasure. As Harrison explained in his article that challenged the idea of a renaissance, black scholars, like Alain Locke, who called attention to what they perceived as a "renaissance" in Harlem, failed to consider that publicity and rhetoric could not be a substitute for artistic talent.[9]

When the white Harlem socialite Carl Van Vechten published his novel *Nigger Heaven*, Hubert Harrison had the evidence he needed to show black scholars and intellectuals that whites closely associated with Harlem during the 1920s would exploit black people for recognition and, perhaps, a fortune.[10] Only a paucity of New Negro intellectuals, like Harrison, had the gall to challenge works like *Nigger Heaven* and those produced by luminaries of the movement that had become known as the "Harlem Renaissance." Indeed, Harrison argued that the most important role of the black intellectual was to confront those individuals, white or black, inclined to trumpet inferior creative works for personal or professional gain. Thus, through an examination of Harrison's caustic review of Van Vechten's novel, one sees the essential elements of his critique of the "Harlem Renaissance" and the atmosphere in which the notion of a renaissance was born.

"When Harlem Was in Vogue"

Hubert Harrison was not alone in his condemnation of the notion that a renaissance was taking place in Harlem during the 1920s. Gustavus Adolphus Stewart in his article "The New Negro Hokum," argued: "What is this renaissance? There have appeared possibly a score of novels, some written by Negroes, some by whites. These range all the way from serious, sympathetic but unsentimental attempts at portrayal of all phases of American Negro life to rollicking profanity and hilarious smut, with here and there a bit of poignant and pregnant expression, a glimpse of searing tragedy, a ray of irrepressible humor, with much conscious propaganda, a large proportion of artificiality and labored 'niggerisms,' and in perspective, all quite unimportant and ephemeral."[11] But as Stewart asserts, the majority of writing in *Opportunity* and the *Crisis* could only be described as "slightly above" mediocre. In regard to the drama of the era, Stewart claimed that the "worthwhile drama [that] has been produced is the work of whites." Indeed, Stewart concurred with Harrison that the persistence of magazine editors and award ceremonies sponsored by whites had fabricated the idea of a renaissance in Harlem.

During the past two decades scholars have acknowledged how contrived the Harlem Renaissance really was. David Levering Lewis, one of the major historians of the period, calls it a "forced phenomenon, a cultural nationalism of the parlor, institutionally encouraged and constrained by the leaders of the civil rights establishment for the paramount purpose of improving 'race relations' in a time of extreme national reaction to and annulment of economic gains won by Afro-Americans during the Great War."[12] More recently, Henry Louis Gates Jr. has claimed that "the Harlem or New Negro Renaissance was born through the midwifery of [Alain] Locke, who edited a special issue of *Survey Graphic* magazine entitled 'Harlem: Mecca of the New Negro' in March of 1925."[13] Locke followed up his issue of *Survey Graphic* with a 446-page anthology, *The New Negro: An Interpretation*. This classic volume presents creative works by most of the writers whom scholars identify as participants in the Harlem Renaissance, writers such as Langston Hughes, Jean Toomer, Countee Cullen, Jessie Redmon Fauset, and Zora Neale Hurston.

Harrison's denial of a renaissance in Harlem was no major conspiracy to thwart the younger generation of writers and artists or the black intellectuals and white patrons who championed its existence. In fact, Harrison had promoted the work of black poets in his *New Negro* magazine and while he was an editor of Garvey's *Negro World.* Furthermore, Charles S. Johnson invited Harrison to a celebration of Jessie Fauset's novel *There Is Confusion,* which Johnson considered a major work of the younger generation of writers who would make up the core group of Harlem Renaissance authors. As David Levering Lewis explains, this gathering at the Civic Club was attended by more than one hundred people, many of whom were white patrons, publishers, and authors, such as H. L. Mencken, Oswald Garrison Villard, and Eugene O'Neill. Although it is unclear whether Harrison attended the gathering, Johnson's invitation illustrates Harrison's stature among those who promoted the Harlem Renaissance and whom Harrison criticized.[14]

Although Harrison did review the poetry of Claude McKay, a friend of Harrison's, and some works of Charles Johnson, W. E. B. Du Bois, Carter G. Woodson, and J. A. Rogers, there remains no record that Harrison reviewed novels such as *Cane* or the works of Jessie Fauset or Nella Larsen. Even Langston Hughes dodged Harrison's critical pen, even though Hughes wrote some of the poems that appeared in Van Vechten's *Nigger Heaven.* Perhaps Harrison's efforts to organize the Unity League, and to address what he believed were more pressing concerns, caused him to ignore those literary works most often identified as prominent within the Harlem Renaissance canon.

But there may be another reason Harrison did not review works from individual authors identified as crucial Harlem Renaissance figures. Through his review of Carl Van Vechten's controversial novel *Nigger Heaven* we gain an important perspective on Harrison's opinion about Harlem Renaissance figures.[15] Thus, it seems appropriate to turn to Harrison's review of Van Vechten's novel that was published in the *Amsterdam News* in September 1926, which Harrison entitled "Homo Africanus Harlemi."[16]

Although George Schuyler proclaimed that Carl Van Vechten had "done more than any single person in this country to create the atmosphere of acceptance of the Negro," Harrison condemned Van Vechten for poor craftsmanship and for exploiting black life.[17] Harrison, however, did not reject the novel out of hand because of its content but instead called it a failed artistic endeavor that, even when placed alongside Van Vechten's own previous works, was unimpressive.

Harrison shared Du Bois's and others condemnation of the title, pointing out that "even a Southerner like Octavus Roy Cohen eschews it from all his writings," and he devoted his attention to the book's "theme and treatment." In true

Harrison fashion the review illustrated his uncanny intellect and grasp of knowledge that some might consider obscure. For example, Harrison called attention to the fact that the publisher mistakenly claimed on the last page of the novel that the book was "set to Caslon type, when it quite obviously isn't." If that was the only bit of sarcastic fault-finding Harrison had offered up, the book's publisher, Alfred Knopf, and its author, Van Vechten, would have been able to draw a long sigh of relief, but they were not so fortunate.[18]

First, Harrison ridiculed the work's "Nigger-dialect," pointing out that "having lived nineteen years in Harlem . . . I can speak, I think, with some authority when I say that Van Vechten's dialect doesn't exist up here." Furthermore, Harrison argued that the plot attempts to present a "love-story with a spoilt rah-rah boy and a sweet little girl as a protagonist, [who] curses him with a college 'education' and an itch to write, and finally whelms him in the rotten results of his own waywardness and asinine incompetence."[19]

Van Vechten, Harrison argues, "can write, or should I say, he could," and this makes *Nigger Heaven* all the more deplorable. Based on Van Vechten's own previous novels, which Harrison calls excellent, this particular novel fails "as literature—as art." In the final four chapters, Harrison claims, the author must have recognized how bad the novel actually was, and thus, attempted to speed "up the pace of his approaching crisis. But that fail[ed] to rescue the thing."[20]

Although Harrison devotes much space to the faults of the novel, he also has "a few good things to say of Van Vechten's novel of Harlem life," yet, as one might suspect, these "good things" do not complement any quality of the actual work. Instead, Harrison argues that the novel's value is that it "show[s] up the present worthlessness of what passes for colored 'society' in Harlem. Its cheap and tawdry assumptions of aristocracy, its reeking but camouflaged color prejudice and its collective crab-barrel tactics are revealed quite as effectively by means of Van Vechten's lay-figures as they would be by genuine characters. In this respect the book is a thinly disguised homily. And, indeed, there is a singular appropriateness in the shoddy quality of the book—a sort of argument-by-example—for it deals with a shoddy social set."[21]

In Harrison's view Van Vechten's novel should be applauded for rising up like a "German submarine to throw the fear of Nigger Heaven" into those black writers "hovering around in Harlem dreaming that they are writing 'Negro' literature, because Van Vechten's kind has coddled them at pink-tea and literary contests." And in paying homage to Walter White's novel *Fire in the Flint*, Harrison called on black writers and artists to abandon their white patrons and "take a leap over the wall of weakness with which they are surrounded and write (with the virile power of Walter White), of the actual lives of actual Negroes in this Harlem, which has been suffering for six years from the blasé neurotics whose Caucasian culture has petered out and who come to this corner of Manhattan for pungent doses of unreality, such as we get in *Nigger Heaven*."[22]

Although Harrison's review in the *Amsterdam News* provoked a flurry of responses, Harrison claimed that his critics misunderstood his review and had lumped it together with other reviews that condemned the novel for presenting black people negatively.[23] In response, Harrison explained, "I must make clear at the outset—in the face of much fog that has been raised—that in my review I did not base my unfavorable opinion of *Nigger Heaven* on the popular ground that it doesn't present the Negro in favorable light." Harrison argued: "It is no part the critic's right to dictate to the creative artist what aspects of life he should select for representation." Instead, Harrison reminded his critics that he "condemned Van Vechten's book as a poor specimen of literary craftsmanship, and on the further ground that it is a viciously false picture of the life which he pretends to depict."[24] Even though Van Vechten's supporters championed the *idea* of the novel, or Van Vechten's courage in trying to depict black life "realistically," Harrison dismissed such tepid responses.

Underlying Harrison's critique of the novel was a critique of white critics and patrons who only seemed interested in black culture and life when it became in vogue. To select a group of writers and artists, label them the best of the race, and tout them to the nation, and even the world, as the pinnacle of black artistic achievement, without acknowledging the great works of previous generations of writers and artists, implicitly denies the greatness of notable literary figures, such as Paul Lawrence Dunbar, and this was, in Harrison's view, disingenuous.

Harrison argued that the public intellectual must guard against this type of artistic and literary hijacking by whites eager to make a quick buck off exploiting the worst aspects of black life to appear "hip." Rather than rely on those from downtown to dictate to the black public which art and literature it should consume, black artists and intellectuals needed to reject white paternalism in literature and the arts and encourage people to decide for themselves which artists, writers, and playwrights they believed produced quality work.

Disappointed but not surprised at how quickly some black scholars, such as Charles Johnson, rushed to the defense of white writers, critics, and patrons, Harrison dedicated articles and editorials to teaching the public how to determine on its own the value of art, theater, and literature. For Harrison the black critic had an essential role, not to those in the "ivory tower" or those eager to run downtown to show and prove to white publishing companies the value of a piece of poetry or a novel, but to the general public. From Harrison's perspective the essential value of the artistic work (and critical interpretation of such work) would be measured by the black community rather than those from outside seeking to associate themselves with the fashion of the day.

Harrison argued that black creative expression of the 1920s did not produce the art, literature, or dramatic production that merited the designation of a "renaissance" in Harlem. He did believe, however, that authentically superb literature, art, and drama were a crucial part of the New Negro movement. In fact, he claimed that the very nature of New Negro social consciousness depended on awakening black people to the achievements of African American artists, as well as those blacks in the diaspora, and he hoped that such works could be a source of pride and inspiration for African people in America and all over the world. When such works were presented to the public, Harrison applauded them. But when other New Negro intellectuals, led by Alain Locke, declared a "renaissance" in Harlem, Harrison challenged the notion that the white literary establishment's newfound fascination with Harlem should warrant a new conceptualization of the achievements of the era.

NOTES

1. "'No Negro Literary Renaissance,' Says Well Known Writer," *Pittsburgh Courier,* March 12, 1927, in Hubert H. Harrison Papers, Box 3, Folder 38, Rare Book and Manuscript Library, Columbia University (hereafter HHH Papers); repr. in Jeffrey B. Perry, *A Hubert H. Harrison Reader* (Middletown, CT: Wesleyan University Press, 2001), 351–54.

2. "An Answer to Dr. Hubert Harrison's Article," *Pittsburgh Courier,* April 2, 1927 (in Perry, *A Hubert H. Harrison Reader,* 449).

3. For biographical information on Hubert Harrison see Jeffrey Perry's first volume of a two-volume biography: Jeffrey B. Perry, *Hubert Harrison: The Voice of Harlem Radicalism* (New York: Columbia University Press, 2008). This book is expanded and revised from Perry's dissertation ("Hubert Henry Harrison, 'The Father of Harlem Radicalism.' The Early Years: 1883 through the Founding of the Liberty League and 'the Voice' in 1917" [PhD diss., Columbia University, 1986]). In 2001 Perry edited a collection of Harrison's writings, and he has offered researchers the most comprehensive analysis of Harrison's work during the 1920s to date; see Perry, *A Hubert Harrison Reader.* Harrison has been central to several studies of the era, but the two

that devote significant space to him are Kevin K. Gaines, *Uplifting the Race: Black Leadership, Politics, and Culture in the Twentieth Century* (Chapel Hill: University of North Carolina Press, 1996); and Winston James, *Holding Aloft the Banner of Ethiopia: Caribbean Radicalism in Early Twentieth-Century America* (New York: Verso, 1998).

4. Perry, *A Hubert Harrison Reader*, 9.

5. "The Greatest American Writer Notes re. Mark Twain. 26 Jan. 1924," autographed manuscript, HHH Papers, Box 4, Folder 64.

6. "Views of Readers on Criticism; Mr. H. H. Harrison Reiterates His Theories," letter to the editor, *New York Times Saturday Review of Books*, April 2, 1907; repr. in Perry, *A Hubert Harrison Reader*, 292–93.

7. "Book Reviewing as a Fine Art," HHH Papers, Box 4, Folder 20.

8. For a clear expression of Harrison's views on white publishers see "On Certain Condescension in White Publishers," HHH Papers, Box 13, Folder 7 (published in *Negro World*, March 4, 1922).

9. For an explanation of the ideological trends of New Negro radicalism see Ernest Allen Jr., "'The New Negro': Explorations in Identity and Social Consciousness, 1910–1922," in *1915: The Cultural Moment*, ed. Adele Heller and Lois Rudnick (New Brunswick, NJ: Rutgers University Press, 1991), 48–68.

10. Harrison gave a lecture entitled "A Reply to 'Nigger Heaven'" in 1926 at the Educational Forum at 200 W. 135th Street. The lecture was held in room 212 of the New York library on Saturday, October 9, at 8 p.m.; admission was 25 cents. See HHH Papers, Box 16, Folder 38.

11. Gustavus Adolphus Stewart, "The New Negro Hokum," *Social Forces* 6, no. 3 (March 1928): 438–45; repr. in *The New Negro: Readings on Race, Representation, and African American Culture, 1892–1938*, ed. Henry Louis Gates Jr. and Gene Andrew Jarrett (Princeton, NJ: Princeton University Press, 2007), 123–29, 128.

12. David Levering Lewis, ed., *The Portable Harlem Renaissance Reader* (New York: Viking, 1994), xv.

13. Henry Louis Gates Jr., "Harlem on Our Minds," *Critical Inquiry* 24, no. 1 (autumn, 1997): 3. See also Gates and Jarrett, *The New Negro*.

14. See Gates and Jarrett, *The New Negro*, 89–90; see also Charles S. Johnson to Hubert Harrison, Esq., March 13, 1924, HHH papers, Box 2, Folder 53.

15. For insight into Carl Van Vechten's novel *Nigger Heaven* and its importance to the Harlem Renaissance see Robert F. Worth, "*Nigger Heaven* and the Harlem Renaissance," *African American Review* 29 (autumn 1995): 461–73.

16. Harrison reviewed this book in several venues, suggesting that his attention to this one work, written by a white author, warrants close analysis. See "*Nigger Heaven*: A Review," an unpublished review on Radio WGL in HHH Papers, Box 5, Folder 57. The text that Jeffrey Perry reprinted in *A Hubert Harrison Reader* was titled "Homo Africanus Harlemi" (*Nigger Heaven* book review, *Amsterdam News*, Sept. 1, 1926) and came from a clipping without page numbers in HHH Papers, Box 4, Folder 71.

17. George Schuyler, "Phylon Profile, XXII: Carl Van Vechten," in *Remembering the Harlem Renaissance*, ed. Cary D. Wintz (New York: Garland, 1996), 154–60, 154.

18. Perry, *A Hubert Harrison Reader*, 341–42.

19. Harrison, "Homo Africanus Harlemi," in Perry, *A Hubert Harrison Reader*, 342.

20. Ibid., 343.

21. Perry, *A Hubert Harrison Reader*, 393.

22. Harrison apparently wrote to Walter White, praising his novel *Fire in the Flint.* White wrote back to Harrison: "You have no idea how happy your letter of September 9th made me. I tried to do an honest piece of work and to know that you with all of your experience felt that I have 'hit the bull's eye' is encouraging indeed" (Walter White to Hubert H. Harrison, Sept. 15, 1924, HHH Papers, Box 3, Folder 52).

23. "*Nigger Heaven*—A Review of the Reviews," *Amsterdam News*, Nov. 13, 1926, in Perry, *A Hubert Harrison Reader*, 344–51.

24. Perry, *A Hubert Harrison Reader*, 344–45.

THREE

It's All Sacred Music

Duke Ellington, from the Cotton Club to the Cathedral

Frank A. Salamone

dward Kennedy (Duke) Ellington (1899–1974) was born in Washington, D.C. He was a gifted artist, turning down a scholarship to the Pratt Institute in New York to pursue a musical career. Ellington was a fine pianist but made his major mark on jazz through his compositions and his orchestra, which partook of Duke's jazz royalty and represented the height of sophisticated music. The nickname was given him by his family when he was a child because of his regal bearing and overall demeanor. It is no accident that Ellington's *Harlem* suite, composed in 1951, is included with his Sacred Concert material and religious works, for there is a direct line in Ellington's music that connects the Sacred Concerts to the Cotton Club days. Ellington took the Cotton Club concepts of elaborate ideas and precision pacing into church. These concerts were, truly, the ultimate in total show-business production, including, as they did, dancing, instrumental and vocal solos, luscious ensemble work, choirs, and, of course, Ellington's signature MC work. Taking the Cotton Club into church, however, was not an attempt to secularize the sacred, for ultimately Ellington viewed all of his music as spiritual at its roots, as his writings demonstrate.[1]

Gary Giddens has a clear understanding of this process and includes this prescient passage in his positive appraisal of the Sacred Concerts. There were three of these concerts: the first was on September 16, 1965, at Grace Episcopal Cathedral in San Francisco. The second was at the Cathedral of St. John the Divine in New York City in 1968, and the third was at London's Westminster Abby in 1973.

Ellington's familiar dictum, "Every man prays in his own language and there is no language that God does not understand," reminds the listener that Ellington did not attempt to apply his genius to an established idiom but rather to bring his own music intact into the church. The difference between playing for people, whether at the Cotton Club or Westminster Abbey, and creating for the greater glory of God was not lost on him. When Fr. Norman O'Connor commissioned a jazz mass (apparently never completed), Ellington pondered the conflict: "'One may be accustomed to speaking to people, but suddenly to attempt to speak, sing, and play directly to God—that puts one in an entirely different position.' He prayed on his own musical terms, and celebrated the talents of his collaborators accordingly; 'All the members of the band played in character,' he said of the first sacred concert. He did not abandon the Cotton Club; he brought the Cotton Club review to the pulpit" (Giddens 1993, 376).[2]

Ellington took the Cotton Club into church because, truly, there was no reason for him to abandon the Cotton Club when entering the church, for he had been conveying a spiritual message through his music from its inception. The Cotton Club was an important element of the Harlem Renaissance, even though it had a strong racist component. In 1920 Jack Johnson, the former heavyweight champion of the world, opened a club at the future site of the Cotton Club. He named it the Club Deluxe. The club was at Lenox Avenue and 142nd Street. In 1923 the English gangster Owney Madden assumed ownership of the club, changing its name to the Cotton Club. Madden brought Duke Ellington to the club. Ellington was involved in producing the shows, which included the racist depiction of African Americans in jungle settings in addition to its color bar, banning all African Americans except staff and performers from entering the club. Moreover, the dancers had to fit the preferred image of being "tall, tan, and terrific" and under twenty-one. The proud Ellington was expected to write jungle music for a white audience. He worked with Jimmie McHugh and Dorothy Fields, learning how to put a show together and write music that was sophisticated and appealing to the discerning public.

Despite its obvious drawbacks, the Cotton Club, with its midnight broadcasts, enabled Ellington to hone his message to its ultimate clarity and precision; namely, that life itself is sacred, that every act of affirmation is an act of love, that no one can love God without loving his or her neighbor, and that his music conveyed that significant message.

Sonny Greer, for example, states that a night at the Cotton Club was "kind of hectic. Harlem was heaven. In those times you had to see that. It was like going to Church. There was a different atmosphere. You could walk up and down the streets all night. There was no molestation. It was a carnival atmosphere. . . . Everybody loved everybody. Love is not a new word in our profession" (quoted in Crouch 1979).

Ellington was keenly aware of the power of music as a symbol of love and saw his music as an appropriate response to prejudice and discrimination. He told Florence Zunser (1930, 45), "I am not playing jazz. I am trying to play the natural feelings of a people. I believe that music, popular music of the day, is the real reflector of the nation's feelings." Ellington told Zunser he was working on an extended work, "The History of the Negro." In 1943 this became *Black, Brown and Beige* and premiered at Ellington's first Carnegie Hall concert. Some mark this work as clearly part of his explicitly sacred works. Mahalia Jackson, for instance, who would only sing sacred music, had no problem performing selections from this Ellington suite.

Ellington rarely, if ever, lost sight of his overall goal of representing his people and presenting positive accounts of their accomplishments. The following excerpt from his seventieth birthday interview underscores this point:

> My eighth grade teacher taught race pride. We've been involved right along. It's a wonder we're still alive. I've been in the theater a long time. I think from the point of drama. A good playwright can say what he wants to say without saying it. . . . I was getting $5000 per week in 1932 but there was a corny cotton field thing in the show. I said the cotton field comes out or we come out. . . . *Black, Brown and Beige* is a tone parallel to a history of the Negro in America. We have always tried to use good grammar, and elegant presentation.

The Sacred

The prevailing view of jazz among the older generation of the American white audience was that it was music of abandon and sin. A number of articles fostered this belief. Anne Shaw Faulkner's (1921) "Does Jazz Put the Sin in Syncopation" typifies this view. It notes that jazz by its very nature stirs up those who listen

and dance to it. It fosters abandonment of moral beliefs and practices and leads
the unsuspecting to do things they should not. It shows a racist bias along the
way, pointing to its low origins and lack of any redeeming musical characteristics.

Of course, not all whites thought this way, but a surprising number of African
Americans did, especially those who held to strong religious convictions. Jazz's
mixing of sacred and profane music tended to be a matter for concern. Many luminaries of the Harlem Renaissance, however, were in harmony with Ellington's
views, including Claude McKay and Langston Hughes, both of whom championed
the spiritual dimension of jazz in their works. Louis Armstrong, among other
musicians, was also quick to note the link between the sacred and jazz, as well as
between humor and the sacred.

For Ellington, then, the sacred and spiritual appear to refer to that which promotes love and in the process provokes a sense of awe. Certainly, the quality of
being life-affirming and inclusive is part of Ellington's conception of the sacred.
Additionally, however, Ellington is aware of the power of ambiguity and humor
in presenting his spiritual message. He is careful to allow dramatic pacing and
juxtaposition of seeming opposites to tell his tale. As noted above, "A good playwright can say what he wants to say without saying it." It was a lesson he had
learned early.

The short movie *Black and Tan Fantasy,* for example, released in 1929, has a
nice little story. The movie opens with Ellington and Artie Whetsol, one of his
trumpet players, rehearsing. They need money, and Fredi Washington, one of the
Cotton Club dancers, informs Ellington and Whetsol that she is going back to
work to help save Ellington's piano. Of course, Washington is in danger of dying
but performs anyway.

The movie features an authentic Cotton Club setting in which there is a brief
but rather complete floor show, featuring the famous Cotton Club Dancers. Fredi
Washington dances, and then she collapses. After a spiritual, *Black and Tan Fantasy* is played. In sum, the movie is programmatic, imitating a Cotton Club performance. This was a pattern that Ellington followed for much of his life.

What is often overlooked, however, is the manner in which Ellington dares
to intersperse the sacred and the profane. There are not only echoes of spirituals
or "church music" in his compositions. There are also outright spirituals used
just before dancing that would offend many traditionally religious people. Moreover, that dancing takes place to a suite that has often been considered more
religious in nature than secular. Ellington was blurring the distinction between
two spheres that many other performers preferred to keep distinct, the sacred

and the profane. By so doing he was placing his music in what he came to call "beyond category." He was also deeply involved in the realm that anthropologists recognize as that of the ambiguous and dangerous.[3]

Steed (1993, 3) notes this Ellington characteristic of avoiding categories. "Although he still personifies jazz for millions of people, Ellington did not even like to use the word unless it was defined simply as freedom of expression." Dance also wrote that "Duke Ellington never ceases to voice his disapproval of categories, which he views as a curb on an artist's right to freedom of expression. He always wants to be free to do what he feels moved to do, and not what someone feels he should do" (Dance 1970, 15).

There is no doubt that Ellington felt that this mixing of categories had meaning beyond the music itself, that it was somehow sacred. He viewed his music as a vocation and as a means for breaking himself and other African Americans out of rigid categories, as his interview with Zunser (1930, 45) makes clear. Ellington frequently noted his belief that music was a vocation, a sacred calling. At the Second Sacred Concert, for example, he labeled himself "God's messenger boy," a phrase repeated in the album notes (Steed 1993, 6).

Steed (1993) includes this important passage from Stanley Dance's eulogy: "Duke knew the good news was Love, of God and his fellow men. He proclaimed the message in his Sacred Concerts, grateful for an opportunity to acknowledge something of which he stood in awe, a power he considered above his human limitations" (quoted in Salamone 2009, 13).[4] For Ellington, attempts to capture that love and awe in his music, a love he viewed as transcending artificial differences and encompassing all life, were attempts at grasping the sacred. It is as if Ellington were saying that God has no limits. Limitations are human. Therefore, attempts to affirm life and love should also know no artificial limits.

Steed (1993, 8) puts this issue in a slightly different, more musicological, manner. At Ellington's funeral, a recording by Johnny Hodges of "Heaven," from the Second Sacred Concert, was played. Steed notes the construction of the melody and some of its notable internal contrasts. One observation is relevant in ascertaining and understanding Ellington's conception of the sacred. "Ellington's favored tri-tone is heard three times, perversely ascending as if he were determined to make what was once called the 'devil's interval' angelic." This desire to force people to reconsider their stereotypical categorizations was a longtime project with Ellington that led logically to the Sacred Concerts.

The Sacred Concerts

Ellington's religious convictions and musical predilections converged in the Sacred Concerts. He had an opportunity to do openly what he had been doing privately. As he put it, "I recognized this as an exceptional opportunity. 'Now I can say openly,' I said, 'what I have been saying to myself on my knees'" (Ellington 1973/1976).

His friends had noticed a growing spirituality about him. Time had, finally, started to take its toll on his energy, and the growing serious illness of his alter ego, Billy Strayhorn, in the middle 1960s was a reminder of his own mortality. Mercer Ellington stated that Duke "always believed in God his whole life. That was always there. It came more to the forefront when Strayhorn got sick. The old man didn't like the whole idea of death or any kind of ending of anything" (quoted in Hajdu 1996, 247).

In 1965 C. J. Bartlett, the dean of Grace Cathedral in San Francisco, the Reverend John S. Yaryan, and James A. Pike, the Episcopal bishop of California, jointly invited Duke Ellington to join their yearlong celebration of the completion of the new Cathedral, a stone structure on top of Nob Hill. Ellington was to write a liturgical work. This work was, as Ellington made clear, not a mass. In a mass the composer addresses God. Ellington intended to address the people (Steed 1993, 12; Hasse 1993, 357–58).

As Giddens (1993, 376) noted, there is a clear connection in Ellington's musical development between the Cotton Club and the Cathedral. As if to emphasize that relationship, Ellington's First Sacred Concert, performed on September 16, 1965, included a number of older works such as "ideas from *Black, Brown and Beige* and *My People,* and included the 1943 piano feature *New World a-Comin'*" (Hasse 1993, 358). These old chestnuts, however, were framed by a new composition, *In the Beginning, God.* In so doing, Ellington reaffirmed the sacredness of his earlier work.

He also harked back to his Cotton Club origins in presenting a sort of floor show at the Cathedral. Ellington imported a tap dancer, Bunny Briggs, choirs, solo singers, and in later concerts various solo musicians. As Hasse (1993, 358) notes, this and subsequent sacred concerts were not quiet intimate music like *Mood Indigo* or *Azure* but celebratory spectacles of the sort that Handel produced.

Predictably, critical reviews were mixed. Throughout his career Ellington received mixed critical reviews whenever he attempted any new endeavor. That the Sacred Concerts suffered this fate is not surprising. Indeed, it would have been surprising if these concerts had not offended a number of people. Hasse provides some insight into the problem: "Traditionally in the African-American community there has been a rather rigid distinction made between sacred religious music—spirituals and gospel—and secular music—blues and jazz—though musically there has been great interchange. For the church, where some were scandalized by the very idea of jazz in a church, it was also a departure from the musical norm" (Hasse 1993, 359–60).

Nevertheless, Ellington was quite pleased with the results of the First Sacred Concert—the Grammy he won for *In the Beginning, God,* the Emmy for the PBS televised version, and the records he sold of it. It was a summation and justification for his work. Ruth Ellington, his sister, spoke to these points in an interview with Janna T. Steed on January 7, 1993:

> The Sacred Concerts expressed his own raison d'etre. We were raised as Christians. . . . The spirituality of his music is why it didn't sound like anybody else's music. . . . The jungle music was not simply that; it expressed the frustration of blacks, male-female relationships, our basic humanity. When Edward was writing music he was expressing love and the emotionality of human experience. . . . When God is guiding you, who can restrict you? . . . He knew his destiny. He didn't act as if he were restricted, and people related to him as if he were equal. He was revolutionary, but not militant, in race; never political. "Show enough love; people will let you in," he would say. (Steed 1993, 22).

It was inevitable that the success of the first Sacred Concert led to two sequels. The Second Sacred Concert was first performed on January 19, 1968, and the Third Sacred Concert was at Westminster Abbey on October 24, 1973 (Steed 1993, 41, 54). In spite of musical, personal, and other problems, there is sufficient excellent music in each of these concerts to compensate for their weaknesses.[5]

It is important to note their relationship with Ellington's overall musical philosophy and persona. Ellington's music was inclusive, a music that Leonard (1987) termed one of "communitas," borrowing the term from Victor Turner. His band was like a family, even a church. Moreover, Ellington hated conflict and sought to avoid it on most occasions. He sincerely believed that love could overcome all obstacles but that if there were any it could not, they were not really worth overcoming.

His musical strengths, as well as weaknesses, flowed from that perspective. At times his music was simplistic; his lyrics could be amateurish. At other times, however, his eclecticism worked, and amazing things ensued. Combinations that others feared to explore revealed unexpected beauty and grandeur. Simplicity and enthusiasm worked more frequently than not. Ellington's belief in his musical vocation as a calling from God produced a high percentage of quality music, whether that music was specifically sacred or not. It is a pantheistic orientation, one common in the 1960s and 1970s but one that also influenced more traditional, established churches. Ellington lent his peculiar genius to something in the zeitgeist and turned it into a thing of beauty.

Ellington's love for things "beyond category" resonates with Lévi-Strauss's notion of anomalous mediating categories as dangerous and sacred (Lévi-Strauss 1967). These anomalous categories, according to Lévi-Strauss, partake of the categories that they mediate and consequently are neither fish nor fowl. They are dangerous and somehow pollute. Mary Douglas (1966) has treated of these categories of pollution, an idea Neil Leonard (1987) has applied to jazz itself.

Leonard (1987, 9–10) notes that Emile Durkheim, who influenced Douglas, indicated not only that there is a distinction between the sacred and the profane but between two kinds of sacredness. There is a sacredness "that produces social and moral order, health, and happiness," and there is a sacredness "that brings disorder, immorality, illness, and death. Though radically antagonistic, these two kinds of sacredness can be highly ambiguous because both stem from similar supernatural sources." Interestingly, however, these types of sacredness appear to be highly unstable, and each can resolve into the other.[6] The musical "purist" seeks to keep them separate. Even in the African American tradition there was a desire to keep the two traditions separate, as some opposition to Ellington's sacred concerts revealed.

There is, however, an older African tradition that understood the unity of the sacred. The variations work together to provide a harmonious whole. Each part both stands alone and yet takes on full meaning only within the context of the entire performance. This perspective is well illustrated in the work of the Nigerian musician Fela Anakulapi-Kuti (1938–97).

Fela was a musician who proclaimed himself "The Black President" and perceived his mission in life to be the restoration of the pride that the black man has had taken from him. He pursued his mission by conveying a spiritual message in his music, which unites every aspect of black music into each performance, including those aspects that white musicians have produced based on black forms. In a sense in his performance Fela added to Gregory Bateson's and Erving Goffman's concept of frames, turning frames into shifting things, ones that almost perpetually transformed themselves into one another. This house-of-mirror image of shifting frames is in keeping with the predominant perspective on African religious and philosophical thought that sees it as positing an ever-changing un-stable reality under the illusory permanent reality of everyday common sense. This skepticism of presented reality and a subsequent search for underlying structures is well-suited to African-derived musical performance. Fela expressed this concept well in an interview with me: "The music is spiritual. . . . I know the music is a gift for me, for the purpose of the emancipation of the black man. It's a spiritual gift. It's a spiritual message" (Anakulapi-Kuti 1989).

Therefore, the incorporation of all varieties of African-derived music is not accidental or haphazard. It served to convey his message of black pride. His point was the unity of black peoples everywhere. Thus, his shifting frames reflect Afri-can religion and philosophy. The manner in which one style of African-derived music melds into another defines their relationship through praxis, not mere dis-cussion. The central role of *jazz*, a word Fela disdains as did Ellington, is demon-strated in its being used as a mediating form. Finally, the continuous transforma-tion of material is also evocative of spiritual matters. Fittingly, the self-proclaimed black president and chief priest leads his people to a better land by invoking spiri-tual images and enacting them on the stage. His entire performance is ritual of a high order. It is a Creole performance that has the "that too" characteristic of all such performances (James Farris Thompson, personal communication).

What is true of Fela illuminates Ellington's mixture of styles and categories. It would be beneficial to explore Ellington's African roots more deeply and to in-vestigate his own reading in greater detail in relationship to his music (Hudson 1991). It is clear that Ellington's religion struck orthodox Christians as pantheistic and idiosyncratic (Steed 1993, 19; and Gensel 1992). His statement that he was "born in 1956 at the Newport Jazz Festival" (Hasse 1993, 322) was often cited but never fully explored. The religious connotations are often noted but the literal sense in which Ellington meant the term has been missed. He believed that somehow he had been literally reborn and called to a vocation.

Seen within the context of African American culture, Ellington's religious be-liefs and practices make perfect sense, even those "superstitious" aspects that so bothered his more traditionally orthodox son, Mercer (Ellington and Dance 1978, 111).[7] The continuity between the Cotton Club and the Cathedral is emphasized by Ellington's very African American philosophy and theology. His mixture of categories of the sacred and profane and various types of sacredness is an affirma-tion of both life and the continuous nature of that life, transcending categories of time and space.

ACKNOWLEDGMENTS

I wish to thank the staff of the Smithsonian Institution Duke Ellington Archives and the staff of the Library of Congress for their aid in facilitating this research.

NOTES

1. See, e.g., Ellington (1931, 15) and Ellington (1973/1976, 25–26). Ellington is quoted in an article carried in *PM* magazine (Dec. 9, 1945): "Religion helps my spirit of independence. . . . [It] helps me do things people call *daring*. For instance, say musicians just don't put in a ninth in a particular place, and we do it. Religion helps me. I guess it gives me the proper inflation when I need it" (Tucker 1993, 254). Steed (1993 and 1999) discusses the role of Ellington's spirituality in his music. She quotes Ellington's sister Ruth regarding the deeper meaning of his "jungle music" in expressing the "basic humanity" of people and the deep love Ellington had for humanity itself.

2. Stanley Dance's eulogy also makes this point: "Duke Ellington knew that what some called genius was really the exercise of gifts which stemmed from God. These gifts were those his Maker favoured. . . . [Duke] reached out to people with his music and drew them to himself" (quoted in "A King Celebration 2001").

3. Claude Lévi-Strauss referred frequently to these ambiguous categories, as has Mary Douglas. These are categories that are neither fish nor fowl and often betwixt and between, as Victor Turner names them. I will address these issues later in the essay.

4. The full text of Dance's eulogy can be found in Mercer Ellington (1978).

5. For in-depth critiques see Steed (1993, esp. 30–77). Steed also offers a detailed discussion of Ellington's theological heterodoxy and his overall influence on church music within the context of the period.

6. See Salamone 2009 and Salamone 1988 for fuller discussion of this concept.

7. For a similar view see Anderson 1995.

BIBLIOGRAPHY

Anakulapi-Kuti, Fela. 1989. Interview by Frank A. Salamone. May 27, Lagos, Nigeria.

Anderson, Paul A. 1995. "Ellington, Rap Music, and Cultural Difference." *Musical Quarterly* 79:172–206.

Crouch, Stanley. 1979. Interview with Sonny Greer. National Endowment for the Arts Jazz Oral History Interview Project. Institute of Jazz Studies, Rutgers University Library.

Dance, Stanley. 1970. Album notes to *Duke Ellington's Orchestral Works,* with Erich Kunzel conducting the Cincinnati Symphony. Decca, reissued by MCA Records, 1989.

Douglas, Mary 1966. *Purity and Danger.* New York: Routledge and Kegan Paul.

Ellington, Edward Kennedy. 1931. "The Duke Steps Out." *Rhythm,* March, 20–22.

———. 1973/1976. *Music Is My Mistress.* New York: Da Capo.

Ellington, Mercer, with Stanley Dance. 1978. *Duke Ellington in Person: An Intimate Memoir.* Boston: Houghton Mifflin.

Ellington, Ruth. 1993. Interview by Janna T. Steed. Jan. 7, New York City.

Faulkner, Anne Shaw. 1921. "Does Jazz Put the Sin in Syncopation?" *Ladies' Home Journal,* August, 16–34.

Gensel, John. 1992. Interview by Janna T. Steed. Nov. 22, New York City.

Giddens, Gary. 1993. "Gary Giddens on the Sacred Concerts." In Tucker, *The Duke Ellington Reader,* 375–78.

Goffman, Erving. 1974. *Frame Analysis.* New York: Harper and Row.

———. 1975. "In Those Days, as Told to Stanley Dance." Album notes, *Ellington Era, 1927–1940.* Vol. 2. Columbia Archive Series.

Hajdu, David. 1996. *Lush Life: A Biography of Billy Strayhorn.* New York: Farrar, Strauss, Giroux.

Hasse, John Edward. 1993. *Beyond Category: The Life and Genius of Duke Ellington.* New York: Simon and Schuster.

Hudson, Theodore R. 1991. "Duke Ellington's Literary Sources (with Appendices)." *American Music* 9:20–42.

"A King Celebration 2001: Composers." NPR online, www.npr.org/programs/specials/mlk2001/composers.html (accessed Oct. 28, 2009).

Leonard, Neil. 1987. *Jazz: Myth and Religion.* New York: Oxford University Press.

Lévi-Strauss, Claude. 1967. *The Savage Mind.* Chicago: University of Chicago Press.

Salamone, Frank A. 1988. "The Ritual of Jazz Performance." *Play & Culture* 1:85–104.

———. 2009. *The Culture of Jazz: Jazz as Critical Culture.* Lanham, MD: University Press of America.

Steed, Janna Tull. 1993. "Duke Ellington's Jazz Testament: The Sacred Concerts." Master's thesis. Yale University.

———. 1999. *Duke Ellington: A Spiritual Biography.* New York: Crossroad.

Tucker, Mark, ed. 1993. *The Duke Ellington Reader.* New York: Oxford University Press.

Zunser, Florence. 1930. Interview with Duke Ellington. *NY Evening Graphic Magazine* Dec. 27, 45.

PART II: Class and Place in Harlem

FOUR

"So the Girl Marries"

Class, the Black Press, and the Du Bois–Cullen Wedding of 1928

Jacqueline C. Jones

At 4 p.m. on Wednesday, April 4, 1928, Nina Yolande Du Bois, the only surviving child of the scholar and activist William Edward Burghardt Du Bois, boarded a special parlor car at Penn Station in Baltimore. Miss Du Bois traveled with several of her sixteen bridesmaids as she made her way to New York City, the site of her wedding to poet Countee Cullen. All teachers in the Baltimore public school system, the women were also members of the Mole, an exclusive African American women's club. Because of the prominence of the father of the bride-to-be and the universal praise for the groom's literary efforts, their nuptials promised to be the most significant social event of the Harlem Renaissance. Unfortunately, the spectacle of the wedding was followed by an unfulfilled honeymoon and a humiliatingly brief marriage. The Du Bois–Cullen wedding, held on April 9, 1928, offers an intimate portrait of New Negro society.

Countee and Yolande were the Charles and Diana of their time—tragically obedient and hopelessly mismatched. As Langston Hughes optimistically built his "temple for tomorrow," so did the leaders of the Harlem Renaissance. The future of the race needed exemplars, and the most promising, according to the bride's father, were produced with the marriage of Countee and Yolande.[1] Yet the potential that a union between Yolande and Countee presented was not and probably could not be brought to fruition. Alain Locke had announced the arrival of the New Negro three years earlier, and a celebration had yet to take place. A social gathering, one of historic significance, would solidify the presence of the New Negro in a way that no work of art could. Nina Yolande Du Bois and Countee Cullen fulfilled the need for visible exemplars of the New Negro. The intense interest of the African American press makes it possible to chart the relationship between Ms. Du Bois and Mr. Cullen and allows for an entree into the social world of the African American middle class during the Harlem Renaissance.

The focus of much of the scholarship on the Harlem Renaissance has been primarily on the public lives and artistic output of those involved. The Du Bois–Cullen wedding offers a look into the private world of the New Negro. Little is known about Nina Yolande Du Bois, and it is my sincere hope that this essay will inspire others to explore the contradictions of her life. Nina Yolande Du Bois was an appealing young woman who was inquisitive and fun-loving. She graduated from Fisk University in 1926, earned a master's degree from Columbia University, and had a long teaching career with the Baltimore public school system. Yet she is most often remembered as the daughter of W. E. B. Du Bois and as the wife of Countee Cullen.

Some close friends of the couple were puzzled about their relationship. Nathan Huggins found the marriage to be representative of the incongruities of the Harlem Renaissance itself:

> The Harlem intellectuals had been anxious to make those class distinctions which would mark them as different from their black brothers further down. So while proclaiming a new race consciousness, they had been wearing the clothes and using the manners of sophisticated whites, thereby earning the epithet "dicty niggers" from the very people they were supposed to be championing. When, for instance, W. E. B. Du Bois's daughter, Yolande, had married Countee Cullen, it had been billed as the marriage of the age. No expense had been spared to make it that. . . . It was a parody or travesty of ceremony . . . a sad pretense . . . made up by the same imaginations that had promoted the renaissance." (Huggins, 306)

Although Huggins and Langston Hughes proposed that class divisions marred the success of the movement, it is possible that colorism was a more important factor. One need only consider that Harold Jackman—a biracial aesthete model, teacher, and society figure—was chosen by Alain Locke to be the physical representation of the New Negro to question the movement's true definition of blackness.[2]

The African American elite traditionally used skin tone and education as two important criteria for membership. Andrew Billingsley argues that professional and social success for African Americans were closely linked to education and skin color. "The data also shows that representatives of old upper class families are much more likely to be highly educated for the professions . . . [and] are more likely to be light in complexion and to have grown up in nuclear families with strong fathers" (Billingsley, 129–30). More recently Lawrence Otis Graham has explored the relationship between class and color among the African American upper class and found similar results:

> Skin color has always played an important role in determining one's popularity, prestige, and mobility within the black elite. It is hard to find an upper-class black American family that has been well to do since the 1950s that has not endured family conversations on the virtues of "good hair, sharp features, and a nice complexion." . . . This is not to say that affluent blacks want to be white, but it certainly suggests that they have seen the benefits accorded to lighter skinned blacks with "whiter features"—who are hired more often, given better jobs, and perceived as less threatening. (377)

Clearly, given Cullen's dark complexion, his academic achievements and family background helped to make him an appropriate suitor. Countee Cullen received his undergraduate degree from New York University and his master's degree from Harvard University. A Guggenheim Fellowship allowed him to study in Paris beginning in the summer of 1928. His poetic success and social standing would, Dr. Du Bois hoped, provide the basis for a productive union with his daughter. Cullen, the adopted son of the Reverend Frederick Cullen and his wife, Carolyn, found himself squarely in the African American middle class. Rev. Cullen, pastor of the majestic Salem Methodist Episcopal Church, located in central Harlem on Seventh Avenue and 127th Street, was well known in social circles. His church was described as "the place of worship for Harlem's black elite" ("Many in Harlem's Easter Parade," 14). Countee's academic success at New York University and, later, at Harvard made him an attractive candidate for marriage.

Educational achievement and, if one merely glanced at the wedding photographs, skin color were clearly part of the stringent criteria for participation in the wedding party. It seemed as if Dr. Du Bois measured pedigree by educational achievement and the social status of one's parents. A list of Yolande's bridesmaids contained the names of the young women, the highest degree each had achieved, and the names of their alma maters. The members of the wedding party exemplified Du Bois's concept of the Talented Tenth: "The Negro race, like all races, is going to be saved by its exceptional men. The problem of education, then, among Negroes must first of all deal with the Talented Tenth; it is the problem of developing the Best of this race that they may guide the Mass away from the contamination and death of the Worst, in their own and other races" (Du Bois, "The Talented Tenth," 842).

A central element of Du Bois's concept of the Talented Tenth is the idea of self-sacrifice for the sake of the advancement of the race. This was just what Yolande did when she married Countee. Certainly, as David Levering Lewis has asserted, Cullen was a surrogate son for Du Bois, who foresaw the marriage as an opportunity to continue his lineage. "Probably no one present at Salem Methodist who knew Yolande thought her possessed of more than average intelligence, yet her father, who shared that opinion, believed that he had engineered the almost certain outcome that his grandchildren would be brilliant and well formed" (Lewis, *W. E. B. Du Bois*, 223). Du Bois's emphasis on the centrality of procreation is ironic as it is a lack of sex that dooms the relationship. Du Bois saw the wedding as the coming-out party (pun intended) for the New Negro: "It was not the mere marriage of a maiden. It was not simply the wedding of a fine young poet. It was the symbolic march of young and Black America. American, because there was Harvard, Columbia, Smith, Brown, Howard, Chicago, Syracuse, Penn and Cornell. There were three Masters of Arts and fourteen Bachelors. . . . But it was not simply conventional America—it had a dark and shimmering beauty all its own. . . . It was a new race; a new thought" (Du Bois, "So the Girl Marries," 208–9).

The issue of the Talented Tenth was not just political; it was personal for Du Bois. He sought to embody its characteristics and wanted his resistant daughter to do the same. Although she eventually capitulated, the process was difficult. Yolande had to be persuaded to attend college, and one got the distinct impression that her marriage to Countee Cullen was an attempt to appease her father. Although Du Bois's correspondence showed him to be a financially strained and exasperated father, he expressed his pride about the wedding in the June 1928 issue of the *Crisis*. Du Bois admitted that he could not control the cost of the wedding, in part because of Yolande's unyielding insistence on having sixteen bridesmaids. Suddenly her powerful and influential father was deflated in the presence of his daughter's strong will.

Often dismissed as the onetime wife of Countee Cullen and the daughter of W. E. B. Du Bois, Yolande is surprisingly silent in many histories of the Harlem Renaissance. Her voice can be found in her letters to Cullen, written from 1923 to 1930, and in her actions. In the letters Yolande referred to herself as a "cry baby," "inconsiderate," and "selfish," and she signed them "Lady." She was discreet, as if she expected others to have access to her correspondence. Yolande's strong personality did reveal itself in her demands for attention. She continually lived her life on her own terms, despite pleas from her parents to adhere to a more chaste mode of behavior, which they believed was expected of middle-class women.

In a particular instance that caused her parents considerable alarm, Yolande developed a relationship with a young man they believed to be unacceptable. In defiance to her parents' wishes she and Jimmie Lunceford, a popular fellow student at Fisk University, did not immediately separate. Du Bois was opposed to her union with the musician suitor and played a pivotal role in the demise of the relationship. Lunceford's biographer asserts that Du Bois's rejection of Lunceford fueled the young man's ambition: "Here Jimmie was in love, deeply, madly, deliriously, with the daughter of his and everybody's hero—only to be rudely embarrassed. It left a bitter spot in his heart and fueled his determination to show his worth to the whole world and Dr. William Edward Burghardt Du Bois in particular" (Determeyer, 22). The romance between Jimmie and Yolande plays a large role in Charles Smith's play about Countee and Yolande, *Knock Me a Kiss.*

Yet some try to rehabilitate Yolande's legacy. Smith's play offers an interpretation of the relationship between Yolande and Countee in which Yolande is depicted as being headstrong, sexual, and spoiled. Yolande is dating Countee and Jimmie Lunceford, a musician whom she loves dearly but who is from a lower social and economic class. Jimmie treats Yolande as a sensual woman. He asks her to have faith in his future success, but she is facing subtle pressure from her father to make a proper match with Countee. Jimmie forces Yolande to choose. "I'm sick of sniffing up behind you like a little dog while you flash your precious little tail all over town. I'm sick of begging you, I'm sick of waiting for you while you try to figure out what you gonna do" (1.6.60). The relationship ends when Yolande decides to marry Countee. Interestingly, Smith's play does not depict the wedding but rather focuses on its dismally brief aftermath. Yolande regrets her marriage and yearns for Lunceford's passion and spontaneity.

In the play Countee admits to Dr. Du Bois his inability to influence his wife. "You know Yolande. Once she makes up her mind to do something, there's nothing I can do" (2.2.69). Du Bois pressured the couple to consider the significance of their union. "This marriage involves more than you and Yolande. The future of practically every Negro in this country is enmeshed in your marriage" (2.2.70). Du Bois was rightly concerned about the coverage of the couple by the African American press. Smith implies that the relationship between Countee Cullen and Harold Jackman was more than friendship. When Yolande decides to go to France earlier than planned, Countee tells her, "I need to spend this time with Harold alone" (2.4.81). He later compares his relationship with Harold to Yolande's relationship with Jimmie Lunceford. *Knock Me a Kiss* is a valuable dramatization of the private lives of Countee Cullen and Yolande Du Bois and ultimately offers a portrait of New Negro society as being overly concerned with appearance.

Yolande was naturally aggressive and passionate, and her parents were powerless to control these inclinations. They had allowed her to be inundated with attention from the Atlanta University community during her childhood, and Du Bois often described a parental relationship in which Yolande had the power. To gain some control over his daughter, Du Bois sent her to Bedale, an English boarding school, so that she would return "armed with manners and knowledge to fight American race hate and insult" (Du Bois, "So the Girl Marries," 193). It was a struggle to get Yolande to agree to attend college for a year and to delay getting married. He described her years at Fisk University in Nashville as "four years of vague uneasiness with flashes of hectic and puzzling vacations" (ibid.). In his letters and published work he reinforced the image of Yolande as spoiled and revealed his lack of interest in parenting. Du Bois described himself as an indulgent and preoccupied parent who was "busy with larger matters and weightier problems" during his daughter's childhood (ibid.).

The powerful and influential father was deflated in the presence of his daughter's strong will. Du Bois eventually agreed not only to an evening wedding but also to the sixteen bridesmaids. The wedding plans revealed the importance of social status and educational achievement. Du Bois saw the wedding as a public acknowledgment of the arrival of the New Negro.

It is not surprising that Yolande Du Bois and Countee Cullen were introduced in July 1923 by Cullen's best friend, Harold Jackman, the most important unknown figure of the Harlem Renaissance. Jackman, a teacher and model known as Handsome Harold, was a well-connected social figure in New York City. Arna Bontemps labeled Countee and Harold the "'David and Jonathan' of the Harlem Twenties" (12), thus memorializing their deep friendship while making subtle reference to their homosexuality. Jackman's central role in the development and demise of the relationship between Countee and Yolande was an indication of the depth of his friendship with Cullen and his influence on some of the major events of the period.

In July 1923 Harold wrote Countee concerning Yolande Du Bois, and apparently Harold's comments piqued Cullen's interests because his responding letter included a request for more information. "Tell me more of Yolande Du Bois. Is she in any way brilliant?" (Cullen to Harold Jackman, July 20, 1923). Evidently the initial attraction between Countee and Yolande was mutual. In his excitement Cullen wrote Jackman and Jessie Fauset about his interest in Yolande and received an encouraging response from Fauset.

The next month, August 1923, Yolande contacted Harold to inquire about Countee's first impression of her. She had been wearing an apron and had her hair in braids when they met, so she feared that she had not made a good impression. The letter was indicative of Yolande's self-deprecating nature. She frequently pointed out and apologized for her perceived inadequacies. Being the only surviving offspring of the best-known African American scholar clearly affected Yolande. She also seemed to fear that she didn't meet the expectations that others had of her because of her father's prominence. Yolande conceded to Harold's urging that she read Edna St. Vincent Millay's poetry, which he mailed her. She went on to downplay her own intellectual abilities to Harold: "I am glad you've found me different enough to think my friendship worthwhile and I hope you won't be disappointed because I'm afraid I'm just a very ordinary frivolous girl" (Y. Du Bois to Jackman, Aug. 6, 1923).

Despite her protestations Yolande's impressions of both Cullen and Jackman were telling. She wrote that she found Cullen to be "young" and that she wasn't surprised to learn that Cullen and Jackman were friends "because you are alike in that way" (Y. Du Bois to Jackman, Aug. 6, 1923). Clearly she was an astute judge of character, yet she seemed to hide behind a kind of pseudoinnocence and lack of self-esteem. Although Harold initially encouraged the relationship between Countee and Yolande, something caused him to change his opinion of her. Except for their initial correspondence I could not locate other epistles between Harold and Yolande. Perhaps her emotional neediness and her willingness to discuss her marriage with members of the press made her an unattractive partner for Countee in Harold's estimation.

Yolande saw the emotional depth of Countee's and Harold's friendship. Scholars, most notably Eric Garber, have maintained that Harold and Countee were lovers, yet an extensive review of the correspondence between the two men and others provides no support for such an assertion. The two men met in high school, and they had a common interest in travel, art, literature, and theater. They also shared a deep sense of decorum and a fierce adherence to privacy. Harold often inquired about Cullen's "special friends," and his primary concern was for Countee's happiness. As a schoolteacher and the primary supporter of his mother, brother, and sisters, Harold Jackman was financially unable to travel except during the summers. His familial responsibilities did not affect his incredibly active social life, however. Operas, theatrical productions, musical performances, and art exhibits sustained Jackman while his friends were abroad. He also kept them informed of these events through his lively letters. Cullen, like many Harlem Renaissance figures, depended on Jackman for his critical assessments of art, theater, and literature, research help, his knowledge of the social and artistic circles, and, most importantly, his friendship.

Yolande was the more aggressive partner in the relationship, as her letters reveal that Countee seemed to pay her little, or simply not enough, attention. Her correspondence with him was filled with appreciation for his taking the time to write her, pleas for letters, requests for visits, or some sign that he was thinking of her. She sometimes wrote him twice a day. In a May 1926 letter Yolande told Countee of her longing to see him, and she admonished, "Don't disappoint me again" (Y. Du Bois to Cullen, May 16, 1926). She addressed Cullen as "dearest" and "beloved" and signed her letters "all my love." David Levering Lewis asserts that Yolande's emotional neediness grew out of her sometimes strained relationship with her distant parents (*W. E. B. Du Bois*, 107). Her parents were no different from many others of her social class who expected their children to marry a socially and intellectually suitable partner. The pressure for both Countee and Yolande to marry well was a considerable factor in their union. Indeed, gossips suggested that the couple *only* married as a result of pressure from their families ("Cullens Plan Divorce," 1).

Why did Cullen, a gay/bisexual man, not only marry a woman but do so in such an ostentatious fashion? In her essay on Richmond Barthe, Margaret Rose Vendryes seems to suggest that Cullen should have felt little pressure to marry: "Common knowledge dictates that no God-fearing black man could be queer, therefore, a religious black man need not construct his closet—it is ready-made" (277). Cullen's religious practice did not protect him from rumors about his relationship with Jackman when they left for Europe a few months after Cullen's marriage. George Chauncey offers a persuasive reason for the marriage: "Countee Cullen, who had begun to identify himself as gay before he turned twenty and was involved in several long-term relationships with men, twice married women in search of respectability" (265). Cullen's inherently conservative nature was perhaps another reason for his marriages. The demands of his public and private lives necessitated a "cover" of some sort. Yet one could argue that Cullen's flourishing literary career produced the kind of acceptance that he sought, but his role in New York society was secured with his marriages. Clearly, given his father's standing in the religious community and his own piety, Cullen was "safe," but he did not have the social standing that a high-profile marriage ensured. In her study of marriage in African American women's texts, Ann DuCille explores the critiques of marriage in the novels of Jessie Fauset, Nella Larsen, and Zora Hurston and offers a plausible explanation for the need both Yolande and Countee share for an appropriate match: "Marriage . . . becomes instead the symbol of material achievement [and] . . . serves as the focal point of at times biting critiques of bourgeois black society and so-called middle class values" (87).

Intelligence and wit were important qualities for a prospective partner for the well-educated poet. Just as important was Yolande's pedigree. A rising New Negro required more than artistic talent; social status was also desired, and that was often gained through marriage. Langston Hughes, Claude McKay, Zora Hurston, and Wallace Thurman proved to be disappointments in this arena, as Aaron Douglas and Arna Bontemps were among the few married members of the New Negro movement.

Yolande and Countee were engaged in December 1927. Correspondence between Countee Cullen, W. E. B. Du Bois, and Yolande Du Bois suggested that the two men planned the wedding with some input from Yolande. Du Bois, a frequent traveler, and Countee both resided in New York City, whereas Yolande lived in Baltimore (and would continue to do so after the wedding). Yolande Du Bois determined the number of bridesmaids, the time of the wedding, the location, and who would perform the ceremony. Despite her father's constant pleas to limit the number of bridesmaids to five or, at most, ten, Yolande succeeded in having sixteen. Her father begged her to consider the financial burden of transporting the bridesmaids and providing bouquets for them, yet she refused to yield. Cullen's ten ushers included a white high school classmate, as well as prominent figures in the arts, such as Langston Hughes, Arna Bontemps, and Edward Perry. Harold Jackman served as Countee's best man, a role he would also perform at Cullen's second wedding in 1940.

There were many lavish events surrounding the wedding, which was hailed as the "grand social, literary and cultural affaire de coeur" ("Society"). The bridesmaids were treated to luncheons, suppers, and bridge parties. Even the results of the bridge parties were reported. Harold Jackman hosted a stag party for the groomsmen at the Dark Tower. Later, the bridesmaids left New York, boarding a train at Pennsylvania Station, where they were sent off with a shower of confetti.

Because the wedding took place on the Monday after Easter, the couple used the Easter decorations that remained in the church. In addition to being filled with flowers, the church was also filled with people. Much was made of the presence of white guests as an indication of the importance of the event. As with Locke's New Negro, the wedding was compared to European models.[3] Apparently Hughes's concern about the "racial mountain" went unheeded. Despite Locke's view that the New Negro no longer wished to imitate white society and took pride in his self-respect, the true sign of the event's significance in the eyes of many was the fact that it was covered by the white press. Articles about the wedding appeared in the *Baltimore Sun,* the *New York Times,* the *World,* the *Journal of Commerce,* the *Providence (RI) Journal,* and the *Dayton Ohio News,* among other publications. Guests hailed from the New York metropolitan areas, forty-eight states, and five countries on two continents.

The wedding and reception were the source of much anxiety for the parents of both the bride and the groom. Du Bois was concerned with the rising expenses associated with the event. The week prior to the wedding the *New York Amsterdam News* ran a headline under Yolande's photograph proclaiming that five thousand people would attend the wedding ceremony. There were actually only twelve hundred invited guests, but three thousand people arrived at the church. Pleas for invitations from Rev. Cullen's congregation led him to renounce responsibility for the wedding: "This is not my wedding! And it isn't Mrs. Cullen's wedding. . . . I am not getting married and Mrs. Cullen is not getting married! So, if there is any member of the Church who feels that he or she has been overlooked in the issuing of invitations, it isn't my fault. Don't blame me!" (Murphy, 4).

Determined attendees began arriving four hours before the ceremony was scheduled to start. Baltimoreans, feeling left out, accused Dr. Du Bois of treating them like "country cousins" for holding the wedding in New York City rather than Baltimore (Matthews). A columnist for the *Afro* asserted that, unlike New Yorkers, Baltimoreans would have acted appropriately. Amid rumors of the police being called, it was reported that two female attendees came close to physically fighting over a piece of left-over wedding cake ("Row over Bride's Cake"). It was the pageantry of the event that attracted much interest.

Countee and Yolande exchanged gifts of jewelry, a platinum diamond bracelet for her and a diamond stud for him. Du Bois presented his daughter with a string of pearls for the occasion. Accounts of the wedding focused on the pomp of the event and its lavishness. The bridesmaids were given sterling silver pins, and the groomsmen received stick pins. The wedding gifts were on display at the Du Bois home.

Despite the expense of the wedding and reception, Du Bois eventually saw the pomp and circumstance as an emblem of the progress of African Americans. He highlighted the nuptials in the June 1928 issue of the *Crisis*. His article "So the Girl Marries" was accompanied by a full-page photo of the bride and photos of the wedding party. More than the proud father, Du Bois was the prophet of the New Negro movement. Lurking beneath the pomp, however, were suspicions that the marriage was doomed.

Every detail of the Du Bois–Cullen wedding was covered by the African American press. The *Baltimore Afro American* (the *Afro*) led the coverage with its numerous articles on the minutiae of the event. With the headline "Cullen Took No Chance on Getting Marriage License Late," the paper reported that Cullen procured the marriage license four days before the wedding ceremony. Gwendolyn Bennett even mentioned the wedding in her "Ebony Flute" column in *Opportunity*. Although Edward Perry noted that reporters from the *New York Times*, the *Herald-Tribune*, the Associated Press, and a Spanish newspaper were present at the ceremony, African American newspapers gave the wedding the most attention. Most assessments of the wedding, such as Langston Hughes's in his autobiography *The Big Sea*, focused on its lavishness.

The most humorous account of the wedding appeared in the *Pittsburgh Courier* and was written by Edward Perry, an actor, writer, and close friend of the groom. Perry's long description of the event is particularly memorable because of his thoroughness and his subtle humor. Perry's standing as a member of Harlem's elite gay community lurked beneath his observations and served to provide a deep sense of sarcasm and irony to his commentary. Taking into account Alden Reimonenq's assertion that Cullen and Perry "were lovers in the late twenties and early thirties before Cullen took his French lovers" (157), one sensed Perry's true feelings in his review of the wedding. Cullen was described as the "noted and brilliant young poet," and the wedding was labeled "one of the most brilliant events in the annals of Negro society"; Perry emphasized Cullen's lack of emotion during the ceremony: "Although both the principals were thrilled over the event, Miss Du Bois was more responsive to the occasion than the gallant young groom." Ironically, the bride merited only one paragraph, in which Perry merely detailed her attire. Despite his description of Yolande as a "beautiful young bride," he went on to note that "the groom did not kiss the bride" and that "there was no excitement of any kind." He was perhaps alluding to the lack of interruptions to the ceremony. He couldn't help noting that "the groom very willingly kissed several of the young ladies."

The honeymoon played a large role in the myth of Harold Jackman's role in the demise of the Du Bois–Cullen marriage. Despite rumors and misleading scholarship, Harold Jackman did not accompany Countee Cullen on either of his two honeymoons. The first honeymoon took place just after the ceremony and foretold the fate of the marriage. The *Afro* proclaimed that "Mrs. Cullen and her husband rode in separate autos on their Atlantic City honeymoon, while friends gasped in amazement" ("Cullens Plan Divorce"). The Cullens traveled together during the week following their wedding. They visited Atlantic City and then Philadelphia, where Cullen, an editor at *Opportunity*, was obligated to attend the Urban League conference. From Philadelphia the couple journeyed to Great Barrington, Massachusetts, the bride's father's birthplace. Much to the surprise of their friends, the trip ended early; and by April 16, 1928, Yolande Cullen was back at work in Baltimore, and Countee had returned to Manhattan. They visited each other on weekends but continued to live apart until they reunited in Paris in August.

The second honeymoon was scheduled to begin at the end of June 1928; Countee and Yolande initially planned to sail to France together, but there were complications. On May 11, 1928, Countee wrote Dr. Du Bois for advice about the travel arrangements. Rev. Cullen would pay for a portion of Countee's fare if they were to travel to France together at the end of June. Much is made of the fact that Yolande did not leave for Europe in June 1928 along with Countee, Rev. Cullen, and Harold Jackman. Yolande decided to go to Europe in August, as she could not be ready to travel by the end of June. She also wanted Countee to upgrade her travel arrangements as her father had done in the past. Because Countee, his father, and Harold had traveled abroad before, this trip was not unusual. The myth that only Harold Jackman accompanied Countee on his honeymoon perhaps was created on the occasion of the divorce. In a front-page article about the divorce, the *Baltimore Afro American* misstated the facts about the honeymoon and misspelled Yolande's name ("Cullens Apart").

Harold and Countee traveled from Paris to Marseilles and then to Algeria. Amusingly, they dressed alike for the trip and even wore matching berets. Harold left France in August just before Yolande's arrival. As a teacher, Jackman had to prepare for the upcoming school year. Yolande addressed the rumor in a front-page article in the *Baltimore Afro American:* "We were married in April, as you know, and Mr. Cullen did go right on to Paris with Harold Jackman . . . because Mr. Jackman was going right at that time on his summer vacation and Mr. Cullen was going to begin his year's work. He wanted to travel a while without being bothered" ("Cullens Not to Seek Divorce"). Why Yolande would characterize her presence with her husband as a bother was certainly a mystery or perhaps just another indication of her canniness.

Fall 1928 found Yolande and Countee living together in Paris, and it was there that the marriage ended. The marriage couldn't have been helped by Harold's input and by the constant coverage by the African American press. When Yolande was seen in public without her wedding ring, the event was given front-page status. By the end of November 1928 Jackman was strongly encouraging Cullen to end the union, saying, "I can see that you two aren't going to 'hit' it no matter how many tears are shed and promises made" (Jackman to Cullen, Nov. 29, 1928). On January 3, 1929, Jackman urged Cullen, who was living apart from his wife, to secure his freedom before he returned to the United States: "So the inevitable has come about! Well, well, well, I didn't think it would be so soon really. Of course the Negroes in America have had it out for a long time. It won't surprise many of them when they learn about it. I don't blame you all the same. You might as well break now and live in peace for the rest of the time you are going to be in Europe than go through a 'more exquisite hell'" (Jackman to Cullen, Jan. 3, 1929).

Yolande attributed their separation to her mother's arrival in Paris in February 1929 and her own prolonged illness. Yet Countee and Yolande separated in October or November of 1928, long before her mother's visit. Dr. Du Bois requested that Countee "keep" Yolande until her mother could arrive. Yolande remained open to a reconciliation but left the matter to Countee to decide (Y. Du Bois to Cullen, April 22, 1929).

Owing to the incessant interest from the black press, the Cullens had a public life and a private life. In public they were amicable, yet they spent much of their time living in separate apartments. It was during this period that Yolande wrote to her father that she had never loved Countee but had instead admired him greatly. She also revealed the true reason for the collapse of the marriage. In his article "Strange Fruits: Rethinking the Gay Twenties" Mason Stokes addresses the effect of Cullen's homosexuality on his relationship with Yolande. Stokes argues that Cullen, by not identifying himself as a homosexual, hides behind a veil of heterosexuality: "By insisting on the language of abnormality rather than identity—of pathology rather than newly liberated homosexuality—Countee and Yolande continue to tell a heterosexual story, though it is a heterosexual story with a twist" (71).

In early March 1929 the *Afro American* carried a front-page headline announcing, "Cullens Plan Divorce: Love Is Cold." The article was full of details, some true and some humorously false. Almost every story about Yolande and Countee included a reference to their nuptials. Of particular interest in the *Afro* account was the characterization of Yolande and Countee. They were described as the "only children of their respective parents and are spoiled" ("Cullens Plan Divorce"). Surprisingly, the article asserted that "Cullen is said to have a girl in the U.S.A. whom he really loves." Clearly friends of the couple provided much of the information as they were quoted as saying that Yolande and Countee did not travel together during their honeymoon and that "they married more to please their parents than to please themselves" ("Cullens Plan Divorce").

By early May 1929 the news was that the Cullens continued to live apart, and Yolande Cullen had ceased to wear her wedding ring. The *Baltimore Afro American* led the coverage with a front-page story titled "Cullens Apart; Bride Removes Wedding Ring." The subtitles of the article left no question about the causes of the disunion. "Poet Leaves Yolande Du Bois and Ma-in-Law in Paris, and Flits to London. MANY STORIES FLY. Paris Recalls Groom Came Abroad with Best Man" (May 4, 1929). The article was seemingly written with the cooperation of one of the parties or at least the aid of their friends.

Yolande and Mrs. Du Bois remained in Paris until August 1929, when they returned to New York City. Mrs. Cullen went to Baltimore the following month, where she attempted to counter the many published rumors by granting an interview to the *Baltimore Afro American* (headline: "Cullens Not to Seek Divorce"). Mrs. Cullen denied removing her wedding ring but suggested that she might do so in the future. She gave the impression that she was in control of the fate of her marriage. She also noted that Edward Perry and Rev. Cullen remained in Paris after she and her mother left in August 1929.

The divorce was negotiated by Cullen and his father-in-law, with Harold Jackman being informed of its progress through timely missives from Cullen. In December 1929 Cullen wrote Du Bois to inform him that Yolande would be notified of the divorce in February 1930. The divorce decree, granted by a French court, stated that Mrs. Cullen found that Mr. Cullen had an "independent and fickle nature" and that he abandoned her. It was gentlemanly of Cullen to acknowledge legal responsibility for the demise of his marriage. His affection for Yolande was also clear in the manner in which he handled the divorce and in the poems that he inscribed to her. "Sonnet to Yolande," "Brown Boy to Brown Girl," and "One Day We Played a Game (Yolande: Her Poem)" all showed the tenderness and disappointment that Cullen experienced during their relationship.

Cullen returned to New York City in late 1930 and, with Jackman's assistance, secured his teaching certification and began working as a French teacher in the public school system. Cullen most notably taught French to novelist, essayist, and playwright James Baldwin at DeWitt Clinton High School. Cullen's only novel, *One Way to Heaven*, was published in 1932. Surprisingly, Countee Cullen married Ida Mae Roberson on September 27, 1940. The couple met through Ida's brother. The ceremony was performed by Rev. Cullen at his home, and Harold Jackman was once again Cullen's best man. Edward Perry also attended the brief ceremony. Cullen's second marriage, seemingly a happy one, lasted until his death in January 1946. Mrs. Ida Cullen was the executor of her husband's estate, but Harold Jackman was given control over Cullen's correspondence. On her death Ida Cullen (who remarried in 1953 to Robert Cooper) left instructions to protect Cullen's literary legacy.

Yolande returned to Baltimore in August 1929 and resumed her position as a teacher of English and history in the Baltimore City public school system. She was known for her unique sense of style. Students admired her and saw her as an important historical figure. "As his [Cullen's] wife and also being daughter of Dr. W. E. B. Du Bois . . . she was to us a direct link to our history" (Phillips).

One of the more detailed sources of information about Yolande was her published obituary, written by her father. Du Bois briefly mentioned Yolande's personal life. She married Arnett Williams in 1932, and they divorced in 1936. Her father noted that "she married a second time, a student of whom I did not choose, but bowed to her wish and helped him through Lincoln [University]. There was one daughter and then divorce" (Du Bois, "Du Bois, 93, Writes Daughter's Obituary"). The brevity and tone of Du Bois's remarks left no doubt about his feelings concerning Mr. Williams. Yolande's daughter is Du Bois Williams, a former professor at Xavier University. Known as Mrs. Williams, Yolande Du Bois Cullen Williams appears to have had a very contented life during her later years.

After providing enormous assistance to Carl Van Vechten as he built the James Weldon Johnson Memorial Collection at Yale, Harold Jackman established a collection of Negro memorabilia at Atlanta University (now Clark Atlanta University) in 1942. The holdings of the collection are on par with the holdings of the

James Weldon Johnson Memorial Collection at Yale University. After Cullen's death, in 1946, the name of the collection was changed to the Countee Cullen Memorial Collection. Jackman continued to teach and model in New York City, where he lived with his younger sister Ivie until his death on July 8, 1961, while vacationing in Maine. The *New York Amsterdam News* announced his death with the headline "The King Is Dead!" that referenced Jackman's customary role as the king of the New York Urban League's Beaux Arts Ball. His sister had the name of the collection changed to the Countee Cullen/Harold Jackman Memorial Collection.

Countee Cullen, Yolande Du Bois, and Harold Jackman are still intertwined after all these years and are essential to any study of the Harlem Renaissance. Looking beyond the myths regarding their relationship, readers are invited into a cloistered class-conscious world of Harlem Renaissance insiders. We learn about the heavy burdens of obligation and legacy, the demands of social class, and the color and class politics of the New Negro society. The wedding of Yolande Du Bois and Countee Cullen serves as a cautionary tale of the sacrifice of love for the price of social status.

NOTES

1. W. E. B. Du Bois's June 1928 essay "So the Girl Marries" chronicles the wedding preparations and what Du Bois saw as its significance.

2. See Winold Reiss's portrait of Harold Jackman, "A College Lad," in the March 1925 special edition of the *Survey Graphic*.

3. Locke compares the movement in Harlem to those in Dublin and Prague (*The New Negro*, 7).

BIBLIOGRAPHY

Billingsley, Andrew. *Black Families in White America*. Englewood Cliffs, NJ: Prentice-Hall, 1968.

Bontemps, Arna. "The Awakening: A Memoir." In *The Harlem Renaissance Remembered*, 1–26. New York: Dodd, Mead, 1972.

Chauncey, George. *Gay New York: Gender, Urban Culture, and the Makings of the Gay Male World, 1890–1940*. New York: Basic Books, 1994.

Cullen, Countee. Letter to Harold Jackman. July 20, 1923. Countee Cullen Collection, Beinecke Rare Book and Manuscript Library, Yale University.

"Cullens Apart; Bride Removes Wedding Ring." *Baltimore Afro American,* May 4, 1929.

"Cullens Not to Seek Divorce." *Baltimore Afro American,* Sept. 21, 1929.

"Cullens Plan Divorce: Love Is Cold." *Baltimore Afro American,* March 9, 1929.

Determeyer, Eddy. *Rhythm Is Our Business: Jimmie Lunceford and the Harlem Express.* Ann Arbor: University of Michigan Press, 2006.

Du Bois, William Edward Burghardt. "Du Bois, 93, Writes Daughter's Obituary." *Baltimore Afro American,* March 18, 1961.

———. "So the Girl Marries." *Crisis,* June 1928, 192–93, 207–9.

———. "The Talented Tenth." In *Writings / W. E. B. Du Bois,* 842–61. New York: Library of America, 1986.

Du Bois, Yolande. Letter to Countee Cullen. May 16, 1926. Countee Cullen Collection, Beinecke Rare Book and Manuscript Library, Yale University.

———. Letter to Countee Cullen. April 22, 1929. Countee Cullen Collection, Beinecke Rare Book and Manuscript Library, Yale University.

———. Letter to Harold Jackman. Aug. 6, 1923. Countee Cullen/Harold Jackman Memorial Collection, Clark Atlanta University.

DuCille, Ann. *The Coupling Convention: Sex, Text, and Tradition in Black Women's Fiction.* New York: Oxford University Press, 1993.

Graham, Lawrence Otis. *Our Kind of People: Inside America's Black Upper Class.* New York: HarperPerennial, 1999.

Huggins, Nathan. *Harlem Renaissance.* New York: Oxford University Press, 1971.

Jackman, Harold. Letter to Countee Cullen. Nov. 29, 1928. Countee Cullen Papers, Amistad Research Center, Tulane University.

———. Letter to Countee Cullen. Jan. 3, 1929. Countee Cullen Papers, Amistad Research Center, Tulane University.

Lewis, David Levering. *W. E. B. Du Bois.* Vol. 2, *The Fight for Equality and the American Century, 1919–1963.* New York: Holt, 2000.

Locke, Alain, ed. *The New Negro.* 1925. New York: Albert and Charles Boni, 1986.

"Many in Harlem's Easter Parade." *Baltimore Afro American,* April 14, 1928.

Matthews, Ralph. "In Darker Baltimore." *Baltimore Afro American,* April 21, 1928.

Murphy, D. A. "1,200 Invited, 3,000 Attended Du Bois Wedding." *New York Amsterdam News,* April 14, 1928.

Perry, Edward. "Yolonde [sic] Du Bois Becomes Bride of Countee Cullen." *Pittsburgh Courier,* April 14, 1928.

Phillips. B. M. "She Remembers Yolande." *Baltimore Afro American,* March 26, 1961.

"Poet Leaves Yolande Du Bois and Ma-in-Law in Paris, and Flits to London. MANY STORIES FLY. Paris Recalls Groom Came Abroad with Best Man." *Baltimore Afro American,* May 4, 1929.

Reimonenq, Alden. "Countee Cullen's Uranian 'Soul Windows.'" *Journal of Homosexuality* 26, no. 2/3 (1993): 143–65.

"Row over Bride's Cake." *Baltimore Afro American,* April 14, 1928.

Smith, Charles. *Knock Me a Kiss.* Woodstock, IL: Dramatic Publishing, 2003.

"Society." *New York Amsterdam News,* March 24, 1928.

Stokes, Mason. "Strange Fruits: Rethinking the Gay Twenties." *Transition* 92 (2002): 56–79.

Tate, Claudia. *Domestic Allegories of Political Desire: The Black Heroine's Text at the Turn of the Century.* New York: Oxford University Press, 1992.

Vendryes, Margaret Rose. "The Lives of Richmond Barthe." In *The Greatest Taboo,* ed. Delroy Constantine-Simms, 274–87. New York: Alyson Books, 2000.

FIVE

The Meaning and Significance of Southern Tradition in Rudolph Fisher's Stories

Aija Poikāne-Daumke

n a 1933 radio interview the African American physician and writer Rudolph Fisher said, "I intend to write whatever interests me. But if I should be fortunate enough to become known as Harlem's interpreter, I should be very happy" (quoted in McCluskey, xxxix). Between 1925 and 1935 Fisher published fifteen short stories, two novels—*The Walls of Jericho* and *The Conjure Man Dies*—and a number of journalistic pieces and scientific articles. Familiar with the complexities of black urban culture in the 1920s, he used Harlem and its codes of behavior as a backdrop for his fiction. In his short stories Fisher shows his love for Harlem, but he does not idealize it. He demonstrates that racism and exploitation are not limited to the South. While Harlem may offer greater freedom and social equality to African Americans, it also engages in racism in more subtle, often even undetectable, ways. Additionally, Fisher reveals a new form of racism: the prejudice of black against black, thus undermining the idea of Harlem as a race capital based on the principles of racial unity. He also elucidates the animosity between African Americans and the immigrants from the West Indies.

The latter conflict has been analyzed in more detail by Margaret Perry, who remarks that "there were several reasons for this real and sometimes imagined dislike between the two groups. To many American blacks it seemed that the West Indians were arrogant about their British background, and many West Indians, like Cyril Sebastian Best in 'Ringtail,' lorded this so-called advantage over American blacks. Also, it appeared that the West Indians who immigrated to the United States fared better economically" (Perry, 5). Perry suggests that the conflict between African Americans and West Indians arose not only because the two communities differed in size and shape, as well as in culture and history, but also because they competed against each other for wealth and position in Harlem.

In his story "Ringtail" Fisher depicts African Americans named Punch, Meg Minor, Red, and Eight-Ball, who harbor feelings of resentment toward the immigrants from the West Indies. Red, for example, says, " 'There ain't nothin' I do like about 'em. They're too damn conceited. They're too aggressive. They talk funny. They look funny—I can tell one the minute I see him. They're always startin' an argument an' they always want the last word. An' there's too many of 'em here' " (McCluskey, 23).

Obviously, Fisher's African American characters believe in their superiority; at the same time, though, they feel insecure about their positions in Harlem. Thus Fisher suggests that if African Americans were truly superior to the immigrants from the West Indies, they would not discuss the presence of West Indians in Harlem so vehemently and view it as a threat to their welfare and success.

Thus, African Americans are afraid that West Indians may succeed in Harlem while they themselves are forced to face poverty and unemployment. Punch, Meg Minor, Red, and Eight-Ball realize that they cannot compete with white Americans because of racism and segregation, but they can and must compete with the West Indian immigrants, whom they tend to view as intruders attempting to usurp the authority in Harlem.

Interestingly enough, West Indians also feel superior to African Americans because of their "British background." The narrator introduces the West Indian immigrant Cyril Sebastian Best: "His self-esteem, his craftiness, his contentiousness, his acquisitiveness, all became virtues. To him self-improvement meant nothing but increasing these virtues, certainly not eliminating or modifying any of them. He became fond of denying that he was 'colored,' insisting that he was a 'British subject,' hence by implication unquestionably superior to any merely American Negro. And when two years of contact convinced him that the American Negro was characteristically neither self-esteemed nor crafty nor contentious nor acquisitive, in short was quite virtueless, his conscious superiority became down-right contempt" (McCluskey, 18).

The description of Cyril Sebastian Best reveals his reluctance to identify himself as a black person because in his eyes "blackness" becomes something undesirable and unpleasant. This might suggest that Best experiences a powerful identity con-flict, but this is not the case. The narrator of the story suggests that Best denies his "blackness" because he does not want to be associated with African Americans. According to Best, African Americans are unworthy people, unable to succeed in anything. Best "dreams big"; he wants to open a restaurant that will bring him prosperity and wealth, but he already sees himself as having made great strides, for he has managed to secure employment as an elevator operator in a respectable apartment building.

Here the narrator shows that Cyril Sebastian Best's perception of reality has been distorted. He does not realize that his appearance and his outfits may seem comic and even ridiculous to other people; he is simply convinced of his "personal excellence" (McCluskey, 18). Certainly, Best's understanding of his "personal ex-cellence" is based on his British background and on his "achievements." Ironically, he never contemplates the fact that white Americans would not perceive him as a British subject.

What becomes clear is that Cyril Sebastian Best's racist prejudices against African Americans arise because of his lack of knowledge, which in turn is gener-ated by his unwillingness to get to know them. Although Best highly values his British heritage, he seems to have forgotten the racism and discrimination prac-ticed by the British in the Caribbean islands. Sadly, neither African Americans nor immigrants from the West Indies seem to realize that they may, indeed, share a common experience—an experience of racism and survival in predominantly white societies.

The subject of the prejudice of black against black leads us to another interest-ing and challenging theme in Fisher's short stories. He emphasizes the importance of rural southern culture that is being preserved in Harlem by the immigrants from the South. Although Fisher never portrays the agrarian South in his prose, the region still plays an important role in our understanding of his work. His short story "The South Lingers On," which consists of five sketches, serves as an extension of the South. Indeed, the title of this story signifies both the presence and significance of rural southern culture in Harlem.

Although Fisher may value southern culture as something precious to the cul-tural scene in Harlem, he also demonstrates that northern blacks view it as "backward" and "primitive." A similar thought is expressed by the historian James R. Grossman: "In the North, even among African Americans, Southerners encountered a contempt for rural Southern culture" (Grossman, 395).

In her study *Looking for Harlem: Urban Aesthetics in African American Literature,* Maria Balshaw talks about Rudolph Fisher's work: "The backdrop to his work is the ongoing New Negro argument about what it means to be black, modern and urban" (30). Balshaw concentrates on the phenomenon of urbanity and its impact on the African American population in the 1920s, arguing that ancestral figures in Fisher's short stories do not attempt to keep southern tradition alive in Harlem but rather redraw it within the urban context. In other words, she suggests that southern tradition has undergone significant changes in order to fit into the cultural scene of Harlem, with the figures of ancestors being responsible for this transformation.

I cannot agree with this statement, since I believe that hardworking and deeply religious elders in Rudolph Fisher's short stories represent the values of rural southern culture. In fact, my argument is that they serve as mediators between rural southern culture and the codes of black Harlem. Young Harlemites, in their turn, face the difficult task of incorporating southern tradition into their daily lives in Harlem; they need to evaluate its importance and understand what role it has played in the formation of their identities. My argument, therefore, is that although many young black Harlemites may find their southern heritage incompatible with the codes of Harlem, in the end they recognize its importance.

Throughout his work Fisher also demonstrates that the development of black urban culture in the 1920s cannot be fully understood without examining the meaning and significance of the Great Migration. Thus, I will briefly evaluate how the Great Migration affected the construction of African American communities in the North. My analysis will be based on "The South Lingers On."

In the early years of the twentieth century a small number of black southerners moved north; their aim was to escape racism and threats of lynching in the South, as well as to find better-paying jobs and provide their children with a good education. These black southerners soon discovered, however, that it was not easy for them to acquire regular employment in the North, since most of the jobs were reserved for white males. This situation changed when World War I broke out in Europe in 1914. The flow of the European immigrants to the United States of America stopped. This led to high labor shortages in northern cities. Despite this fact, many railroad companies and factories were not willing to employ African Americans. According to Grossman railroad companies would "exhaust other alternatives" (Grossman, 385) before they employed African Americans. The stories of high wages and better living conditions, however, traveled to the South. Many black southerners readily embraced the opportunity to move north. They first sought information and then headed to the cities where their friends or relatives had already established themselves. Unfortunately, the information about the living conditions in the North proved to be false and misleading.

Between 1916 and 1919 approximately five hundred thousand black southerners moved north, with twice that many following during the 1920s. In his famous anthology *The New Negro* Alain Locke claims that the Great Migration should not be viewed as "a blind flood started by the demands of war industry coupled with the shutting off of foreign migration" (6) but rather as a deliberate movement inspired by new visions of social equality and freedom. It also marks a transformation of the African American population from agrarian workers into city dwellers.

In the northern cities black southerners faced numerous challenges. They found themselves in a new and strange environment. Fisher reveals in his stories that black southerners were both mesmerized and paralyzed by the pace of city life. For the first time in their lives they saw trains and fire engines rushing past, the horrible noise hurting their ears. The bucolic South remained a distant memory, while overcrowded apartment buildings with dirty air shafts became their reality.

In "The South Lingers On" Fisher depicts the difficulties of southern blacks looking for regular employment in Harlem. He draws a portrait of a young man named Jake, who has just arrived in Harlem from Virginia. Jake's conversation with the job agency clerk provides valuable insights into the ordeals of black southerners in Harlem:

> What kind of work are you looking for, buddy?
> No purtickler kin', suh. Jes' work, dass all.
> Well, what can you do?
> Mos' anything, I reckon.
> Drive a car?
> No suh. Never done that.
> Wait table?
> Well, I never is.
> Run elevator?
> No, suh.
> What have you been doing?
> Farmin'.

Farming? Where?

Jennin's Landin', Virginia. 'At's wha' all my folks is fum. (McCluskey, 33)

Thus Harlem's utopian patina is shattered by the harsh reality of poverty and unemployment.

Jake is proud of his southern heritage; it does not even occur to him that the clerk views him as a primitive. When the clerk tells him to "come in later in the week" (34), Jake does not realize yet that he is not wanted there. He seems to believe in the goodness and honesty of black people. In a sense this shows his perception of blackness; Jake regards blackness as something that may unite all African Americans. He has apparently come from a small community in the South where African Americans have lived closely together, worked in the fields side by side, and shared joy and sorrow.

The situation in Harlem, however, is different. One can hardly speak about a singular united African American community; it is more appropriate to recognize the existence of several African American communities. In his short stories Fisher demonstrates that many black northerners tend to think in terms of money and power. They take advantage of the inexperienced and naive black southerners in order to accumulate more wealth.

Such an idea would not be acceptable to Jake. In fact, he would not believe that black people can mistreat one another. Here Fisher shows that the minds of the northerners have been corrupted by money and power, whereas the southerners have remained kindhearted and genuine. This particular thought is emphasized later in the sketch when Jake walks out of the job agency and is approached by the applicant who has preceded him. He tells Jake that the only way to succeed in Harlem is to either become a pimp or a pickpocket, but Jake refuses to accept this point of view; he "had greater faith in Harlem. Its praises had been sounded too highly—there must be something" (34).

Through characters like Jake, Fisher suggests that no matter how difficult the lives of black southerners in Harlem may have been, they did not lose their hopes. Jake has not come to Harlem to become a pickpocket or a pimp. Like so many black southerners, he is attracted to Harlem by its charismatic power, and because Jake believes in a better future, he is determined to overcome any difficulties that may lie ahead.

The old preacher Ezekiel Taylor, the protagonist of the first sketch in "The South Lingers On," stands in sharp contrast to Jake. He does not resemble those cheerful black southerners who have come to Harlem to better their lives. His shabby clothes and his musings about his life back in the South imply the hardships he has endured. He has watched many members of his little southern congregation leave for Harlem. This makes Ezekiel sad and lonely: "But he was old and alone and defeated. The world had called to his best. It had offered money, and they had gone; first the young men whom he had fathered, whom he had brought up from infancy in his little Southern church; then their wives and children, whom they eventually sent for; and finally their parents, loath to leave their shepherd and their dear, decrepit shacks, but dependent and without choice" (McCluskey, 30).

Ezekiel fails to appreciate the courage and desire of his fellow southerners to leave their familiar but oppressive surroundings behind and start a new life in the North. He does not see the importance of the idea of movement that is crucial to the African American experience. During the slavery era and Reconstruction whites tried to keep blacks as ignorant as possible of outside opportunities. And it seems that Ezekiel has absorbed this ignorance, which later results in his reluctance to leave the South and in his negativism when he sees Harlem. His decision to leave his hometown is not his own; he has been swept away by the flow of migrants. This shows both the dependency and the insecurity of Ezekiel.

Ezekiel sees Harlem as a "city of the devil—outpost of hell" (McCluskey, 30), a "barren place" (31) where God is absent. Even children here have become sinners, and they must be brought to salvation. Ezekiel does not realize, however, that he must be saved himself from his inability to adjust to life in Harlem and to determine his own fate. The irony is that he first understands his powerlessness in Harlem. His life in the South may have seemed difficult for him, but at least there he wielded some power, since he was a preacher and was supposed to guide the members of his church through life. Ezekiel acknowledges that poverty is a driving force that pushes his fellow southerners to leave their homes and seek better lives in the North, but he never thinks in terms of racial oppression and discrimination. Ezekiel has learned to live with these racist attitudes, unconsciously accepting them as part of his everyday life.

When Ezekiel walks through Harlem, he silently sings an old, religious hymn. Suddenly he realizes that he does not sing alone. He follows a chorus of voices until it leads him to a house whose windows resemble church windows. He walks in, and in this moment we meet the Reverend Shackleton Ealey:

The Reverend Shackleton Ealey had been inspired to preach the gospel by the draft laws of 1917. He remained in the profession not out of gratitude to its having kept him out of war, but because he found it a far less precarious mode of living than that devoted to poker, blackjack and dice. He was stocky and flat-faced and yellow, with many black freckles and the eyes of a dogfish. And he was clever enough not to conceal his origin, but to make capital out of his conversion from gambler to preacher and to confine himself to those enlightened groups that thoroughly believed in the possibility of so sudden and complete a transformation. (McCluskey, 32)

Thus, the narrator reveals the reverend's true nature. Ealey resembles a dogfish, a predator, taking advantage of naive and good-natured black southerners. Throughout this particular passage we hear his voice, full of contempt for black southerners and their cultural values. He views preaching as a means to better his financial situation, not as a sacred connection between heaven and the secular world. He notices Ezekiel and defines him as a "Perfect type—fertile soil" (32), calculating the profit he may realize if the old man joins his church. Ealey does not succeed with his devilish plan, however. The members of the congregation recognize their old, dear preacher, and before the prayer is over, they start talking about the need to found their own congregation. In this moment Ealey understands his defeat, and this enrages him. The only words he manages to utter, however, are "bless you my brother" (33).

This scene marks a turning point in Ezekiel's experience of Harlem. On the one hand he starts to appreciate what Harlem has to offer, but on the other hand he cannot fully come to terms with the codes of Harlem. His perception of Harlem as a place of unmitigated wickedness reveals his inability to recognize its importance for black southerners. He fails to understand that both the growth and the development of Harlem have been influenced by the northern migration of black southerners. Consequently, black southern culture has penetrated the cultural environment of Harlem. Finally, Ezekiel does not realize that he himself could contribute to Harlem's development by establishing a church of his own and thus reviving the values of southern tradition. Instead, he expects his fellow southerners to do this work for him.

An interesting aspect of this story is Ezekiel's name. Ezekiel was a prophet in the Bible. Although the book of Ezekiel provides little information about his life, it purports that he possessed an ability to resuscitate the dead. His name means "God will strengthen." In this particular sketch Ezekiel is depicted as a weak man who wishes to be found and saved from the evils of Harlem. The fact that he finds the Reverend Shackleton Ealey's church appears at first to be a mere coincidence.

I believe, though, that Ezekiel was predestined to "see the power of God" in Harlem and reevaluate his opinions on the lives of black Harlemites. Before he undertakes this task, however, he must overcome the barriers he has constructed himself. Ezekiel has to contemplate what he can do to improve his situation. He also needs to explore and understand Harlem's meaning and significance for black Americans.

In describing the lives of black Harlemites, Rudolph Fisher shows that the demand for jobs in the North was often far greater than their supply. The lack of jobs bred urban criminality and poverty in Harlem. In "The South Lingers On" Fisher illustrates that many black southerners have lost their hope in Harlem and have chosen to earn their money dishonestly.

In the fifth sketch he introduces the protagonist, Lucky, a former black southerner who has now become a bootlegger. Lucky's friend Pete urges him to come to the church tent that is set on the opposite side of the street. At first Lucky refuses: "I'm a preacher's son—got enough o' that stuff when I was a kid and couldn't protect myself" (McCluskey, 38). Eventually, however, Lucky agrees to accompany his friend. When they enter the church tent, Lucky and Pete are enveloped in the musty heat. Voices, clear and old, high and low, sweet and mellow, fill the tent. The preacher starts to describe hell, enumerating the horrors that befall unrepentant sinners. His voice is strong and deep. Suddenly the preacher stops; he is waiting for the voices to fade away. The shouting and the cheering of the members of the little congregation are replaced by a brief moment of silence. Then the preacher resumes his sermon, turning once again to the subject of hell. At this point Lucky hastily leaves the tent.

This particular episode is of great importance to our understanding both the encounter with and the experience of black southerners in Harlem. Grossman states, "Other than the family, the oldest African-American institution was the church. By the beginning of the twentieth century the church brought together African Americans as no other institution possibly could" (Grossman, 367). African American churches served not only as places where people practiced religion but also as community centers where they shared their experiences about difficulties in their lives. This endowed the churches with a sense of unity and strengthened their position as communal watering holes.

Thus, it became one of the primary goals of black southerners to establish their churches in Harlem. The church helped them preserve their cultural heritage and create new communities in northern cities. The church performed two functions in the North: (1) it served as an extension of southern tradition, providing the elderly immigrants from the South with a sense of togetherness; and (2) it widened the gap between the elderly and the young Harlemites.

In the fifth sketch of Fisher's "The South Lingers On" the narrator points out that the people who have gathered to pray are old. Pete calls them "old-time sisters" (McCluskey, 38) and perceives the religious service as a good circus. In his eyes such a form of praying—clapping hands, getting excited, and emphasizing the significance of worshipers' personal experiences with God—is archaic and amusing.

The absence of young people in the church tent implies the discontinuity and ephemerality of southern tradition in Harlem. Obviously, the young Harlemites have other priorities in their lives. In fact, their lives have been shaped by Harlem itself. This becomes a bone of contention between the elderly southerners and the young Harlemites. While the elderly immigrants from the South find it difficult to accept the fact that the younger generation does not show piety and respect for rural southern culture, the young Harlemites wish to concentrate on their lives in Harlem, not on their southern heritage. Another important aspect is, of course, that many young Harlemites have never been to the southern states, and because of this they are not familiar with rural southern culture and its traditions.

Throughout this particular sketch Fisher weaves a theme of the presence of southern tradition in Harlem and reveals the uneasiness it evokes in the minds of former southerners. In the case of Lucky it becomes apparent that despite his inability to combine his southern cultural heritage with his life in the North, he silently recognizes its significance. The narrator discloses that it is not resentment that animates Lucky but rather a carefully developed strategy to protect himself from his own thoughts. It appears that the religious service revives his memories about his home in the South. His southern upbringing conflicts with his current life in Harlem. Lucky did not come to Harlem to become a bootlegger. He begins to see how his dreams have perished in Harlem. His name, "Lucky," underscores the irony of his situation because he is unhappy and does not know how to cope with his life.

By creating the characters of Jake, Ezekiel, and Lucky, Rudolph Fisher demonstrates both the heterogeneity and the complexity of the African American experience in 1920s Harlem. Black southerners' responses to the codes of Harlem were very diverse. For instance, if Lucky succumbs to the evils of Harlem, Jake refuses to believe that Harlem is merely a place for bootleggers, pimps, and pickpockets. For Jake Harlem embodies the ideals of freedom and equality. Ezekiel, in his turn, lets out all his frustration when he sees Harlem for the first time. He fails to acknowledge the presence of God in Harlem, which in a sense implies that he has lost faith in God.

Throughout his writings Rudolph Fisher urges black southerners to preserve their cultural heritage because it may serve as a means of strength and vitality to many African Americans in Harlem. Fisher tends to romanticize southern migrants (also southern tradition itself) by portraying them as virtuous, industrious, and pious people. Their naivety about Harlem's criminal activities makes them vulnerable and at the same time attractive to those northern blacks who take advantage of their inexperience. But even in the situations when the southern migrants have been unjustly accused of some criminal activity, they retain their dignity and honesty. Fisher does not seem to condemn northern blacks for misusing both the trust and the inexperience of southern immigrants. In fact, he suggests that Harlem is an evil place, giving it a shape of a villainous beast that swallows up the virtues of people, but never mentions that it could have been people who transformed Harlem.

By introducing black characters from the South into his short stories, Fisher suggests that southern tradition is crucial to our understanding both the development and the uniqueness of black Harlem in the 1920s. Despite the fact that the black population in the North has undergone important changes, including its transformation from agrarian workers into city dwellers and the emergence of new cultural identities, lifestyles, and needs, southern tradition is revived and reinforced by the arrival of new migrants from the South.

BIBLIOGRAPHY

Balshaw, Maria. *Looking for Harlem: Urban Aesthetics in African-American Literature.* London: Pluto, 2000.
Grossman, James R. *A Chance to Make Good.* New York: Oxford University Press, 2000.
Locke, Alain. *The New Negro: Voices of Harlem Renaissance.* New York: Touchstone, 1999.
McCluskey, John, Jr., ed. *The City of Refuge: The Collected Stories of Rudolph Fisher.* Columbia: University of Missouri Press, 1987.
Perry, Margaret, ed. *The Short Fiction of Rudolph Fisher.* New York: Greenwood, 1987.

SIX

Back to Harlem

Abstract and Everyday Labor during the Harlem Renaissance

Jacob S. Dorman

> At least a nigger a week is being lynched in the South this season, the color line is getting tighter and tighter, even in New York, but in books and the theatre the Negro is still muy simpatico. Dance, damn you, dance! You're awfully strange and amusing! —LANGSTON HUGHES

Claude McKay wrote the novel *Home to Harlem* when he was a hungry, broke, and somewhat desperate writer "at the end of my rope," struggling to get by in Marseilles and having dropped the writing of poetry in 1925 to "get in on the Negro vogue," as he called it.[1] After many months of chasing fruitless leads, he received a letter from his agent, Louise Bryant Bullitt, in December of 1926: "Dear Claude: I think I have good news for you at last. The Boni's turned the short stories down but are very much interested in having you do a novel called 'Back to Harlem.'"[2] When the book finally appeared, in 1928, it was well received—the *New York Times* extolled its "more authentic flavor," compared to Carl Van Vechten's *Nigger Heaven* of the same year, saying "it is the real stuff, the low-down on Harlem, the dope from the inside."[3] F. Scott Fitzgerald particularly liked the "Harlem motif of dissipation," as he confessed in a letter to McKay, who was in residence across the Atlantic, where he remained from 1919 to 1934. McKay might have set out to write a book called "Back to Harlem," but the man who inspired much of the New Negro literary renaissance remained outside the United States during its "Negro vogue."[4]

In the early 1920s Harlem surpassed the South Side of Chicago and all others as the most famous black city in America. It was a neighborhood that rapidly gained international notoriety as the home of African American poets, playwrights, and jazz musicians, and it boasted many nightclubs, cabarets, and speakeasies. Yet McKay's physical dislocation from New York as he helped to create the literary idea of Harlem is only one example of such geographical displacement and abstraction: the Harlem Globetrotters began shooting hoops in the 1930s not from New York but from Chicago; Langston Hughes wrote most of the Jessie B. Semple tales, depicting the wisdom of a Harlem rube, while living in Chicago in the 1940s. In the 1920s Alain Locke and Hughes lived in Washington, D.C., the home of Duke Ellington; Hughes, Wallace Thurman, Aaron Douglas, and Fletcher Henderson were westerners; Chicago's black business community far outstripped Harlem's. And yet it was Harlem, not Chicago or Kansas City, that became synonymous with the African American literary and artistic production of the 1920s. Harlem became a symbol and a metonym by which all black American cities were known, but, curiously, scholars have paid little attention to the masses of people who lined its streets, as opposed to the few people who lined its poems.[5] To the extent that it has been written at all, the history of Harlem in the decade of its renaissance has become largely the story of poets, artists, religious eccentrics, political activists, and exclusive clubs and cabarets—essentially, the face that Harlem presented to the outside world.

Examining everyday life and work patterns in 1920s Harlem illustrates that the abstracted Harlem of the literary imagination is an inadequate replacement for the knowledge of Harlem to be gleaned through social history. Harlem's black workers inspired and helped create the abstraction of Harlem, but discrimination prevented them from earning their due; in theoretical terms one could say that their labor never became fully abstracted.[6] Whereas the abstract image of Harlem became a commodity to be sold in the primary market of publishing and the secondary market of academe, laboring Harlemites were unable to gain adequate compensation for their labors, cultural or otherwise, so living in Harlem not only systematically impoverished them but distanced them from the abstraction of Harlem that was their original creation. Yet it is the abstract Harlem, not the street-level version of living laborers, that has come to stretch its mantle across the entire era of the "Harlem Renaissance." A close examination of the working life of 1920s Harlemites both retrieves and destroys different versions of Harlem: bringing into focus Harlem at the level of lived experience makes it clear that the

"Harlem" in the designation "Harlem Renaissance" is not a place but rather is a symbolic abstraction. Appreciating this duality allows us to have our "Harlem Renaissance" and understand Harlem, too.

If everyday Harlem was not the land of leisure and fast living, of hooch, hookers, and "Jungle Alley," then what was it? How did its people live, work, play, and pray? Harlem in the 1920s was Janus-faced, home of glittering jazz clubs, famous poets, and a few African American multimillionaires, while simultaneously home to disease-ridden slums and desperate poverty. In Harlem the acclaimed artists and writers of the Harlem Renaissance met the working-class intellectualism of street-corner orators; the imposing preachers and edifices of established black churches met the robust enthusiasms of stepladder preachers and storefront houses of worship; the politicking of the black bourgeoisie met the striving militancy of black nationalists. Harlemites generally lived in overpriced but substandard housing; the majority worked in backbreaking and poor-paying jobs; most businesses, including almost all of Harlem's nightclubs, were owned by nonblacks; time off spent in the home, in church, or in casual settings like pool halls and street corners was more common than nights in cabarets; and Harlem's many mainline churches were often packed yet did not serve the entire community. Harlem in the 1920s was a highly class-conscious society, where pedigree, dress, behavior, and skin tone mattered. It surely attracted bohemian poets and painters, but its hegemonic social standards were those of the middle and upper classes, who continually tried to get their working-class compatriots to comport themselves according to bourgeois standards of conduct.

African American tenants began moving to Harlem in 1904, and their numbers had reached 22,000 by 1910, 84,000 by 1920, and almost 190,000 by 1930, roughly two-thirds of the total black population in all boroughs and 80 percent of Manhattan's total black population. Yet in 1930, New York City's 327,706 blacks were only 4.7 percent of the total population. By 1930 less than a quarter of New York City's African American population had been born in New York State, with another quarter hailing from the Caribbean and most of the rest from Virginia, South Carolina, North Carolina, Georgia, Florida, and a dozen other states.[7] Harlem also attracted blacks from other, older black neighborhoods within Manhattan, such as the "San Juan Hill" or Columbus Hill neighborhood on the lower West Side, near Hell's Kitchen.

Although today the abstraction of Harlem has become synonymous with black Harlem, the neighborhood had a complex racial geography in the 1920s. Early in the decade an Irish group occupied a wide band between 116th and 126th streets, all the way from St. Nicholas Avenue in the west to Lenox Avenue in the east. That section abutted a Russian-Jewish section from Lenox to Park avenues and from roughly 110th to 126th streets. Italians lived from 120th to 124th streets, from Fifth Avenue to Park Avenue. Near the river between 109th and 130th streets lived Hungarians in the upper section and Italians in the lower. African Americans lived from 130th to 146th streets, between Seventh and Lenox avenues, and spread outward from that core. There was even a large Finnish community in Harlem, living in the area east of Lenox between 120th and 128th streets, with a social focal point in Finnish Hall at 13 West 126th Street. Harlem as a whole had gained 14,522 inhabitants from 1910 to 1920, but the total increase of the black population was 52,795, meaning that 38,273 white inhabitants were replaced by black ones.[8]

The 1920s saw a remarkable socioeconomic diversity within African American Harlem: professionals and poverty-stricken laborers frequently could be found in the same block, often in the same building. Yet at least by the end of the decade a socioeconomic geography had emerged. "The Valley" was a slum area, from 130th to 140th streets, east of Seventh Avenue. Once the black population spread below 125th Street to the edge of Central Park, the "Golden Edge" apartments facing the park housed "colored" professionals. The wealthy lived in comparative splendor on the heights of "Sugar Hill." "The Market" was the segment of Seventh Avenue from 110th to 115th streets, where prostitution flourished.

One of the main thoroughfares of the community was Lenox Avenue, a wide, slightly shabby, boulevard with shops, lunchrooms, pool parlors, restaurants, speakeasies, and pushcart food vendors who sold popcorn, baked sweet potatoes, peanuts, jam, sausages, pigs' feet, and other refreshments heated by kerosene lamps. Street speakers lectured from stepladders and boxes to crowds of pedestrians on topics ranging from politics to occultism to science and religion. One block to the west was Seventh Avenue, Harlem's widest street, running from 110th Street to Washington Heights, at 155th Street, with a median strip planted with trees running down the center of the stately boulevard. Seventh Avenue was classier than Lenox and featured slightly more upscale apartment buildings, retail stores, beauty parlors, restaurants, nightclubs, and saloons. A key artery running crosstown, 125th Street became enveloped by black neighborhoods to the north and south. Throughout the 1920s the street remained an exclusionary racial zone that was used as a shopping district by the white residents of Manhattanville and Morningside Heights. The thoroughfare featured many hotels, stores, movie theaters, real-estate offices, banks, and restaurants, almost all of which were owned by whites and employed no blacks, a cause of much resentment to Harlem's African American community. The transformation of 125th Street's Apollo Theater into a mecca of black entertainment would not occur until 1934. Additional shopping but few employment opportunities could be found in the many white and Jewish-owned shops along 135th and 145th streets.

Working

The mandarins of respectable opinion in Harlem tried to reinforce a strong work ethic among the masses of laboring people, sometimes lecturing them on the merits of labor and fidelity to their jobs. An editorial in the *Amsterdam News* read, "If you work for a man, in heaven's name work for him! If he pays you wages that supply your bread and butter, work for him—speak well of him, stand by him and the institution he represents." Similarly, opinion-makers challenged Harlem's women to apply themselves dutifully to their work: "What does your job mean to you?" asked Edith McAllister, a columnist for the women's section of the *New York Amsterdam News*. "As is the case in most lines of endeavor, one gets little more out than one puts into a thing," McAllister preached. "Clock watchers, readers, and office ornaments are a few of the things that a self-respecting, one might say a job-respecting woman, avoids even the semblance of."[9]

Yet despite what their social betters preached, the majority of black New Yorkers faced a work world of toil and drudgery. Although a handful of New York blacks worked in skilled trades such as carpentry, they were excluded from white unions and found well-paying jobs hard to come by. It was not unusual for qualified teachers to work as cooks or laborers, instead, unable to find work in their chosen profession. "In New York as in all large cities the Negro does not only encounter greater difficulty in getting jobs than does the white, but he is forced to accept the menial jobs and meager salaries," wrote a contemporary observer.[10]

A rough idea of the class structure of black Harlem is revealed by a 1927 Urban League study of 1,765 male heads of household. On the whole Harlem incomes were low: 16.7 percent of Harlem households were struggling along, making less than $75 a month at a time when less than $100 a month was considered poor and $133 a month was the minimum required to maintain a "fair American standard" of living for a family of four in Manhattan. The great majority, 70.8 percent, earned between $75 and $125 a month. A thin band at the top of the pay scale, 11.5 percent, earned incomes between $125 and $175, and less than 1 percent earned more than that. By the end of the decade there were fewer than twenty people in Harlem making more than ten thousand dollars a year.[11] Discrimination and poor education were both part of the picture. The paucity of African Americans at the top of the pay scale can be explained in part by the fact that in the last quarter of the nineteenth century there were only 2,313 black college graduates in the entire country, so that twenty years later the population of college graduates who had reached the peak of their earning power in middle age was quite small. In 1910 only 60 percent of black children in southern states were able to attend school. Yet an even greater factor was the fact that African Americans routinely were refused employment in jobs for which they were qualified or were paid less than whites when they were hired. And despite the low incomes, between 75 and 80 percent of African American Harlem residents paid monthly rents from $32.23 to $51.52. To help pay for expensive apartments, nearly a third of Harlem families took in lodgers.[12]

Greater than two-thirds of black Harlem men worked in manual labor, as longshoremen, janitors, waiters, elevator and switchboard operators, porters, day laborers, or some other similar occupation. In most parts of Harlem the percentage of manual laborers was much higher: an Urban League study of the block bounded by 133rd, 134th, and Lenox and Fifth avenues found 120 porters and 81 laborers among the 242 male breadwinners, and 104 domestics and 35 laundry women among the 156 female workers. Remarkably, for a city as large as New York, close to 70 percent of all working black women in Manhattan worked in domestic and personal service as laundresses, hairdressers, domestic day workers, maids, waitresses, or seamstresses. Black women also had a much greater rate of participation in the labor force than their white female peers. Another Urban League study found that 58 percent of married women worked outside their homes, four times more than the percentage of native-born white women and five times more than that of foreign-born women.[13] Wages for black domestic workers increased substantially while the eight-hour day became standardized because of labor shortage during World War I, falling only slightly after hostilities ended. Still, wages for all domestic servants were low. Among male domestic servants, cleaners could earn $15 a week, while cooks earned from $15 to $25 a week. Dishwashers earned between $10 and $30 a week, and doormen and elevator operators earned from $10 to $20. Apartment-building elevator operators who also ran switchboards earned more, from $14 to $18. Doormen and elevator operators who worked in hotels could expect to earn substantially more through tips—sometimes as much as $40 or $50 a month. Firemen who stocked the coal furnaces in apartment buildings earned between $20 and $30 a week. Janitors, whose functions included those of a building superintendent, were surprisingly well-paid, making the princely wage of between $20 and $60 a week. Some janitors also had lower-paid assistants, who labored for $10 or $15 a week. Waiters could make anywhere from $10 to $21 a week. Chauffeurs commanded $25 a week.[14]

The labor shortages of the First World War had led to more opportunities for African Americans in industrial jobs, some of which they retained after the war. The industries opened to African Americans during the war years included freight handlers, mechanics, and firemen on the Lackawanna and Pennsylvania railroads. Foundries, quarries, and shipyards all kept black workers in roughly the same proportions in their reduced workforces as they had during the war. In New York, Downey's Shipyard, Standard Ship Building Corporation, and Submarine Boat Corporation all used black laborers. In addition, blacks were working in sugar refineries, meat-packing houses, and jam-making plants. Although many unions in the building trades excluded blacks, jobs were available in lower-skilled positions, although the economic slump following the war meant that work was scarce.[15]

Longshoremen and Pullman porters were the best paid positions of New York's black working class, yet Pullman porters earned only $67 a month, though that may not include the substantial amount they earned in tips. A Pullman porter work song testified to the status, freedom, and high pay of the position:

Braid on the cap an'
Buttons in a row,
On that blue uniform
Right down the fo'.
Chorus:
In Pullman train
Pullman train,
Is a Negro porter
On de Pullman train.
It's a tip right here
An' a tip right tar,
Tip all along
Up an' down de Pullman car.

. . . .

Pocket full o' money,
Stomach full o' feed,

What next in the worl'
Do a fellow need?[16]

Blacks were excluded by most labor unions in the 1920s and thereby were kept out of the higher-paying trades. Instead of being carpenters and plumbers, many found work as day laborers doing the hardest and poorest paying work. Overall, two-thirds of working-blacks in New York worked in unskilled occupations. Recent European immigrant men had higher rates of illiteracy than African American men, yet they quickly moved into higher occupational categories than most black men, while black men remained for the most part in the least appealing service sector and industrial jobs.[17]

Physical labor in this era was literally backbreaking, and job titles alone do little to describe how difficult such jobs could be. The term *stationary* engineer is particularly deceptive. So-called stationary engineers were responsible for a building's furnaces, boilers, and elevators. One such engineer earned only $14 a week, with which he tried to support his wife, child, and four unemployed younger sisters from Barbados, who lived in a dark basement apartment on East 10th Street. The man was paid poorly despite the fact that he had ten years' experience and had even served an apprenticeship to learn his trade. In exchange for his meager salary he worked nine hours a day in the summer, ten hours a day in winter, and shoveled an astounding twenty tons of coal a week into two furnaces, by himself. He also had to remove the ashes, adjust the boiler pressure, clean and service the furnaces, and maintain the elevators. This man was no giant either: he was thirty-one years old, short, muscular, and weighed only 134 pounds. His workplace was a saunalike cellar where the heat was always intense and the walls and floor damp with condensation. Not surprisingly, he suffered from signs of depression: "he is nervous and has the characteristic diminished appetite, loss of weight, lack of interest in life, and desire for stimulants that so frequently result from over-exacting work."[18]

Even a job that sounded more manageable could be physically taxing. A night watchman in the same building took home $12 a week and worked seven nights a week, twelve hours a night. He had to walk the halls and stairs constantly, punching in at time clocks at various stations in addition to attending the furnaces and shoveling some coal. The watchman, who was fifty-nine years old, completed the equivalent of hiking a small mountain every single night of the week.[19]

Working Women

Female domesticity was a cultural ideal in the 1920s, but most unmarried black women, struggling to make ends meet, were part of the workforce. A 1925 report on English women entering typically male professions was greeted dismissively in the black press. "Sour grapes! This is no new discovery so far as we are concerned. Although some of the trades and professions are new to our group, the gentle African women, after their Americanization, forced and otherwise, carried on men's work for years and years, not by invasion, but by conscription."[20] More black women than white women worked in the New York of the 1920s, but black women generally performed different jobs than black men. Black women were split between clerical, factory, and domestic service jobs in the ratio of 9.9, 28.6, and 61.5 percent, respectively. Unlike black men, black women were able to find jobs in factories, mostly in the needle trades, and such industrial jobs paid 75 percent to 100 percent more than jobs in domestic and personal service.[21]

Female domestic servants made less on the whole than their male counterparts. But domestic workers frequently also received money to cover transportation expenses, as well as one or two meals, while men received only the wage, presumably because their wives were thought to prepare their meals for them.[22] Almost all black women in domestic service (96.5 percent) were in general housework and laundry, which suggests that women of other races were commonly used to fill the domestic service roles that required more direct service and interaction with employers.[23] Germans, Irish, and other northern European immigrants were generally preferred to fill such higher-status and higher-paying positions.

When women could get it, domestic labor was one of the most grueling and least remunerative forms of work. A task as simple as washing clothes was a major enterprise. At the beginning of the decade only half of homes had washing machines of some kind. Even a sink, or "stationary tub," was a relative luxury, available in less than 40 percent of early-1920s homes. Doing laundry involved lifting water into either heavy wooden or lighter zinc tubs, then lifting the water out again after washing. A rubber tube to drain the tubs was a luxury not always available to laundresses. The wet laundry was then placed on a dry goods box or a wash bench and scrubbed, after which it was set out on lines to dry. Stationary drying machines had been invented but were available in less than one percent of homes. Laundry was ironed with either electric or gas irons, which made it possible to do bed linens at home rather than sending them out to steam laundries.

Yet black laundry workers received only $8.85 a week for their grueling labors and were often cruelly exploited. One large Harlem laundry fired its white workers who had worked five and a half days a week with an hour off for lunch and replaced them at the same wage with black workers who worked six days a week with only forty-five minutes for lunch.[24]

Domestic labor was one of the most common occupations among Harlem's African American residents, but it was one of the lowest-status forms of employment in the black community. People generally disliked the social isolation and close supervision of working for a white housewife, and their peers scorned them for accepting such positions. Domestic labor brought with it a foul taste of subservience and memories of slavery, which the black community was doing its utmost to transcend and leave behind. Yet other work was difficult to find: during the 1920s department stores barred black women as saleswomen or clerical workers, and other companies barred them entirely.[25]

With such poor wages and such hard work, most women could not earn enough to support both themselves and their dependents. Stenographers were the highest-paid female office workers, with a third taking home $20 to $21 a week. Most other office jobs averaged roughly $15 a week. Factory jobs likewise varied by skill level, with most of them paying between $12 and $16 a week, but the top tier of workers earned up to $25 a week.[26] Overall, women's wages in industrial and clerical jobs had advanced from 1919 and were much higher than wages for jobs in housework.

Yet many women were unable to find positions in office work even though they were well qualified for such jobs. A sewing-machine operator who manufactured underwear related: "I trained for a typist, but was unable to get work. The work that you train for is hard to get. Very few colored girls get office jobs unless their own color employ them." A domestic servant testified that though she was trained and experienced working as a dental assistant, she was not even considered for an interview at the telephone company.[27] Black women also faced discrimination in hiring for domestic service positions. Half of the newspaper ads for female help specified white women or gave nationality preferences that excluded blacks. Only 5.7 percent of black female domestic servants found their positions through newspaper ads; 51.5 percent found jobs through friends and relatives and 31.4 percent by going door to door in person.[28] The Urban League also ran an employment bureau out of its Brooklyn office, by which workers were placed in private homes and businesses.

Light-skinned blacks were able to use their social capital or skin privilege to find jobs, sometimes by "passing" for white, but when their race was discovered, they often were demoted or dismissed. One light-skinned young woman related: "I secured a position as a wrapper at a Department Store through a white school friend. When the forelady discovered I was colored she gave me a job dusting furniture, and when I protested, I was dismissed." Other light-skinned women had similar experiences, being dismissed from jobs as theater ushers or fur workers. In other cases where black women were hired, they were paid as much as $5 less a week than white women, even though the black women were graduates of the Pratt Institute or Manhattan Trade School and better qualified than European immigrants who had not attended trade schools.[29]

The difficulty in getting by and providing for extras like medical care, education, recreation, and travel can be seen when we compare wages to the cost of living. In 1921 food, shelter, and clothing cost a family with three children between $20.15 and $24.05 per week. The Urban League sociologist George Edmund Haynes wrote, "It begins to dawn upon one why more married colored women work than white women, either foreign or native born or both, why children leave school as soon as they get working papers and why family life is menaced by the lodger evil."[30]

Economic necessity forced many mothers to return to work soon after childbirth, and the practice of leaving one's children with a neighbor developed into a cottage industry of "baby farms" in which Harlem women charged a few dollars a week to look after infants. A survey in 1927 discovered 123 baby farms advertised in local newspapers; only sixty-one of these had applied for permits, and only nineteen had received them. In the words of Edward Grey, a contemporary with a low regard for the value of domestic labor, the proprietors were either "old decrepit and sickly women," young women who themselves had children and took on others to earn more income, or young women "too lazy to work regularly and who take in children as a means of earning a living." Working with a representative of the New York City Health Department, Grey discovered numerous cases of unsanitary conditions, in which attendants suffered from everything from contagious lung diseases to scalp infections and one case in which an attendant even suffered from leprosy yet worked for three years caring for children. In other cases children as young as five years old provided most of the care for the babies. Not infrequently, baby farms were used as fronts for criminal activities. At Fifth Avenue and East 134th Street prohibition agents broke into a day nursery and arrested the husband and wife who used it as a front for manufacturing moonshine. Local gamblers also were known to use childcare facilities as convenient fronts. One Saturday night in June of 1927 the police raided a baby farm in the basement of a building around the corner from Harlem Hospital. The cops escorted forty gamblers and the woman who ran the dice game into a waiting paddy wagon, while the infants were left overnight in the care of a seven-year-old child.[31] The high cost of living and low wages forced women to work and leave their children in the care of others, but when women chose reproductive over productive labor they were accused of being "lazy." There were few good options for people struggling to get by on their labor in Harlem.

The Great Migration is usually said to have introduced a black rural and agricultural population into the regimes of industrial labor in the North.[32] Yet one of the things that created the conditions for the abstraction of Harlem in the "Harlem Renaissance" is that New York followed a different course. Unlike Chicago, Detroit, or Kansas City, New York was the nation's capital of publishing, fashion, and finance and did not have large manufacturing industries or packing plants.[33] New York's location as the center of the finance, fashion, and publishing industries meant it was possible in New York for a boundary-crosser like the writer Carl Van Vechten to introduce uptown friends to wealthy downtown patrons and publishers. What industrial jobs were available to men were almost entirely monopolized by exclusionary unions that did not allow blacks to enter. Black women had a slightly better time of it, working in large numbers in the needle trades, thanks to the more welcoming stance of the relevant unions. Yet the vast majority of black women and men worked in service industries and in the most physically demanding labor. As others have argued, the concentration of black workers in service industries such as domestic service brought African Americans into contact with upper-class whites and promoted the circulation of expensive fashions and tastes.[34] Then there is the very visual quality of New York itself, where promenading was a many-hours-long pastime and where the subway served as a social panopticon, allowing its riders to view people of every race and class, from street urchins to businessmen and even perhaps the occasional grandee.

The cultural labor of black workers created the glamorous abstraction of "Harlem"—it was black brains, muscles, synapses, and sinews whose labor created the Lindy Hop, black societies, jazz, and the blues.[35] But over time, as whites systematically excluded blacks from New York's best jobs and underpaid them for the work they could find, and as the artificially high demand created by the segregated housing market allowed Harlem's landlords to charge the highest rents in the city, Harlem systematically impoverished its workers. By the end of the decade, a newspaper writer could justifiably write that Harlem "is the poorest, the unhealthiest, the unhappiest and the most crowded single large section of New York City."[36] As the decade wore on, few black laborers could afford the glittering nightclubs of Harlem that feature so prominently in the abstraction of Harlem—and in any case they came to be excluded from them, just as they had always been excluded from the most prestigious jobs. As Langston Hughes wrote to his friend Claude McKay in the year of the publication of *Home to Harlem,* "Harlem cabarets are disgracefully white. The only way Negroes get in nowadays is to come with white folks, whereas it used to be the other way around."[37]

This chapter's tale of the two cities of Harlem is also a story of abstraction and commodification: the successful abstraction and commodification of the literary image of Harlem, and the largely unsuccessful abstraction and commodification of the labor power of Harlemites. These differing histories helped establish two divergent trajectories for studies of each topic. In contrast to the large and rich scholarship on the Harlem Renaissance, equality for the black workers of 1920s Harlem remains an abstraction—in scholarship as in the past.[38]

ACKNOWLEDGMENTS

My thanks to the Donald C. Gallup Fellowship in American Literature at Yale University's Beinecke Rare Book and Manuscript Library and the New Faculty General Research Fund at the University of Kansas for support that aided the preparation of this chapter.

NOTES

Epigraph. Langston Hughes to Claude McKay, Sept. 30, 1930, Claude McKay Papers, Box 4, Folder 99, James Weldon Johnson Collection, Beinecke Rare Book and Manuscripts Library, Yale University (hereafter JWJC).

1. Claude McKay (Marseilles) to Louise Bryant Bullitt (New York), June 24, 1926, Claude McKay Papers, Box 1, Folder 26, JWJC.

2. Louise Bryant Bullitt to Claude McKay, Dec. 18, 1926, Claude McKay Papers, Box 1, Folder 27, JWJC.

3. John R. Chamberlain, "When Spring Comes to Harlem: Claude McKay's Novel Gives a Glowing Picture of the Negro Quarter," *New York Times Book Review,* March 11, 1928.

4. F. Scott Fitzgerald to Claude McKay, June 5, 1928, Claude McKay Papers, Box 3, Folder 80, JWJC. McKay's absence from Harlem was not entirely of his own choosing, although his foot-dragging frustrated James Weldon Johnson, who was attempting to put his diplomatic connections to use in getting McKay back into the United States. The passage of restrictive immigration legislation in 1924 and McKay's leftist political sympathies made it difficult for him to acquire a reentry visa for the United States. Yet of perhaps even more importance was McKay's extreme poverty, his ability to live cheaply in Marseilles and Morocco, his fascination with both places, and his reluctance to return to the racism of the United States. See Claude McKay Papers, Boxes 1–4, various correspondence, 1925–34, JWJC.

5. The extensive literature on the Harlem Renaissance includes Nathan Irvin Huggins, *Harlem Renaissance* (New York: Oxford University Press, 1971); David Levering Lewis, *When Harlem Was in Vogue* (New York: Penguin, 1979); Jervis Anderson, *This Was Harlem, 1900–1950* (New York: Farrar, Straus, Giroux, 1981); and Ann Douglas, *Terrible Honesty: Mongrel Manhattan in the 1920s* (New York: Farrar, Straus and Giroux, 1995). For an excellent overview of this literature see Eric J. Sundquist, "Red, White, Black and Blue: The Color of American Modernism," *Transition* 6, no. 2 (1996): 94–115.

6. See Karl Marx, *Grundrisse: Foundations of the Critique of Political Economy*, trans. Martin Nicholas (New York: Penguin Classics, 1993), 295–97; and Karl Marx, *Capital: A Critique of Political Economy*, trans. Samuel Moore, Edward Bibbins Aveling, and Ernest Untermann (New York: Modern Library, 1906), 45, 51–67, 84–93. In these two works Marx developed a distinction between the "use value" of labor, concrete labor, and labor in the abstract. A prerequisite for the concept of abstract labor is equality of legal, social, and political freedom: "all kinds of labour are equal and equivalent, because and so far as they are human labour in general, cannot be deciphered, until the notion of human equality has already acquired the fixity of a popular prejudice" (*Capital*, 69). See also Moishe Postone, *Time, Labor and Social Domination: A Reinterpretation of Marx's Critical Theory* (Cambridge, UK: Cambridge University Press, 1993), 123–70; Dipesh Chakrabarty, *Rethinking Working-Class History: Bengal 1890–1940* (Princeton, NJ: Princeton University Press, 1989), 225–26; and idem., "The Two Histories of Capital," chap. 2 in *Provincializing Europe: Postcolonial Thought and Historical Difference* (Princeton, NJ: Princeton University Press, 2000), esp. 50, 52–55, 58.

7. The population figures come from Cheryl Lynn Greenberg, *Or Does It Explode? Black Harlem in the Great Depression* (New York: Oxford University Press, 1991), 15. I have also used Gilbert Osofsky, *Harlem: The Making of a Ghetto: Negro New York, 1890–1930* (New York: Harper Torchbooks, 1963), 113, 128–30, 141; Seth M. Scheiner, *Negro Mecca: A History of the Negro in New York City, 1865–1920* (New York: New York University Press, 1965); Ira Rosenwaike, *Population History of New York City* (Syracuse: University of Syracuse Press, 1972), 141; Jeffrey S. Gurock, *When Harlem Was Jewish, 1870–1930* (New York: Columbia University Press, 1979), 147; Winston James,

Holding Aloft the Banner of Ethiopia: Caribbean Radicalism in Early Twentieth-Century America (London: Verso, 1998); and Anderson, *This Was Harlem, 1900–1950*, 301.

8. Harold Cooke Phillips, "The Social Significance of Negro Churches in Harlem" (master's thesis, Columbia University, 1922), 20; Works Progress Administration, Federal Writer's Project, *New York City Guide* (New York: Random House, 1939), 260; Edward M. Gilliard, "The Housing Problem in Harlem" (master's thesis, Columbia University, 1926), 11. This essay relies heavily on Harlem newspapers, especially the *New Amsterdam News*, and the collection of master's theses written by Columbia University students in sociology and political science, which are neatly indexed and stored in Columbia's archives in Harlem. Theses obviously reflect the biases of their authors, and I have attempted to mine them for specific data rather than for narrative or value judgments. Despite their limitations they are invaluable sources for the student of the 1920s, a decade before the Works Progress Administration's Writer's Project created a repository of observations on daily life.

9. "How to Make Good," editorial, *New York Amsterdam News*, Dec. 2, 1925; Edith M. McAllister, "What Does Your Job Mean to You?" *New York Amsterdam News*, Aug. 4, 1926.

10. "Twenty-four Hundred Families in Harlem," unpublished mss., New York Urban League Files, 19–20, cited in Barrington Dunbar, "Factors in the Cultural Background of the American Southern Negro and the British West Indian Negro That Condition Their Adjustments in Harlem" (master's thesis, Columbia University, 1935), 15; Greenberg, *Or Does It Explode?* 21.

11. Beverly Smith, "Harlem's Distress Intensified as Growing Property Values Threaten Impoverished Tenants," *New York Herald Tribune*, Feb. 10, 1930.

12. Greenberg, *Or Does It Explode?* 251; Phyllis A. Stancil, "Trends of Opinion among Negroes in the United States" (master's thesis, Columbia University, 1932), 22.

13. Greenberg, *Or Does It Explode?* 24.

14. Elizabeth Ross Haynes, "Negroes in Domestic Service in the United States" (master's thesis, Columbia University, 1923), 27–28.

15. George Edmund Haynes, "Report Impressions from a Preliminary Study of Negroes of Harlem, 1921" (unpublished report produced for the National Urban League), 22, George Edmund Haynes Papers, Box 1, Folder: 1921 Report, Schomburg Center for Research in Black Culture, Astor, Lenox and Tilden Foundations.

16. "Pullman Porter," in Howard Odum and Guy B. Johnson, eds., *Negro Workaday Songs* (Chapel Hill: University of North Carolina Press, 1926), 186.

17. In 1920 blacks made up less than 1 percent of all machinists in New York and less than 2 percent of all carpenters and masons. Somewhere from 17 to 21 percent of Manhattan's black men worked in industrial jobs, a figure that increased only 1 percent by 1930. The higher number comes from Greenberg, *Or Does It Explode?* 21; the lower figure is from Haynes, "Impressions, 1921," 26.

18. Russel Sage Foundation Building Employees Study, November 15, 1916, George Edmund Haynes Papers, Folder: "Russel Sage Foundation Employees Study,"

Schomburg Center for Research in Black Culture, Astor, Lenox, and Tilden Foundations, 4.

19. Ibid., 5.

20. "Woman! Why Weepest Thou?" *New York Amsterdam News,* Feb. 4, 1925.

21. Haynes, "Impressions," 41.

22. For women general housework earned them from $10 to $18 but averaged around $14. Chambermaids-waitresses earned $12 to $18 a week. Cooks averaged $16.50 a week, but could command anywhere from $15 to $21, while their kitchen helpers earned from $9 to $17 a week. Maids made an average of $13 a week. Nannies and nurses earned from $10 to $15, and waitresses earned $7 a week plus tips that would be between $5 and $7 a week. Haynes, "Negroes in Domestic Service in the United States," 39, 41.

23. Haynes, "Impressions, 1921," 31.

24. Ibid., 54; Greenberg, *Or Does It Explode?* 24.

25. Frances Gunner, "A Study of Employment Problems of Negro Women in Brooklyn" (master's thesis, Columbia University, 1923), 6.

26. Haynes, "Impressions, 1921," 47.

27. Ibid., 32.

28. Ibid., 7.

29. Ibid., 33.

30. Ibid., 62.

31. Edgar M. Grey, "Harlem's 'Baby Farms,'" *New York Amsterdam News,* Sept. 7, 1927.

32. See, e.g., James R. Grossman, *Land of Hope: Chicago, Black Southerners, and the Great Migration* (Chicago: University of Chicago Press, 1991); and Milton Sernett, *Bound for the Promised Land: African American Religion and the Great Migration* (Durham, NC: Duke University Press, 1997).

33. Kenneth T. Jackson, "The Capital of Capitalism: The New York Metropolitan Region, 1890–1940," in *Metropolis 1890–1940,* ed. Anthony Sutcliffe (London: Mansell, 1984), 319–54.

34. George Hutchinson, *The Harlem Renaissance in Black and White* (Cambridge, MA: Harvard University Press, 1995), 5–6; Michelle Birnbaum, *Race, Work, and Desire in American Literature, 1860–1930* (Cambridge, UK: Cambridge University Press, 2003), 100.

35. For other instances of black cultural production as forms of labor see Robin D. G. Kelley, *Race Rebels: Culture, Politics, and the Black Working Class* (New York: Free Press, 1994); and Davarian L. Baldwin, *Chicago's New Negroes: Modernity, the Great Migration, and Black Urban Life* (Chapel Hill: University of North Carolina Press, 2007).

36. Beverly Smith, "Harlem's Distress Intensified as Growing Property Values Threaten Impoverished Tenants," *New York Herald Tribune,* Feb. 10, 1930.

37. Langston Hughes to Claude McKay, Sept. 13, 1928, Claude McKay Papers, Box 4, Folder 99, JWJC.

38. An Australian team is currently at work on a promising "ethnographic study of everyday life in Harlem," the first part of which to appear is Shane White, Stephen Garton, Stephen Robertson, and Graham White, "The Envelope, Please," in *The Cultural Turn in U.S. History: Pasts, Presents, Futures*, ed. James W. Cook, Lawrence Glickman, and Michael O'Malley (Chicago: University of Chicago Press, 2008), 121–52.

PART III: Literary Icons Reconsidered

SEVEN

Jessie Redmon Fauset Reconsidered

Claire Oberon Garcia

Many readers have viewed Jessie Redmon Fauset's works as "minor" texts in the Harlem Renaissance canon and regarded her most significant contribution to black literary history as her role of literary editor of the NAACP's *Crisis* magazine and mentor to younger male writers such as Langston Hughes and Countee Cullen. Since the 1990s, however, feminist scholars have turned their attention to Fauset's long-out-of-print novels, appreciating their engagement of the intersections of race, class, and gender. The four novels represent only a small portion of Fauset's written legacy, however, which comprises dozens of book reviews, travel essays, journalistic reporting, translations, poetry, and short stories for children, as well as for adults. An examination of the entire corpus of Fauset's work reveals that she was concerned with exploring modern African American experience—especially women's experience—in a broad context that was global, modern, and cross-cultural. These shorter pieces, which to date have received little critical attention, look rich, complex, and much more important when viewed from a perspective that regards the Harlem Renaissance as part of a transnational phenomenon of black cultural and political affirmation and links Fauset's work to her francophone contemporaries Suzanne Césaire and Paulette and

Jane Nardal, whose writing also articulates a diasporic black feminist consciousness. Fluent in French, an avid traveler, and widely read, Jessie Redmon Fauset was a black cosmopolitan according to Ifeoma Nwankwo's definition: "Black cosmopolitanism is born of the interstices and intersections between two mutually constitutive cosmopolitanisms—a hegemonic cosmopolitanism, exemplified by the material and psychological violence of imperialism and slavery (including dehumanization), and a cosmopolitanism that is rooted in a common knowledge and memory of that violence. . . . The desire to be recognized as an agent is interwoven with the desire to be a citizen, and both desires determine both individual identity and textual and ideological engagements with people of African descent in other sites" (Nwankwo, 13).

An examination of the entire body of her work reveals a writer who was not afraid to engage the problems or possibilities of articulating a diasporic black consciousness and political agenda. Fauset often used the semantic and ethical problems posed by translation as a means to address three political concerns central to the New Negro woman's literary discourse: the critique of the dominant culture's representation of black women; the nature of the bonds between African Americans and "darker peoples" in other countries; and the possibilities of artistic expression as a means of social change. I discuss here a travel narrative and two early short stories that originally appeared in the *Crisis*. These pieces illustrate how deftly Fauset uses the idea of France and French culture to articulate an aesthetic and political liberation agenda for African American women that situates their struggles in a global context. An examination of these and other texts from Fauset's large and varied oeuvre reveals a writer who, far from being the genteel chronicler of the northern African American bourgeoisie—a mischaracterization that persists to this day—or the mere "midwife of the Harlem Renaissance"[1]—made important contributions to the transnational New Negro discourse of the early twentieth century. Her writing affirms the authority of a black, female imagination and perspective while radically critiquing the dominant narratives of race, gender, and class that constrained black women—especially those with creative desires—in early-twentieth-century America.

An active member of W. E. B. Du Bois's American delegation to the Second Pan-African Congress in 1921, whose reports on the multicity conference appeared in several installments in the *Crisis,* Fauset wrote extensively on global racial issues in other articles such as "Nationalism in Egypt" in 1920 and "The Emancipation of Brazil" in 1921. Several of her book reviews and translations also focused on anti-imperialist struggles by people of color around the world. Like other New

Negro–era writers, Fauset raised and confronted questions of racial identity across national borders and cultural boundaries. While Erica Griffin argues that Fauset explores the world outside the United States as an "invisible woman" writing from a position within the "veil" to "unit[e] black American women with European and North African women through their shared status as invisible members of patriarchal culture" (Griffin, 76), I believe that Fauset's focus on Europe, Africa, and Latin America in both her fiction and her nonfiction is a bold, high-visibility claim to her right, as a black woman, to actively and self-consciously participate in a critique of imperialism and creation of a transnational black political agenda. Her construction and examination of her own multilayered subjectivity (a race woman, an artist, an American, a bilingual person, a writer, a tourist, a single working woman, to name but a few of those layers) challenges the deterministic notions of racial and gender identity that fundamentally structure the America in which she lived. Her writing, anchored in the perspectives of a cosmopolitan woman of color, evokes, rather than evades, the profound complexities inherent in trying to both posit and exploit the idea of a common consciousness uniting oppressed people, especially women, of color.

Fauset, like other New Negro–era writers, used the rhetoric of black internationalism to support claims for African Americans' rights to the privileges and opportunities of American citizenship. The five Pan-African congresses between the World Wars, the social experiences of African American soldiers in Europe during the Great War, Marcus Garvey's calls for a return to Africa, and ever-increasing resistance to European colonial power—all contributed to New Negro–era writers' perceptions of the African American condition in a context that extended well beyond the borders of the United States. Attempts to construct and politically deploy a black identity across national, cultural, and sometimes religious lines, however, posed both rhetorical and political challenges.

Brent Hayes Edwards, in *The Practice of Diaspora*, proposes the concept of "décalage" as a tool for understanding the rhetoric of black internationalism and its inevitable misreadings and mistranslations. Problematizing Léopold Senghor's assertion that the differences between "Negro Americans" and "Negro Africans" is a matter of "a simple décalage—in time and in space," Edwards asserts that the fundamental relationship among members of the black diaspora is always "haunted" by that which can't be translated or understood, and that articulations of racial unity (such as Senghor's concept of Négritude or Du Bois's of Pan-Africanism) are always rhetorical artifices predicated on difference and disarticulation: Edwards notes, "Articulation is always a strange and ambivalent gesture, because, finally, in the body it is *only* difference—the separation between bones or members—that allows movement" (14).

This concept of décalage and its attendant rhetorical and political challenges are dramatically illustrated in Jessie Fauset's international pieces. A paradigmatic essay is her "Dark Algiers the White," an account of her visit to the French colonized city of Algiers in 1925. Published in the *Crisis* in April and May of 1925, and illustrated by her traveling companion and fellow *Crisis* contributor, Laura Wheeler, this piece richly presents the questions and cross-currents of "décalage" from a perspective that explores the inflections of national identity, language, race, and class on the notion of a common bond between nonwhite people subject to white power. Alain Locke claimed that the "growing group consciousness" of the "darker peoples of the world . . . is making the Negro international" (Locke, 7). How, this essay asks, are the similarities and differences among "the darker peoples of the world" articulated, and how may they be mobilized to battle the white world's exploitation and persecution of the nonwhite world? Fauset also inquires how gender inflects the experiences of people of color across national borders and cultural practices. How is it possible for a black, American, educated woman to "see" and represent "the real "Algiers, and how can the representation of her experiences there support the NAACP's cultural and political commitments? In "Dark Algiers the White" Fauset's attempts to construct, authorize, and deploy a feminist writer's subjectivity to address these questions results in a text décalagé.

At the time that Fauset wrote "Dark Algiers the White," the North African city had been under French colonial rule for more than a century, and Fauset was well aware that her encounter with "Africa" was mediated by French colonial power. The first installment of this illustrated personal memoir appeared between E. Franklin Frazier's account of a humiliating Jim Crow experience in a white southern eye doctor's office and a biographical sketch by Maud Hare about an Arabian slave poet and dramatist born in the sixth century. The placement of the essay implicitly links the black Americans' suffering under Jim Crow to a diasporic black history that is characterized as long, noble, and neglected. The title of Fauset's piece alludes to the French nickname for the city, "Alger la blanche," which refers to the fabled tiers of white buildings around the artificial harbor (depicted in Wheeler's pen-and-ink view that illustrates the first page of the article), but Fauset's single-word addition to the moniker—placed on a separate line above the words, "Algiers the White"—draws the reader's attention to the North African inhabitants of the city and Fauset's own "colored" subjectivity. Although French writers have referred to North African colonized lands as "France in Africa," Fauset's Algiers is emphatically an African city, not a French outpost: "For a few days we would be residents of Algiers," she writes enthusiastically, "dwellers in Africa." She delights in the prospect of being part of "a moving picture of brown and black faces" (255). Fauset's opening lines serve to reorient the reader from a European perspective on the city. Her north-south migration from "sunless Paris" is met by a dynamic presence that originates deep in the African interior: "All the strangeness and difference of that life which, starting far, far in the interior of Africa, yet breaks off so abruptly at the southern edge of the Mediterranean, rose instantly to meet us" (255).

Curiosity about the nature of the cross-cultural bonds between women is a central focus of Fauset's experiences in Algiers. She immediately notices the absence of women in the streets: "This street and all the streets in Algiers swarm with people—children, boys, and men, men, men!" (257). Fauset is entranced by the "mysterious figures of women clothed in white and numerous garments, a white face veil covering mouth and nose, cheeks and hair, all but two dark impenetrable eyes and a triangle of creamy forehead" (256), and disturbed by "the misshapen bodies, broken and distorted by neglect, abuse and much bearing of children" that the burkas and veils can't hide. One young woman on a bus captures Fauset's attention: she sits silently beside her husband "like an automaton beside her lord—there was no conversation" (256). When the young woman dismounts the trolley, however, and Fauset catches a glimpse of her "dainty" ankles in pink-colored stocking and russet shoes beneath the burka, Fauset is reassured by what seems a sign of the young woman's impulse to self expression, despite what appear to Fauset to be the suffocating social constraints of a patriarchal society.

An idea of common femininity is also reinforced during Fauset's visit to the Frenchwoman's "Moorish friend" Fatmah. Fauset marvels that the encounter with the Moorish women, following a journey through labyrinthine streets and embedded interiors, is so familiar: they talk, "after the fashion of ladies calling the world over," of children, pets, food (18), she writes. Yet this commonality is subverted by the very scenario: the white Frenchwoman has offered her "friend" as an exhibit to the American tourist, and the American tourist responds as if she is presented with a rare object for appreciation and consumption: "Her hair dyed a dark henna is perfection with her mat skin. I stare at her in such complete absorption that her glorious eyes finally question me and I blurt out: 'You are so beautiful, Madame; I wish my artist friend could see you'" (18). Afterward, Fauset thanks the Frenchwoman for "a rare afternoon that [is] such as [she] could never have procured from a guide" (18)—the rareness and authenticity of the experience is enhanced by the fact that it was not purchased from a professional but offered by a woman who originally stepped in to protect Fauset in a gesture of a woman looking out for another woman. The Frenchwoman politely rejects the equivalent of a tip—Fauset's offer of a present to her little girl—and the two women part "with the glance of people whose lives for an hour have touched deeply at their only possible tangent" (18). But when the policeman's wife shows up the next day—following what Fauset imagines are her husband's orders: "She was an American and you showed her about all afternoon and didn't get a penny from her!" (18)—it is clear that Fauset's experience with the Algerine has been as much a commodity as the rugs and bangles the salespeople in the bazaar offer to her and the other tourists. The "only possible tangent" is not a felicitous chance encounter but a meeting made possible by deep structures of nation, class, gender, and economic power. "The little idyll," writes Fauset, "has a tarnished ending" (19).

As an American in Algiers for a few days, what more could she have? What could she really see? The question of whether an American, despite her racial identity, education, and political allegiances, could ever perceive "the real Algiers" invokes the paradoxes of "décalage." Fauset seems to suggest that the Algiers of her imagination—the African frontier, the "gateway to the deepest mysteries of Africa and the East" (19), "the real Algiers," the unmediated perception or the experience that occurs outside the relationship of tourist/consumer and native/commodity—is not accessible to her, indeed, has actively eluded her.

Fauset's visit to Algiers also challenges her hopes for the commonalities of color, as well as gender. A pair of East Indian shopkeepers insists on treating Fauset and her companion as "friends" rather than customers, welcoming the African American women into their private quarters with effusive hospitality. The brothers treat Fauset's party as if there were some bond between them, yet Fauset reflects with a wistful wonder: "I notice a curious phenomenon: the brothers are brown, we are brown, but there is a difference in our brownness, so much that clad all of us in Western dress each would shortly be able to discriminate" (258). This encounter raises the prospect of a bond between nonwhite people but simultaneously acknowledges the difficulty of constructing anti-imperialist alliances across culture, gender, and national boundaries, especially those that lay some claim to transcending economic (in this case, commercial) relationships.

Though Fauset from the outset positions herself as a Western traveler seeking alliances with the black and brown Algerines, the French colonizers see her as completely different from the North Africans, though what she is they are not quite sure because she doesn't fit into any of the categories of colonial society. The misreadings and disarticulations of race and gender that Fauset's presence—as an educated, relatively wealthy, African American woman—generates are dramatized when Fauset asks a local French woman if it is safe for her to walk around unaccompanied in a certain quarter. The woman responds, "'You may go anywhere, anywhere, Mademoiselle, and then besides one sees you are from Martinique (Martiniquaise) and there is no danger here for a French woman!'" (16). This comment contains many layers of irony. At the time, Antilleans were legally French citizens, while the North and West Africans in French colonies were French subjects. This was a source of friction among Francophone blacks, even as they were attempting to formulate the political and cultural basis for the Négritude movement. And, of course, Fauset herself is neither French nor Antillean, but the local woman seems to have no other category for the well-mannered black woman who spoke fluent French. Fauset's very presence in Algeria subverts the categories imposed on her. Fauset's identity is a modern identity—fractured, ambiguous, and elusive. Yet any notion of common bonds of consciousness must by necessity rely on nineteenth-century concepts of race and identity still bearing the aroma of racial essentialism, a problem that Senghor and other proponents of Négritude encountered as they began to try to articulate its ideology and aesthetic.

What is the nature of the bond that connects what Du Bois referred to as "the darker peoples of the world"? Is it a matter, as Locke asked, of common condition or common consciousness? What are the differences, what are the similarities, Fauset asks in "Dark Algiers the White," between the modern American "race" woman and the black and brown Algerines? What are the differences, what are the similarities, among the "shrouded" Arab women, the young white Frenchwoman who warns Fauset that it is dangerous for a "lady" to walk alone in the Arab quarter, and the African American woman who wandered, with the freedom of a tourist or a Martiniquaise, through that very same quarter the day before the warning? All of these questions lead up to the most important one confronting Fauset as a writer: How can a black woman writer in 1925 frame her first experiences in an African country for the readers of the NAACP's monthly magazine in a way that creates a political relationship between the Algerines and *Crisis* readers in Harlem, Oklahoma City, and New Orleans? As "Dark Algiers the White" makes clear, it is all a matter, as Senghor says, of "décalage"—though certainly not a simple one, as he had hoped. This text exposes and explores the fissures, as well as the possibilities, of a transnational racial consciousness that doesn't shirk the ambiguities and complications of gender, class, and national identity on the part of both beholder and beheld. The décalage of "Dark Algiers the White" enacts both the difficulties and the hopes of the black internationalist project.

Although a knowledge of French, for so long a lingua franca of sophisticated cosmopolitans, was a sign of status for the white American middle class, it is not a class marker in Fauset's work. In one of her earliest short stories, "'There Was One Time!' A Story of Spring," which was published in the *Crisis* in two installments in April and May 1917, French serves to unite two young African American lovers not only to each other but to a diasporic consciousness that unites oppressed African Americans to colonized people around the globe. Issues of translation in this story and another early story, "Emmy" (published in the *Crisis* in 1913), also raise questions about how black women read and resist society's often vicious representations of both their gender and their racial affiliations. Both stories use the protagonists' associations with French as a means of exploring racial and gender societal constraints and of allowing the heroines first to imagine and then to live a more satisfying counternarrative.

"Emmy," which appeared in two installments, opens with a schoolgirl, Emilie Carrel, being asked to identify her racial affiliation from a choice of five visual representations. Although to her teacher's relief Emmy chooses the "correct" image, the "Hottentot, chosen with careful nicety to represent the entire Negro race" (51), Emmy's logic is definitely countercultural and, in a country governed by white supremacy, subversive and irrational, though the narrator declares that Emmy is "always severely logical" (53). To Emmy the Hottentot "had on the whole a better appearance" (51),[2] and when her white friend expresses sympathy after Emmy's public declaration of blackness, Emmy retorts, "'We're just the same, only you're white and I'm brown.'" Her response is similar when her biracial friend wishes that he "'were a good sure-enough brown like you'" (52): "'But what difference does it make?'" (52).[3] Although as Emmy grows up and learns "what color means" to other people, she manages to graduate from high school "mak[ing] them see she was perfectly satisfied with being colored" (56). The opening scene is the first of several in the story in which Emmy is confronted with a representation of "blackness" and forced to position herself in relation to that representation.

Emmy's nonconformance to the racial norms and attitudes of her central Pennsylvania village is attributed by its citizens to her "foreignness": her mother "used to live in France" (53), has a French maid, and makes a good living by translating ("'Seems so funny for a colored woman to speak and write a foreign language,'" asserts one of Emmy's teachers. "'I like colored people to look and act like what they are'" [53]). Emmy and her mother's association with French language and culture, like her friend Archie's olive-skinned racial ambiguity (he is often taken by white people for a "foreigner," and when a white colleague discovers his liaison with a "colored lady friend," his taste is attributed to his "foreign notions" [72]), is a cause for suspicion, not privilege, in their community. Their "Frenchness" is bound up in the history of slavery and the social and legal constraints against miscegenation: Emmy's grandmother was a slave woman. In one instance Emmy's knowledge of French is a currency that might allow her to buy off some of the stigma of blackness—a classmate offers to allow Emmy to join her club if she helps her with her French verbs, asserting to Emmy that "'colored folks can't expect to have what we have, or if they do they must pay extra for it'" (56)—but Emmy's racial pride prevents her from acquiescing to the rules of that game.

The story is permeated by problematic tropes of representation in the verbal and visual arts. In a misguided attempt to help Emmy learn her place in American society, her teacher, Miss Wenzel, gives Emmy a copy of a Robert Louis Stevenson poem entitled "A Task." Emmy's instinctive racial pride and self-satisfaction cause her to misunderstand her teacher's purpose, however, and read the poem's message to suit her own life and perspective on her dilemma. In rejecting her classmate's racist invitation to exchange her French skills for a discount in the social cost of her blackness, Emmy declares that she finally understands a line in the poem. According to the white supremacist mores of American society, Emmy has not only misread the poem, but she has also misread her place in the world.

By contrast, her friend Archie is all too eager to accept others' representations of him. Archie decides to pass for white after he allows his imagination to be sparked by a "quixotic" young white man's construction of a racial narrative for him. The wealthy white man, interested in Archie's "history" spins a fanciful tale of Archie's present and future life:

> A guest at one of the hotels one summer had taken an interest in the handsome, willing bellboy and inquired into his history. Archie had hesitated at first, but finally, his eye alert for the first sign of dislike or superiority, he told the man of his Negro blood. . . .
>
> "By George! How exciting your life must be—now white and now black—standing between ambition and honor, what? Not that I don't think you're

doing the right thing—it's nobody's confounded business anyway. Look here, when you get through, look me up, I may be able to put you wise to something. Here's my card. And say, mum's the word, and when you've made your pile you can wake some fine morning and find yourself famous simply by telling what you are. All rot, this beastly prejudice, I say." (58)

The first conflict that Emmy and Archie experience as a courting couple occurs in a theater after Archie has decided to pass,[4] and the second confrontation— a scene where Emmy expects a marriage proposal and Archie expects her acquiescence to a two-year deferral of their wedding date—is full of imagery from the visual and the performing arts. As Emmy waits for her lover's visit, she prepares herself as if for a role in a performance: she chooses an appropriate costume (a symbolically red dress) and decides to pretend to resist his entreaties ("'Well, I'll tell him I will [marry him] Christmas. Dear old Archie, coming all this way to tell me that. I'll let him beg me two or three times first, and then I'll tell him. Won't he be pleased? I wouldn't be a bit surprised if he went down on his knees again'" [68]). In the midst of Archie's agitated visit, Emmy visualizes herself as a figure in a sentimental picture: "The grey mist outside in the somber garden, the fire crackling on the hearth and casting ruddy shadows on Archie's hair, the red of her dress, Archie himself—all this was making for her a picture, which she saw repeated on the endless future Sunday afternoons in Philadelphia" (69).

When she realizes that Archie is suggesting putting off the marriage because he can't be associated with a woman of color at this point in his career, Emmy pretends that she never wanted to marry him, and even after he leaves the house, she is aware of the theatricality of the incident, experiencing an uncharacteristic sense of self-division: "She crossed heavily to the armchair and flung herself into it. Her mind seemed to go on acting as if it were clockwork and she were watching it. Once she said, 'Now this, I suppose, is what they call a tragedy'" (69). Later, in Philadelphia, Archie is unmasked as a "Negro" when his employer confronts the melodramatic scene of Archie "mooning" over Emmy's photograph. To the white male spectator, Archie's performance of a young white gentleman in love becomes a performance of sexual perversion when the object of his romantic yearning is a black woman, and then becomes a major disruption of the order of things—both in his office and in the larger social world—when Archie reveals himself as a black man.

The moral crisis in the story surrounds Emmy's reaction to—or reading of— her mother's cautionary tale, based on her own experience of love and marriage, about the perils of misreading a situation based on the lexicon of racial and sexual exploitation, violence, silence, and pride. Mrs. Carrél relates how her husband, coming home unexpectedly, found her in the arms of a white man. He accused his wife of infidelity, and struck her "'—you mustn't blame him; child. Remember it was the same spirit showing in both of us, in different ways. I was doing all I could to provoke him by keeping silence and he merely retaliated in his way. The blow wouldn't have harmed a little bird'" (141). Insulted by his accusations, Mrs. Carrél banned him from her house and her life rather than explain that the white man was her father, her own "mother's guardian, protector, everything, but not her husband" (141). The Carréls' reconciliation is aborted by a shipwreck, which kills Emmy's father en route back to his wife; "his body was so badly mangled, they wouldn't even let [her] see him" (141). The irony of the chapter from family history lies in the fact that Mrs. Carrél's father, on his fateful visit to her, "'had come after all these years to make some reparation. It was through him that I first began translating for the publishers. You know yourself how my work has grown'" (141).

Emmy, however, characteristically misreads this didactic tale, which, in its nineteenth-century prescription of womanly sacrifice ("'If you really loved Archie . . . you'd let him marry you and lock you off, away from all the world, just so long as you were with him'" [141]), only increases her "gloom" and bitterness about the poisonous role of "color" in black women's relationships. While her mother ascribes Emmy's romantic dilemma to Emmy's "pride" and "talk of color," Emmy has a different interpretation of both her mother's romantic tragedy and her own: "'It wouldn't have happened at all if we hadn't been colored,' she told herself moodily. 'If grandmother hadn't been colored she wouldn't have been a slave, and if she hadn't been a slave—That's what it is, color—color—it's wrecked mother's life and now it's wrecking mine'" (141).

Emmy goes as far into her depression to wish, for a moment, that she were white, before she "check[s] herself angrily" (141). Although she rejects her mother's advice of self-suppression and self-silencing and refuses to crawl back to Archie, Emmy does resolve to adopt the nineteenth-century woman's mask of "cheerfulness" before her mother. Fortunately for her, and crucial to the ideology of race pride that the story affirms, Emmy does not have to resort to that. Archie returns to her, full of apologies, and asks her to marry him and join him in the Philippines, where he finds a job through Emmy's mother's connections, as it seems impossible for him to pursue his career as a black man in the United States. Unlike the racial outsiders in nineteenth-century novels such as George Eliot's *Daniel*

. Helen Hunt Jackson's *Ramona,* the couple need not leave their native
_y to live a fulfilling life: a Christmas Eve change of heart on the part of
.rchie's white employer ensures that he can pursue his career and their class-appropriate marriage there in Pennsylvania.

Despite its coincidences and conventional language, the story is radical in its insistence on Emmy's rejection of nineteenth-century racial and gender identities and life plots available to black women, as well as its rejection of the notion that African Americans must expatriate themselves to find professional and personal freedom. Another early story, "'There Was One Time!' A Story of Spring," also ends with a black couple eschewing an easier career in another country—this time, France—and resolving "to live that wonderful fairy tale" in New York ("'There Was One Time!' A Story of Spring," 15).

The protagonist, Anna Fetters, is a "typical American girl done over in brown" who graduates with "the quota of useless French—or German—vocabulary which the average pupil brings out of the average High School" (ibid., 273). She "must teach foreign languages—always her special detestation" (272)—because of intractable discrimination in the job market of her small Pennsylvania town. Trained in a business school and excelling in mechanical drawing, Anna bitterly "realize[s] the handicap of color" when she discovers that no business will hire her and that the only employment opportunities open to a black woman are teaching or domestic service. Deeply angry, frustrated, and resentful, Anna has spent two years working as a waitress, and her mother, who takes solace in the delusions of religion, worked as a maid while Anna attended night school for teacher training. Anna is finally hired to teach at a "colored school," "but Fate, with a last malevolence, saw to it that she was appointed to teach History and French" (272). At the opening of the story the French language, rather than being a marker of education and class status, is for Anna a symbol of discrimination, humiliation, and "the merciless indifference of life" (272).

The French fairy tale romance that she tries to get her students to understand is far removed from her life and theirs, and when a brief bolt for temporary freedom is cut short by a white tramp's attempted sexual assault on her, Anna concludes, "This is what could happen to you if you are a colored girl playing at being a French shepherdess" (275). A Prince Charming does rescue her, but irony permeates her own version of the fairy tale of the shepherdess and the prince. Her nameless savior's bout with malaria contracted in colonized Guiana makes him a weak and apparently fearful defender of his damsel's virtue. As part of a series of "anti–fairy tale" turns of the plot, the potential prince then disappears from Anna's life for several weeks. While many critics have identified the fairy tale plot structure in Fauset's novels,[5] this story, which features a prince whose spring fever is diseased ("'I get it every spring, darn it!'" [277]) rather than romantic, suggests that Euro-American fairy tale tropes are inappropriate for "two young colored people" (275) in America. In fact, when several weeks later Anna (whose French language skills are rudimentary, keeping her only a few pages ahead of her pupils) returns to her laborious translation of the fairy tale, which had been interrupted by a period of what is described as typical, for "colored" schools, curricular disorganization, she speculates that it will end with the prince giving the shepherdess a job rather than making her queen: "Perhaps, she thought fancifully that Thursday evening,—the shepherdess meets the prince again and he gives her a position as court-artist" (11). When Anna does finish the story, her translation is woefully inadequate; the narrator describes it as a "mutilation" (12) rather than a translation of the story.

Her Prince Charming also has connections to the French language, but that language for him is a sign of his migratory life in the colonized black diaspora. The nameless stranger is a foreigner yet American—born in New Jersey, he spent his childhood in British Guiana and then ran away and lived a vagabond life in England and France before making a kind of reverse migration "home to Harlem." A critic of the white imperial "cold-bloodedness which enables a civilized people to maim and kill in the Congo and on the Putumayo, or to lynch in Georgia" (276), his politics of racial uplift is informed by his transnational experiences and diasporic consciousness.

Translation and mistranslation, reading and misreading, are tropes that course their way through the story, from the students' insistence on mistranslating the conventional opening lines of French fairy tales to Mrs. Fetter's habitual misuse of biblical phrases and her propensity to turn common phrases "upside down" (12). It is the effort of translation and deferral of comprehension that unites the lovers at the end of the story—Anna's thick-headed pupil in French class miraculously starts turning in apt translations, thanks to his uncle's help. His uncle, ironically bearing the name "Winter" in "A Tale of Spring," had misinterpreted his nephew's interest in his German books, thus not realizing that Tommy was one of Anna's pupils until several weeks after meeting her. Although Anna and Richard plan a future together involving a return to the freedom of Europe, where Richard would "build bridges and [Anna could] draw the plans" (14), they must wait until after the war, in the meantime "liv[ing] that wonderful fairy tale" in Harlem.

Fauset's multilayered identity as both implied and explicit narrator in these short early works questions the ontological status of the categories of nation, race, and gender that are fundamental to any black diasporic political project. Emmy's— and later in *Plum Bun*, Angela's—recurring question, "What's the difference?" haunts these early narratives with the possibility of the unthinkable response that finally, there might only be "difference" and thus the political and cultural project, which depends on cross-cultural and transnational articulation, is doomed to failure. These stories' depiction of disappointed idealism, vignettes of misreading, as well as being misread, and deft evocation and debunking of stereotypes reminds us of the difficulties of creating a black feminist rhetoric in the New Negro era. In Fauset's texts the black woman narrator's creative subjectivity dramatizes the problems of modernist ideas of the self as a fragmented, fluid consciousness negotiating a world whose only coherence is that imposed on it by the imagination. The New Negro, and then the Négritude, writers later discovered the difficulties inherent in delegitimizing essentialist ideas of race left over from nineteenth-century pseudoscience while trying to identify qualities of "negritude" that could transcend national and social identities on which modern black people could build a global agenda for liberation.

Edwards's iteration of Senghor's concept of décalage may also help to explain contemporary readers' (including his own) enduring uneasiness with Fauset's work, even as we acknowledge its complexity and range. Despite his invitation to appreciate Fauset, on the basis of her essays, as more than "solely an apologist for the urban U.S. black bourgeoisie" (Edwards, 135), even he is disappointed with the ultimate value of her literary and political contributions, which he attributes to her ladylike qualities (as Fabre, Wall, and Sato do): "self-effacement," "reticence," and "her cloistered upbringing" (138–40). His discussion of her focuses on missed opportunities and her failure to fulfill postmodern readers' expectations:

> Unfortunately, whereas Fauset's essays are unprecedented in the ways they introduce gender issues, they never sustain this approach toward an articulation of diaspora which would combine anti-imperialism with a Feminist critique. In one sense, this is due to Fauset's habitual self-effacement. . . .
>
> . . . This kind of reticence carries over into Fauset's essays on poverty and everyday life in Europe: the portraits of women in her articles . . . never push issues of gender as far as they might.

. . . Fauset's work tends to retrench its own limitation and to reproduce its own injunctions, especially by a recourse to sentimentality. Her vision of black internationalism, as sharp-sighted as it can be in her essays on the Pan-African Congress, curdles into a discourse of *nostalgia* as it strains to elide and compensate for the very gaps and discrepancies it uncovers. (138, 141)

From the earliest criticisms of Jessie Fauset's work, as not working-class enough and not "black" enough, to the late-twentieth-century criticisms of her work, as not going "far enough" into feminist territory, to postmodern complaints that her writing looks back rather than forward, it is clear that we still have problems reading and appreciating it. Could it be we, the readers, who are stuck in our conventions of understanding "feminism," "modernism," and liberation writing rather than Fauset herself? Could readers—whether in the 1920s, in the 1960s, or at the opening of a new century—be resisting the disorientation of perspective that Fauset's work imposes on her readers? This discussion is only the beginning, I hope, of an era of new analyses and fresh appreciation of Fauset's rhetorical and political challenges to her readers, challenges that may broaden our understanding of her contributions to the canon of American modernist texts.

NOTES

1. Though this phrase, so often uttered or written in the same breath as Fauset's name, has been attributed to Langston Hughes, I have been unable to determine its origin.

2. It is difficult not to also read into this vignette an allusion to the Hottentot Venus, Sarah Baartman.

3. This question is also a major ground note of *Plum Bun*, as the protagonist, Angela, realizes that racial identity is in the eye of the beholder and not inherent in any physical or internal characteristics.

4. From Du Bois's heavily ironic scene in "Of the Coming of John" to scenes in Johnson's *Autobiography of an Ex-Colored Man*, Chesnutt's *House behind the Cedars*, and Gwendolyn Brooks's *Maude Martha*, African American writers in the early twentieth century used theaters as settings for dramas of racial performance and representation on the audience's side of the footlights, milking the ironic tensions between discourses of culture and civilization and the brutality of racial injustice.

5. See, e.g., McDowell, "Introduction," xxx.

BIBLIOGRAPHY

Edwards, Brent Hayes. *The Practice of Diaspora: Literature, Translation, and the Rise of Black Internationalism.* Cambridge, MA: Harvard University Press, 2003.

Fabre, Michel. *From Harlem to Paris: Black American Writers in France, 1840–1980.* Urbana: University of Illinois Press, 1991.

Fauset, Jessie Redmon. "Dark Algiers the White." *Crisis,* April 1925, 255–57; and May 1925, 16–20.

———. "Emmy." *Crisis,* Dec. 1912, 79–87; and Jan. 1913, 134–42.

———. *Plum Bun: A Novel without a Moral.* Boston: Beacon Press, 1999.

———. " 'There Was One Time!' A Story of Spring." *Crisis,* April 1917, 272–77; and May 1917, 11–15.

Griffin, Erica. "The 'Invisible Woman' Abroad: Jessie Fauset's New Horizon." In *Recovered Writers/Recovered Texts: Race, Class, and Gender in Black Women's Literature,* ed. Dolan Hubbard, 75–89. Knoxville: University of Tennessee Press, 1997.

Locke, Alain. "The New Negro." Introduction to *The New Negro,* edited by Alain Locke, 3–16. New York: Atheneum, 1968.

McDowell, Deborah. "Introduction: Regulating Midwives." In Fauset, *Plum Bun,* ix-xxxiii.

Nwankwo, Ifeoma Kiddoe. *Black Cosmopolitanism: Racial Consciousness and Transnational Identity in the Nineteenth-Century Americas.* Philadelphia: University of Pennsylvania Press, 2005.

Sato, Hiroko. "Under the Harlem Shadow: A Study of Jessie Fauset and Nella Larsen." In *Remembering the Harlem Renaissance,* ed. Cary D. Wintz, 261–87. New York: Garland, 1996.

Wall, Cheryl. *Women of the Harlem Renaissance.* Bloomington: Indiana University Press, 1995.

EIGHT

Speak It into Existence

James Weldon Johnson's God's Trombones *and the Power of Self-Definition in the New Negro Harlem Renaissance*

McKinley Melton

When the writers of the New Negro Harlem Renaissance (NNHR) conceived of a "rebirth" of African American cultural expression, they understood all too well the role and significance of language in defining who they were and what their experience had been as the sons and daughters of Africa now living in America. In the foreword to *The New Negro: Voices of the Harlem Renaissance*, the editor and project initiator, Alain Locke, writes that "of all the voluminous literature on the Negro, so much is mere external view and commentary that we may warrantably say that nine-tenths of it is *about* the Negro rather than of him, so that it is the Negro problem rather than the Negro that is known and mooted in the general mind" (xxv). The only remedy for this "problem," Locke argues, is an unrelenting concentration "upon self-expression and the forces and motives of self-determination. So far as he is culturally articulate, we shall let the Negro speak for himself" (xxv). Locke argues that the record of American cultural production has denied the Negro a voice, making him a subject rather than a source. Thus, one of the first challenges to the NNHR writers was to take ownership of the dominant society's definition of black people and offer new definitions of their own.

These writers understood the need to incorporate elements of the historical tradition into the artistic production of the NNHR, regardless of how much they looked to the future. As much as they wanted to advance the status of Negro people by taking charge of their own representations and charting their own course, they understood that without recognizing their roots, the transformation they so desperately craved would inevitably falter without a solid foundation for support. Rather than abandon those cultural roots in favor of conforming to parameters imposed by mainstream white America, these writers embraced a "reimagining" of the way the story had previously been told.

James Weldon Johnson was writing out of this particular moment when he published *God's Trombones: Seven Negro Sermons in Verse* in 1927. Johnson powerfully utilized the traditions of black religious expression and biblical interpretation to present poetic sermons that both reflect those African-derived oral and performance traditions and address the specific contemporary concerns of the NNHR. Looking to the future for motivation and culling the richness of the past for inspiration, he sought to define the New Negro as one created by the legacy of the past, as well as by the imperatives of the present.

In the NNHR writer's quest to mine African American culture for examples of the authentic voice and cultural expression of "the Negro," speaking on his own behalf and out of the resources of his cultural legacy, Johnson's selection of the "song sermon" was an absolutely inspired one. Johnson's work clearly advanced the argument that, as articulated by Ekwueme Michael Thelwell, "the song sermon of the black preacher is the earliest, most original, most powerful poetic form created in American culture." The black preacher "expropriated the legends of the ancient Hebrews, rendered in the magnificent English poetry of the King James Version and elevated into a new art form by the performance conventions of the African griot: rhythm, melody, chant, mime and dramatic impersonation" (Thelwell). This marriage of Christian doctrine and African performance styles resulted in the song sermon, which would have an enduring legacy as "the highest expression of the African American oral tradition" (Thelwell).

Johnson felt a tremendous responsibility to honor the cultural significance of the song sermon, and he clearly recognized the inadequacy of the literary form to capture many important dimensions of the art form. Properly understood, the art form herein referred to as "the song sermon" is a collective, collaborative enterprise involving the full participation of preacher, congregants, choir, and musicians. There was no such phrase in Johnson's day as "performance art" and the text of these sermons—which Johnson has so skillfully reduced to literary poetry on the page—is only one element, albeit a crucial one, of the form. Johnson writes that "there is, of course, no way of recreating the atmosphere—the fervor of the congregation, the amens and hallelujahs, the undertone of singing which was often a soft accompaniment to parts of the sermon" (*God's Trombones* [hereafter *GT*], 10). The magnificent music, the absolutely necessary musical responses of the congregation, the dramatic rhythms and emphases of the preacher's oratory, the melodic cadences of his song, and the ecstatic musical shouts of members moved by the spirit all combined to create a unified work of performance art with discernible structure, aesthetic conventions, and a power and beauty not seen before on these shores.

The black preacher, who was heir apparent to the cultural figure of the griot, was as much a part of the African cultural inheritance as the art form of the song sermon that he delivered. The griot was the oral historian of the Mandingo peoples, who recited and sang the story of the ancestors and the deeds of kings to the music of a chorus. All the varied cultures of West Africa, out of which the African American community was plucked, however, can be seen as contributing to the repertoire of the African American preacher. The African tale-teller, the supreme artist of the oral tradition, was as multifaceted as he was eloquent. He was actor, singer, dancer, composer, director, mime, and a supreme virtuoso on his vocal instrument. In a performance, for example, of an animal fable, his voice would approximate a roar in the role of lion as quickly as it would answer timorously in the higher registers of the hare; when the sly fox entered the tale, the voice would resonate with guile and treachery. All good African tales have a song, which the tale-teller sings and directs the chorus as the audience responds. His movement and body language reflect the action and drama of the story with extraordinarily precise mime. When dances were incorporated (as they frequently were), the griot would perform the steps with grace and elegance. A superior African tale-teller was a consummate artist, commanding many skills, and anyone fortunate enough to see a good black preacher in the rural South deliver one of these sermons would immediately recognize the entire repertoire of skills at work.

Johnson lauded the black preacher's oratorical skill, painting a portrait of the folk preacher that was a near mirror image of the griot who preceded him. Acknowledging the daunting task of capturing the preacher figure through words on the page, Johnson describes his own witnessing of the preacher in action: "He strode the pulpit up and down in what was actually a very rhythmic dance, and he brought into play the full gamut of his wonderful voice, a voice—what shall I say?—not of an organ or a trumpet, but rather of a trombone, the instrument possessing above all others the power to express the wide and varied range of emotions encompassed by the human voice. . . . He intoned, he moaned, he pleaded—he blared, he crashed, he thundered" (*GT*, 6–7). Johnson, in large part, was driven to produce this literary effort by his own recognition that the preacher, "a man of positive genius," had "not yet been given the niche in which he properly belong[ed]" (*GT*, 4, 2). Johnson crafted his poetic sermons to reflect the preacher's genius, understanding that his words must leap from the page and exist beyond the text in such a way as to honor the legacy of a cultural hero who had never received the respect he was due.

While *God's Trombones* is, by Johnson's own acknowledgment, limited in its ability to capture fully the art form of the song sermon or the power of the preacher's delivery, the text provides a powerful example of NNHR literature precisely because of Johnson's ability to focus on language, a focus that serves to highlight the cultural traditions that inform the NNHR movement. A principle aim of this collection—that of defining the New Negro by reclaiming power over language—has its roots in the spiritual ancestry of the New Negro, reaching back to the African Continent. Janheinz Jahn, in *Muntu: An Outline of the New African Culture*, explains this significance of language in terms of the prominent Dogan cultural concept of "nommo": "Nommo is water and the glow of fire and seed and word in one. Nommo, the life force, is a unity of spiritual-physical fluidity, giving life to everything, penetrating everything, causing everything. . . . And since man has power over the word, it is he who directs the life force. Through the word he receives it, shares it with other beings, and so fulfills the meaning of life" (124). It is important to recognize that the New Negro movement was driven by the desire to reclaim basic humanity and its attendant rights, such as those held by their ancestors over "the word" itself.

Jahn's recognition of the power of the word should prove significant in a literary movement. The example that he offers as a follow-up, his description of conception, which is effected "not only through the seed, but at the same time through the word" (124), has, however, a particularly strong connection to the project of the NNHR writers, who were literally endorsing a "rebirth" by categorizing their efforts as a renaissance. Jahn writes that "this Nommo, which effects conception and then calls forth birth, is not sufficient to produce a complete human being, a personality, a muntu. For the new-born child becomes a muntu only when the father or the 'sorcerer' gives him a name and pronounces it. . . . Before this the little body is . . . a thing; if it dies, it is not even mourned" (125). Jahn concludes that "all the activities of men, and all the movement in nature, rest on the word, on the productive power of the word, which is water and heat and seed and Nommo, that is, life force itself" (125).

While it is unlikely that NNHR writers such as Johnson were grounding their efforts in a deliberate engagement of "nommo," the concept of language power was certainly a significant aspect of the spiritual traditions of the African American community. A consideration of other African-descended peoples provides evidence of the significance of this word power in the oral traditions of diasporic communities. In discussing the rituals of the Candomblé in Brazil, for example, José Flávio Pessoa de Barros acknowledges that "the word has a special place . . . possessing the power to animate life and stimulate the Ashe [again, life force] contained in nature. The intentions, petitions, and desired outcomes of religious practice should be verbalized. It is unthinkable to ask the òrìṣàs anything in silence" (404). Indeed, according to Pessoa de Barros, in order for any desires or appeals "to reach the gods, the word should be movement" (404). Writers of the NNHR such as Johnson selected language as the tool for channeling their own collective "life force" to effect change, directly engaging the very same distinct and distinguished cultural heritage that served as a foundation for patterns of cultural expression throughout the diaspora.

To engage this diasporic cultural heritage, there was perhaps no better source than the religious and cultural figure of the preacher and the oral tradition from which he emerges, as Johnson does. Johnson crafts his own representations of sermons against a poetic backdrop, attempting to capture the power of the slave preacher, whom he recognizes in the preface as "above all, an orator . . . a master of all modes of eloquence" (*GT*, 5). Johnson admits the complexity of the preacher's language, describing it as "saturated with the sublime phraseology of the Hebrew prophets and steeped in the idioms of King James English, so when they preached and warmed to their work they spoke another language, a language far removed from traditional Negro dialect. It was really a fusion of Negro idioms with Bible English; and in this there may have been, after all, some kinship with the innate grandiloquence of their old African tongues" (*GT*, 9). Thus, Johnson's preacher stands where the influence of the "old African tongues" meets with a second tradition where language is a defining and creative force: that of Judeo-Christianity.

For acknowledgment of the power of the word within the Judeo-Christian tradition, we may consider the themes of naming and claiming that run throughout the Bible, which emerge from the very beginning, specifically Genesis. Genesis 1:3 explains the process of creation: "and God said, let there be light: and there was light." The idea that the Lord, in his role as creator, had but to speak in order to create the world resonates with traditional West African cultures that position the "Great Creator" as occupying the same sphere as humankind. Distinctly, however, the "Great Creator" possesses the greatest life force, which in turn endows his words with the greatest power. The idea that humankind shares in the power to create by declaration is reflective not only of traditional West African cultures but of a Judeo-Christian tradition that acknowledges human beings as made in the image of God and likewise recognizes the power possessed by those who allow God's words to abide in them.[1]

Thus, as we consider the importance of Johnson's *God's Trombones*, we must acknowledge that the work functions on multiple levels. Johnson argues and demonstrates that the preacher's repertoire of poetic language, rhythm, and musical elements and the deployment of black idiom are among the finest and most original artistic accomplishments of the Negro race. In making this claim, he answers Alain Locke's call to the NNHR writer: "For the present, more immediate hope rests in the revaluation by white and black alike of the Negro in terms of his artistic endowments and cultural contributions, past and prospective. It must be increasingly recognized that the Negro has already made very substantial contributions, not only in his folk-art, music especially, which has always found appreciation, but in larger, though humbler and less acknowledged ways" (Locke, 15).

Johnson works to elevate the "less acknowledged" figure of the preacher, fully participating in what Anne Carroll refers to as "a far-reaching project that engaged many of the participants of the Harlem Renaissance," the hope "that texts showing African Americans' accomplishments might contribute to a reassessment of African Americans, and that such a reassessment might help undermine the racism that was still prevalent in American society in the 1920s" (Carroll, 57). More than providing a showcase for the artistic accomplishments of the Negro, Johnson's text also harnesses the power of the word to directly engage the imperatives of social and political equality, which were central not only to the NNHR but to the art form of the song sermon itself.

The poetic sermons presented by Johnson in *God's Trombones* raise significant claims regarding the Negro's place within the Judeo-Christian tradition, and the themes likewise address the aims of the NNHR. The sermons simultaneously redefine biblical narratives and reposition the Negro within these narratives, the historical record, and contemporary society as well. While Johnson clearly draws on the cultural heritage of the African and African American oral tradition through the style in which he writes, the sermons also contain important messages about what direction this "New Negro" should take to carve out his or her own niche in the world. The New Negro must not continue in what Locke describes as his or her previous role of being "more of a formula than a human being—a something to be argued about, condemned or defended" (Locke, 3). The sermons in *God's Trombones*, anchored in a religious foundation with far-reaching cultural goals, function on several levels, reflecting and compounding much of the other literary work being done during this critical period.

To fully understand the cultural work that *God's Trombones* does within its particular historical moment, one must also appreciate the central importance of biblical interpretation within African American culture, which is as central to the sermons' effectiveness as the preacher-figure's linguistic and performance skill. For many African Americans the Bible is not a static document but a living and breathing text that speaks directly to the circumstances they face on a daily basis. Indeed, "to a remarkable degree, there is a spirit of collective engagement with the biblical text in the black community" (Felder, 7). This collective engagement was largely due to the shared sense of oppression that blacks felt with the struggles of biblical figures such as the Israelites, long held in Egyptian bondage. Being instantly drawn to those biblical tales that positioned the Lord as defender and liberator of the oppressed and imprisoned, blacks "heard and read the Bible through the existential reality of their own oppression in America, and that reality allowed them to readily identify with the historical oppressions recorded in Scripture" (Hoyt, 28). Thus, blacks were inspired to consider each incident of biblical oppression "in terms of an analogous, concrete, historical event within their own experience" (Hoyt, 28). Beyond the theme of oppression, however, biblical narratives also resonated tremendously in times of triumph, as well.

God's Trombones builds on the tradition of African American biblical interpretation as Johnson's sermons solidify the relationship between biblical and African American history by locating African Americans firmly within the Judeo-Christian tradition, offering distinctly African American language to frame the sermons and placing African American characters within them. Compounding the power of self-definitive written language, Johnson's sermons are complemented by the inclusion of African American subjects within the illustrations by Aaron Douglas that punctuate the text. The text and the artwork operate in concert to achieve a common goal, as was the expectation of NNHR leaders for all artistic production of the time. This African American presence is evident in the first sermon included in the text, which was also the first sermon written by

Johnson in 1917, ten years before the collection's publication. Although the sermons in *God's Trombones* are not organized in chronological order of subject, as is the Bible, Johnson still chooses to begin the collection of sermons, following an opening prayer, exactly where the Bible begins, with "The Creation."

The biblical account of the creation is, of course, a central element of the Judeo-Christian tradition, forming the foundation for the religious practitioners of every race. The creation myth holds particular significance for African Americans, however, as is the case with many of the sources that Johnson draws on for this collection. He begins his sermon by offering a humanized God, an important aspect of the African American religious experience:

> And God stepped out on space,
> And he looked around and said:
> I'm lonely—
> I'll make me a world (*GT*, 17)

Robert Fleming explains: "The anthropomorphic God who appears in these lines is maintained consistently throughout the poem. He is not the remote, formal, all-knowing God of the Scriptures so much as an approachable, questioning, evolving Being with whom the listener could identify. Creation is an act of problem-solving, as God seeks to remedy the loneliness that has plagued Him; thus He is not only an understanding but an understandable Being" (55). Johnson's portrait disallows the conception of God as a distant, shadowy figure sheltered in the far-removed spiritual world of heaven. Furthermore, Johnson's preacher describes a process by which humankind is created to fulfill the needs of God and establishes a symbiotic relationship that allows black listeners to see themselves as more than a ward of a powerful God. Rather, the text promotes the black community's view of God as personally connected to them by virtue of being not only involved in their struggle but invested in their very existence.

The conception of God as an approachable being is important because of the African American need to see God not simply as a protector and liberator, nor simply as a friend, but also as a father figure, a position that was vital because "the universal parenthood of God implied a universal kinship within humankind" (Hoyt, 32). This biblical understanding was in large part what allowed religious African Americans to dismiss society's imposing of inferiority upon them and encouraged them to lay claim to their rights as Americans, secured under the doctrine that "all men are created equal."

Johnson further advocates for the rights of African Americans to embrace their position as children of God by including specific African American sensibilities within the sermon of the "The Creation." Not only does he offer the figure of a humanized God, but Johnson "uses folk idioms such as 'I'll make me a world'" and "the description of God making man 'like a mammy bending over her baby'" to allow black listeners to visualize themselves as a part of the story (Collier, 359). The recognition of the black presence at the very creation of the world was significant not only for African Americans' religious identity but for their secular self-conception as well. Similar themes are expressed throughout the NNHR period, as writers sought to reclaim a distinguished cultural past that the dominant society attempted to deny them. There was no stronger argument for the rights of humanity than the declaration that blacks were present from the very beginning.

Langston Hughes offers a similar conception in his famous poem "The Negro Speaks of Rivers," as his narrator speaks of knowing "rivers ancient as the world and older than the flow of human blood in human veins" and having "bathed in the Euphrates when dawns were young" (lines 2, 4). Placing the Negro at the moment of creation allows for a certain longevity and depth of African American culture, but it also makes a very strong claim on the right to equality that was central to the work of the NNHR. Johnson's and Hughes's inclusion of black voices within the conversation of creation serves not only to define the moment of creation as a genesis for "All God's Chillun" but also to firmly position blacks as the rightful heirs to the power that enables a reality to be created through the invocation of the spoken word.

Johnson continues the theme of locating an African American presence within the Judeo-Christian tradition in the next sermon included in *God's Trombones*, "The Prodigal Son." He begins the sermon by addressing the prodigal son figure directly:

Young man—
Young man—
Your arm's too short to box with God. (*GT*, 21)

In addition to once again invoking African American idiom, Johnson capitalizes on a recurring theme within the black sermon, explained by Henry Mitchell in a chapter of his *Black Preaching* titled "The Black Bible." Mitchell asserts: "The Black imagination adds appropriate dimensions and details to the biblical protagonist, whether individual or group. It is common in Black sermons to hear lengthy and gripping discussions of Bible characters. The instinctive attempt is made to speak of the biblical person as one who might have known him. . . . In other words, the sketch is intended to be intimate and thus more influential on the hearer from the speaker's having been closer up" (123). As both speaker and hearer are immersed in the performed sermon, they become more than eyewitnesses to biblical proceedings and position themselves as active participants, so much so that the narrative takes on the quality of firsthand testimony.

The intimacy between the listener as reader and the protagonist is later intensified through Douglas's illustration. Apparently inspired by Johnson's description of the prodigal son's time in Babylon as being filled with "dancing and gambling," "wine and whiskey," and "hot-mouthed women" (GT, 25), Anne Carroll observes that "Douglas moves beyond Johnson's rendering of the parable to set it in Harlem in the 1920s" (70). While this capitalizes on the tradition of reimagining biblical events in concrete terms reflective of the black experience, Douglas's illustration of a young man dancing to the sound of trombones and surrounded by money, liquor, and cards "hints at the importance of imagining stories in different settings and with different characters than they usually include" (Carroll, 71).

Douglas not only provides a setting reminiscent of 1920s Harlem in order to draw the parallels with the Babylon in which the prodigal son finds himself lost; his illustrations throughout the text decidedly render the characters identifiably African American. With the illustration accompanying "The Prodigal Son," as with all of the other illustrations that include human figures, Douglas uses "styles of representation that echo Egyptian and African art for the eyes of the figures," using "not only the slit eye from Dan masks, but also a rendering of the human form common in Egyptian art, with the shoulders and hips in the picture plane, facing the viewer, but the head turned at a right angle" (Carroll, 71). The reimagining and redefining of these characters' racial identity was in direct support of the aims of the NNHR, particularly with the goal of revitalizing the landscape of American cultural traditions in order to recognize the Negro as an equal participant in the diasporic community. "In American culture, Biblical characters are depicted, most often, as white. But Douglas's illustrations suggest that the white identity of those characters is not necessarily a historical truth but a construction of illustrator and viewer" (Carroll, 73). Taking this argument outside the parameters of a religious context, Douglas's renderings of biblical characters as African American had significant implications in encouraging viewers to "reconsider their assumptions about historical narratives, particularly black people's roles in them" (Carroll, 72). The ability to reconsider these assumptions was a natural result when black writers took control of the language that had been used to define them for generations, creating these historical narratives in the first place.

Similar work is done by Johnson through the actual texts of the sermons—not only when he provides African American sensibilities to these biblical protagonists but also when he directly acknowledges one of those figures as being black, such as with the figure of Simon in "The Crucifixion." Johnson writes of Simon, most widely known as the man who helped Christ carry his cross:

> And then they laid hold on Simon,
> Black Simon, yes, black Simon;
> They put the cross on Simon,
> And Simon bore the cross." (*GT*, 41)

The inclusion of Simon, a central figure in the story of the Crucifixion, and the significant emphasis that Johnson places on his blackness are not only for the purpose of showing "Blacks as part and parcel of Biblical events" (Carroll, 72). Rather, it is important to note the role that Simon is playing: that of burden-sharer in the pains and crucifixion of Christ, a role reversal given the Lord's reputation as a "burden bearer and heavy load sharer."[2] Simon's effort to help carry the load after Johnson's preacher narrates "I see him sink beneath the load, / I see my drooping Jesus sink" (*GT*, 41) recognizes the humanity of Christ and allows for the same accessibility that Johnson previously ascribes to God the Father in "The Creation."

Furthermore, the inclusion of a sympathetic black presence, easing the suffering of Christ, renders Christ's sacrifice that much more immediate and identifiable for the congregation. Whatever the textual origin or the accuracy of historical evidence, the identification of Simon of Cyrene as "black" or African is a long-held, widely distributed, deeply embedded element of the liturgical and commonly held oral tradition of the black church. In the 1923 "A Prayer for Good Friday" George Alexander McGuire, founder and head of the black-nationalist African Orthodox Church in America, addresses the crucifixion: "Almighty Saviour, whose heavy Cross was laid upon the stalwart shoulders of Simon the Cyrenian, a son of Ham, in that sad hour of thine agony and mortal weakness, when the sons of Shem delivered thee into the hands of the sons of Japheth to be crucified, regard with thy favor this race still struggling beneath the cross of injustice, oppression, and wrong laid upon us by our persecutors" (133).

As McGuire discusses the details of the Crucifixion, he refers to the popular lore regarding the biblical origin of the races, acknowledging the roles played by the sons of Ham, Shem, and Japheth, thus racializing not only Simon but all of the participants in Christ's crucifixion. Notably, McGuire places Christ's blood on the "hands of the sons of Japheth," Japheth being the son of Noah widely regarded as the ancestor of the peoples of Europe, the same group responsible for placing generations of heavy loads on African Americans. What is important in Johnson's poetic sermon, and McGuire's prayer, is not the historical "accuracy" of the biblical figures' race but the place and role of racial lore in the black liturgy, hence in the religious sensibilities of the congregation.

Even without the direct references to race, however, Christ's endurance of oppression and crucifixion held tremendous resonance within the African American religious tradition. Robert Fleming points out that "at first there is no attempt to relate the sufferings of the Savior to those of the black people of the United States—sufferings of which Johnson was all too aware after his years of service with the NAACP—but a black congregation hearing such a sermon, like the black reader, would not need to be reminded of the parallel" (Fleming, 57). This concept is key not only to sermons that narrated the crucifixion but to all sermons whose subjects, heightened by the performance style in which they were delivered, spoke directly to the conditions faced by African Americans.

The reference to black Simon is not essential in drawing a parallel between the crucifixion and the oppression of blacks, but it is nevertheless valuable. After the reference to Simon's blackness "the connection has become explicit, and, along with Jesus, the black listener could shudder at the sound of the hammer and feel the pain being inflicted" (Fleming, 58). Even without Simon's carrying his share of the burden, the "aspect of a suffering messiah, like Jesus, especially serves as an analogue to black suffering. In their suffering, blacks have identified with the birth, life, death, and resurrection of Jesus, and hence in Jesus blacks have found a true friend" (Hoyt, 29). Significantly, the relationship between the black listener, or reader, and the crucified Christ is more than that of witnesses to each other's pain. Rather, friendship is possible because each feels empathy for the other, having been placed in analogous positions of persecution.

The expansion of one oppressed victim's pain into a shared experience with a black audience through literature is certainly not unique to Johnson's God's Trombones, and "The Crucifixion" reverberates quite prominently with another important literary genre of the NNHR—lynching literature. The parallels between the Crucifixion and the act of lynching are highlighted throughout the sermon, as Johnson refers to the very public ritual fueled by the humiliation and mutilation of Christ. The resonance with other lynching literature appears, as well, at moments such as when Johnson writes, "They crucified my Jesus. / They nailed him to the cruel tree" (*GT*, 41), a moment that recalls Angelina Weld Grimké's personification of the tree from which a man is lynched in her "Tenebris," also published in 1927. Other writers make the connection more explicit. Countee Cullen, in his 1922 poem "Christ Recrucified," writes, "The South is crucifying Christ again / By all the laws of ancient rote and rule" (lines 1–2). The significance of lynching literature itself is certainly worth noting, as a major aim of this genre was to provide a voice for the victims of lynching, who had been previously relegated to the silenced position of visual spectacle.

Furthermore, Johnson's condemnation of the "they" who crucified Christ is echoed through Cullen's palpable contempt for the spectators of the lynching:

> They kill him now with famished tongues of fire,
> And while he burns, good men, and women, too,
> Shout, battling for his black and brittle bones. (lines 12–14)

Further drawing the parallel between those who crucified Christ and the lawless lynch mobs that terrorized blacks is Johnson's inclusion of Pontius Pilate, "the mighty Roman Governor" to whom the mob dragged "blameless Jesus." Pilate declares, "In this man I find no fault," yet the mob cries out to "Crucify him!" anyway (*GT*, 40–41). This is a direct commentary on the manner by which mob justice operates outside of the boundaries of the legal system that is supposed to be in control. In much the same way that the declaration of innocence in Pilate's court could not save Christ, neither were lynch mobs willing to bend to the will of legal rulings. Here we see Johnson carrying out one of his most aggressive acts of language power. He not only redefines these biblical moments in terms of the black experience, and redefines the position and role of blacks within those moments, but he also redefines the position that whites held in both the biblical and contemporary narratives.

The NNHR writers' usage of the crucifixion as a prominent trope also illustrates a classic, indeed central, process in the evolution of Afro-Christian preaching: that of selecting, adapting, and redeploying biblical characters, themes, and stories in ways accessible to the imagination of the congregation and in service to black psychic needs, spiritual aspirations, and political necessities. It should not surprise us that, for example, the early slave "exhorters," the spiritual descendants of the African griot and the ancestor of the contemporary preacher, were selective—and very tellingly so—in their appropriation of ancient Hebrew texts. The books that spoke most urgently to African Americans' perception of their circumstances were the apocalyptic books prophesying the destruction of a sinful world; the prophets Ezekiel and Jeremiah denouncing oppression, exile, dispersal, and wickedness in high places; and—perhaps most often referenced—the narrative of Exodus, recounting the deliverance of the Children of Israel, bearing obvious parallels to the African American experience in slavery.

Johnson's collection would be incomplete without the inclusion of a sermon that revolves around the Exodus narrative. In what is perhaps the strongest exercise of language power in *God's Trombones*, Johnson addresses the collective voice of an oppressed people in "Let My People Go." Although the themes of the Lord as protector of the oppressed run throughout "Let My People Go," the strength of Johnson's sermon lies in his discussion not of the Israelites' oppression but of their liberation. Alain Locke addresses the historical representation of the race, arguing that "hitherto, it must be admitted that American Negroes have been a race more in name than in fact, or to be exact, more in sentiment than in experience. The chief bond between them has been that of a common condition rather than a common consciousness; a problem in common rather than a life in common" (Locke, 7).

While the biblical story of Hebrew bondage could allow for what Locke considers a loosely constructed unity based on common oppression, Johnson's version of the story provides a different reading altogether. "Let My People Go" is a directive that demands obedience, with dire consequences for the Pharaoh should he refuse, as he does. It is the voice of the powerful, not the plea of the oppressed, that sets into motion this tale of liberation, suggesting to Renita Weems that "what one finds in the entire saga of Israel's Exodus from Egypt and its earlier attempts in the wilderness recounts the details of a social revolution. It tells of Israel's efforts to constitute itself as a theocratic community that would be the voice of an oppressed people who sought intentionally to stand in radical contradistinction to the elitist, despotic, totalitarian, oppressive values and policies of neighboring societies" (Weems, 74), The artists of the NNHR saw themselves as facing similar circumstances, acknowledging that a rebirth was necessary not only for the "New Negro," but for a nation that had failed to live up to its purported ideals of democracy and freedom.

In addition to the command that forms the sermon's title, the concluding lines also provide a decidedly political bent that connects quite well to the struggles of the NNHR:

Listen!—Listen!
All you sons of Pharaoh.
Who do you think can hold God's people
When the Lord God himself has said,
"Let my people go?" (*GT*, 52)

These lines strike a powerful chord with readers to remind them that they are indeed in the midst of a social revolution. Furthermore, the ending of this sermon, with its warning to those who wish to "hold God's people," is made that much more powerful by the fact that the following and final sermon in the collection is "The Judgment Day," a brazen challenge that informs all that the day of reckoning is at hand.

Johnson makes it clear that he writes with a particular purpose in mind, with a full awareness of the goals of the NNHR. His expressed desire to secure a newfound respect for the preacher within the context of African American cultural history is significant because of the contemporary agenda of proving Negro worth through cultural production. The NNHR was about more, however, than bringing about revolution by proving artistic merit. For Johnson the artistic movement was fueled by reaching back to the folk, honoring the folk preacher's skillful use of language that had been denied the praise it deserved. In much the same way the political and social agenda of the NNHR utilized the foundation already laid down by the folk, and the historical and cultural traditions of the Negro past, demanding the proper use of language to communicate the New Negro identity rather than simply his or her condition. *God's Trombones* laid bare the repository of religious beliefs that had sustained the Negro people. Now that "Judgment Day" was here, those beliefs needed to be employed not just to sustain but to empower and to drive forth the transformation that is at the core of exactly what a renaissance, a "rebirth," is supposed to be.

In the effort to utilize African American beliefs based on race-conscious biblical interpretation, Johnson necessarily turned to the church as a social and political body that could use the religious ideology that permeated the black existence as a means of effecting change. Thus, while "Johnson himself rejected the notion of a personal God, identifying himself as an agnostic" (Spencer, 455), he maintained a certain respect for the black church, as evidenced by his respect for the black preacher. This respect was accorded, however, only so long as they did not spout empty and static doctrine used to placate the masses rather than energize them. As Johnson wrote in his 1934 essay "The Negro Church": "The Negro church is the most powerful and, potentially, the most effective medium we possess. The whole Christian church stands at this period in need of another Reformation: a sloughing off of outworn creeds and dogmas, and an application of its power to the working out of the present-day problems of civilization and of social and spiritual life. . . . The Negro church, notwithstanding, is the most powerful agency we command for moving forward the race as a mass" (Johnson, *Negro Americans, What Now?* 20, 25).

God's Trombones, published only a few years prior to this essay, seeks to tap into the transformative energy of African American religious beliefs and rhetoric. Indeed, part of this call to the black church is Johnson's own call to the black preacher. Even as he praises the artistic and imaginative skill of the old-time folk preacher in the preface to *God's Trombones,* he reminds his readers that the "power of the old-time preacher, somewhat lessened and changed in his successors, is still a vital force; in fact, it is still the greatest single influence among the colored people of the United States" (*GT,* 3). Johnson argues that putting the preacher, and the congregation under his sway, to the most effective use in the struggle for equality should be a principal aim of the NNHR.

Once again, in this particular effort, though Johnson's work stands out as uniquely praiseworthy for his use of poetically political biblical interpretation, he was working well within the greater agenda of the NNHR. In fact, though little scholarly attention has been directed toward the religious movements within the NNHR, there was distinctly political activity occurring throughout the black church at this time. Encouraged by the likes of Johnson and Locke, who also "viewed 'Social Christianity,' as he termed it, as a possible rubric under which a new and more just social order could be worked out to benefit blacks, the poor, and women" (Spencer, 457), black ministers such as Reverdy Ransom and Adam Clayton Powell Sr. embarked on a struggle similar to the artists in their desire to bring about a redefining of the Negro presence in America. As much as Johnson admired the black preacher's skill at storytelling and oratory, he also fully understood and advocated the idea that, as Henry Mitchell argues, "the story must never be told for the sake of mere entertainment. The Black preacher, like the writer of a play, has a message. Plays and stories are processes which engage the vital emotions of an audience, making possible new understanding and a new orientation and commitment. No matter how charming the story or how captivated the audience, the Black preacher must take care of business and lead the hearer to do something about the challenge of this part of the Word of God" (Mitchell, 133).

Johnson took extreme care that *God's Trombones* would not blast out "obsolete doctrine" packaged in poetics but that the sermons would be as powerfully influential with regard to their message, as the artful way in which that message was communicated. In redefining and repositioning African Americans within a narrative as powerfully evocative as the biblical narrative, James Weldon Johnson used his poetic voice to sound an alarm notifying all who were under the sound of that voice that a new dawn had arrived in which the labels previously used to define this space and the people within it had to be questioned because of the introduction of the long absent voice of the Negro. In reclaiming that voice, NNHR writers such as Johnson engaged in the process of speaking a new reality into existence. The fact that they had confidence in their power to do so speaks to the very heart of those traditions that imbue words with transformative power, be they steeped in concepts of the life-force-affirming Nommo, Judeo-Christian creationism, or otherwise. Believing in one's own power to speak revolution into existence points to the power of faith, in one's principles, in one's strength, and in one's language, a power that, even in doses the size of a mustard seed, can command the movement of mountains.

NOTES

1. This idea runs throughout the Bible but is particularly evidenced in the book of John, where Jesus declares himself to be "the true vine": "If ye abide in me, and my words abide in you, ye shall ask what ye will, and it shall be done unto you" (John 15:1, 7).

2. Explicit reference to the burden-sharing role of the Christian God can be found in Psalms 55:22: "Cast thy burden upon the Lord, and he shall sustain thee."

BIBLIOGRAPHY

Carroll, Anne. "Art, Literature, and the Harlem Renaissance: The Messages of *God's Trombones*." *College Literature* 29, no. 3 (2002): 57–82.

Collier, Eugenia W. "James Weldon Johnson: Mirror of Change." *Phylon* 21, no. 4 (1960): 351–59.

Cullen, Countee. "Christ Recrucified." In *Witnessing Lynching: American Writers Respond*, ed. Anne P. Rice, 221–22. New Brunswick, NJ: Rutgers University Press, 2003.

Felder, Cain Hope. Introduction to *Stony the Road We Trod: African American Biblical Interpretation*, ed. Cain Hope Felder, 1–14. Minneapolis: Fortress, 1991.

Fleming, Robert E. *James Weldon Johnson*. Boston: Twayne, 1987.

Grimké, Angelina Weld. "Tenebris." In *Double-Take: A Revisionist Harlem Renaissance Anthology*, ed. Venetria K. Patton and Maureen Honey, 174. New Brunswick, NJ: Rutgers University Press, 2001.

Hoyt, Thomas, Jr. "Interpreting Biblical Scholarship for the Black Church Tradition." In Felder, *Stony the Road We Trod*, 17–39.

Hubbard, Dolan. *The Sermon and the African American Literary Imagination*. Columbia: University of Missouri Press, 1994.

Hughes, Langston. "The Negro Speaks of Rivers." In *Double-Take: A Revisionist Harlem Renaissance Anthology*, ed. Venetria K. Patton and Maureen Honey, 460. New Brunswick, NJ: Rutgers University Press, 2001.

Jahn, Janheinz. *Muntu: An Outline of the New African Culture*. Trans. Marjorie Grene. New York: Grove, 1961.

Johnson, James Weldon. *God's Trombones: Seven Negro Sermons in Verse*. New York: Penguin, 1927.

———. *Negro Americans, What Now?* New York: Da Capo Press, 1973.

Locke, Alain, ed. *The New Negro: Voices of the Harlem Renaissance*. New York: Touchstone, 1997.

McGuire, George Alexander. "A Prayer for Good Friday." In *Conversations with God: Two Centuries of Prayers by African Americans*, ed. James Melvin Washington, 133. New York: HarperCollins, 1994.

Mitchell, Henry M. *Black Preaching*. New York: Harper and Row, 1970.

Pessoa de Barros, José Flávio. "Myth, Memory, and History: Brazil's Sacred Music of Shango." Trans. Maria P. Junqueira. In *Òrìṣà Devotion as World Religion: The Globalization of Yorùbá Religious Culture*, ed. Jacob K. Olupona and Terry Rey, 400–415. Madison: University of Wisconsin Press, 2008.

Spencer, Jon Michael. "The Black Church and the Harlem Renaissance." *African American Review* 30, no. 3 (1996): 453–60.

Thelwell, Ekwueme Michael. "The Cultural Legacy of the African Griot." Lecture, Amherst, MA, April 15, 2008.

Weems, Renita J. "Reading *Her Way* through the Struggle: African American Women and the Bible." In Felder, *Stony the Road We Trod*, 57–77.

NINE

Border Crossings

The Diasporic Travels of Claude McKay and Zora Neale Hurston

Myriam J. A. Chancy

Claude McKay and Zora Neale Hurston escaped the disciplining (imperial) gaze of their time and deployed a subjectivity that, far from subaltern in its constitution, was fully humanist and pluralist. McKay's *A Long Way from Home*, for instance, provides a glimpse of a thoroughly cosmopolitan figure able to move as easily between "white" and "black" worlds as he does continents (the Americas, Europe) and nations (Russia, Germany, France, England, Morocco). Hurston's *Their Eyes Were Watching God*, published in the same year as McKay's novel (1937), is an encoded, creolized text marked by her passage in Haiti, during which time she researched her anthropological text *Tell My Horse* (published in 1938), in Port-au-Prince while writing *Their Eyes*, in its entirety, in a feverish six- to eight-week sprint. How could the text have escaped the author's geographical resettlement, however brief, in a culture saturated with storytelling and a rich folkloric history and language? *A Long Way from Home* and *Their Eyes Were Watching God* do not "speak back" to empires, nor do they correspond to what would later be termed "resistance literature" (to invoke Barbara Harlow's text of the same name). They do not resist; they participate, engaging preexisting traditions of embodied subjectivity that neither deny the fact of slavery, and the marking of history by the

Middle Passage, nor glory in it. This subjectivity participates within the parameters of dominant discourse at the same time as it encodes competing philosophical perspectives. In reconciling opposing epistemologies, McKay and Hurston demonstrate a nascent erasure of hegemonic binaries that enshrine the artistic production of said-subalterns to a subordinate discourse of resistance that can never escape the powerful discourse of otherness that subsumes it.

Koppi Sree-Ramesh and Kanudula Nirupa Rani assert in *Claude McKay: Literary Identity from Jamaica to Harlem* that McKay's *A Long Way from Home* "records his ideological evolution from being a British colonial writer in exile to being a black writer in search of identity" (177), concluding that McKay, as a Caribbean exile, "embarked on a long and torturous search for viable native roots" (178). Though Sree-Ramesh's and Rani's attempt to situate McKay in a broader African diasporic context is refreshing, they nonetheless continue to understand McKay in African American terms, suggesting that what has been called McKay's "autobiography," and which I will refer to as a "memoir," participates in an African American literary tradition: "African American scholars trace the roots of African American autobiography to the slave narratives, which were primarily produced to prove their humanity and to claim a historically denied voice" (7). Though the authors suggest that there is more to McKay's memoir than this, they are hesitant to situate the memoir in that space of otherness, whether that space be defined as Caribbean or, in our present-day lexicon, as global or as transnational. Why not read McKay's text as having resonance with texts by other Jamaican writers with whom he would have been familiar, such as Mrs. Seacole[1]—texts that advanced memoir narratives from the position of free subjectivities *during times of slavery* and that were, thereby, not participating—at least not explicitly so—in the politics of demonstrating black humanity?

To define *A Long Way from Home* not as "autobiography"—that is, as a "true" account of McKay's life—but as a "memoir" facilitates, I believe, a broader assessment of the text as an artistic work. Unlike autobiography, the memoir, as genre, does not attempt to be "factual." It renders a representation of lived experience that readers recognize as fallible, as accurately impressionistic as opposed to accurate in its details. As McKay himself notes at the end of the memoir, "All I offer here is the distilled poetry of my experience" (270), a phrase that denotes poetic license in choosing and shaping the retelling of key episodes (from McKay's perspective) from the author's traveling and most productive writing years in the late 1920s and early 1930s. For instance, much of the memoir grapples with McKay's attempts to develop as an artist, to find publishing outlets for his work, as well as reaching a wider readership in the face of implicitly racist assessments of his writing. Indeed, McKay's ruminations on this latter issue reflect more recent assessments by African postcolonial critics such as Chinua Achebe, who, in the mid-1970s, reflected on the reception of his 1958 first novel by (white) British critics; Achebe found that it was the practice of such critics to undercut the literary and intellectual achievements of increasingly visible (black) African writers by claiming that their higher-class status derived from the colonial and therefore invalidated their authenticity. Achebe summarizes: "the colonialist devised two contradictory arguments. He created the 'man of two worlds' theory to prove that no matter how much the native was exposed to European influences he could never truly absorb them . . . clearly inspired by the desire to undercut the educated African witness" (73).[2] Some twenty years prior, McKay had expounded: "Now it seems to me that if the white man is really more civilized than the colored . . . then the white man should take Negro poetry and pugilism in his stride, just as he takes Negro labor in Africa and fattens on it" (73). Anticipating late-twentieth-century critiques of imperialism in Africa from Mudimbe to Achille Mbembe, McKay connects the reduction of black artistry to mimicry or entertainment as a condition of the distortion of imperialist history that deflects critical gazes on the African continent away from the exploitation of African human labor and resources in the project of "civilizing" Africa. Jennifer Wenzel, in her incisive, recent essay focusing on imperialism in the Congo, says it best when she begins her discussion by stating, "If the Congo did not exist, it would be necessary to invent it. Time and again, whatever natural resource became indispensable to European capitalist expansion and technological innovation was to be found in the Congo in vast stores, beginning with slave labor in the sixteenth century" (1). Wenzel then proceeds to posit an "anti-imperialist nostalgia" (set against the imperialist nostalgia yearning for the good old colonial period and complicit with processes of domination) that "move[s] through and beyond the past into the future, trapped neither by forgetting the past nor by romanticizing it" (15).

Interestingly, following the discussion of his reviewers, McKay launches into a lengthy appreciation of a first-century pre-Islamic poet, Antara Ibn Shaddād al'-Absi, the son of an Arabian and an African slave woman, whose poetry apparently "produced the model for the earliest of the romances of chivalry" (McKay, 73). McKay reflects on the irony that a precursor of European chivalric poetry should be an African Arabian and concludes that a miseducation of both white and black children has obscured this history; this is owing to the invention of Africa as an uncivilized terrain in need of disciplining and an imperialist nostalgia that must reimagine Africa (much like America) as either un-peopled or inhabited by "savages" (74). He ends on a point of irony: "Perhaps if black and mulatto children knew more of the story and the poetry of Antar, we might have better Negro poets. But in our Negro schools and colleges we learn a lot of Homer and nothing of Antar" (75). Such "miseducation" stems from what Mudimbe has termed the violent, "missionary language of derision" as a "cultural position, the expression of an ethnocentric outlook" (52).

McKay pursues the thread of miseducation in the subtext of the memoir; that thread eventually asserts itself as a subversion of the proposed or perhaps obvious short-changing of black children in the educational markets of Europe and America. When pressed on the "Negro" issue during his travels in Russia, McKay defers to the director of the Eastern Bureau, a Japanese American named Sen Katayama, who had been educated in Negro colleges. McKay relates: "Sen Katayama had no regard for the feelings of the white American comrades, when the Negro question came up, and boldly told them so. He said that though they called themselves Communists, many of them were unconsciously prejudiced against Negroes because of their background. He told them that really to understand Negroes they needed to be educated and among Negroes as he had been" (141).

McKay does not elaborate on this point; still, his lack of comment is a comment in itself: it suggests that the truly miseducated are the former imperialists and their progeny and suggests implicitly that the "Negro" has an alternative epistemological reality from which something can be gleaned. His admiration for Katayama demonstrates McKay's desire to see a shared intellectual intercourse between the races that would acknowledge and valorize black intellect, much like what Achebe will advocate some twenty years into McKay's future. In this McKay deploys an anti-imperialist nostalgia grounded in a (dismissed) history of precolonial African civilization posited in the service of a hopeful future.

In reproducing his encounters with figures from Shaw to Trotsky to Alain Locke, among many others, McKay presents himself as a figure who can circulate freely, if not expansively, from one country to another, crossing open seas, and having the doors to elite literary and political figures open to him as if by magic. Perhaps McKay constructs within the pages of the text a myth of himself. But whether his self-portrayal is mythic or not, it creates an alternative sign system by which we are meant to read him as an actor in his own life rather than as a subaltern fighting his way through a marginal existence. In compelling analysis Gary Edward Holcomb argues for reading McKay's work against that of T. S. Eliot and Whitman, but even as he does so, he claims for McKay an oppositional black

Atlantic, creolized voice (after Glissant). Is it not possible that the reality of McKay's raced existence would necessarily mean that his art would be marked by different literary choices, choices that do not necessarily relegate him to the margins of modernity or to an "other" modernity but that speak to the modernity of the black subject within the construct of Western modernity? So, when McKay produces the cynical and bitter Shakespearean sonnet "America" (1921) in advance of T. S. Eliot's "The Waste Land" (1922), it is possible to read the poem, as Holcomb does, as racial allegory by which "the poem undoes the racist sexual certitude by making the white female the antagonist . . . identifiable in the shape of the Statue of Liberty" (28). Though from a Black Nationalist perspective Holcomb's analysis is compelling, his invocation of the Statue of Liberty suggests an alternative reading. The Statue of Liberty was originally conceived by its sculptor, Frederic-Auguste Bartholdi, as a black woman freeing herself from chains of bondage;[3] this is something McKay would certainly have known, or at the very least suspected, from his peregrinations to France. When McKay states in the poem, "I love this cultured hell that tests my youth," he speaks as an American subject critiquing the nation from within, not from the margins; the form of the poem invokes this Janus face well. He utilizes a conventional form to make an unconventional commentary derived from both European and black Atlantic traditions and histories and the shadow sign of the Statue of Liberty invokes the irony of simultaneous racial erasure and presence. McKay attempts to transcend his time and to view a future in which the "Negro" might participate in the world economy (269). In this he presciently engages notions of globalization and transnationalism.

If McKay engages the modern on its own grounds, refusing to be marginal in a Eurocentric discourse, Zora Neale Hurston similarly but differently engages notions of black subjectivity by pursuing the collection of African gnosis in the Americas both as an anthropologist and as a storyteller. If we were to read *Their Eyes Were Watching God* as an encoded travel narrative of Hurston's confrontation with the Haitian landscape and geography in which the text was written, as I can only begin to sketch briefly here, then we would understand the text as engaging in a dialectic relationship not between "white" and "black" but of "black" *to* "black"—not in resistance but in acknowledgment of the store of knowledge embedded in the black diasporic experience. Though Hurston commonly acknowledged the site in which she wrote *Their Eyes Were Watching God*, it has been of less interest to critics of her writings until, in the most recent reprinting of the novel, populist Haitian American writer Edwidge Danticat was asked by series editor

ıry Louis Gates to pen a foreword situating the novel's relevance in personal
tɛıms to Danticat's own self-affirmation as an African diasporic writer. Danticat
discovered the text in a high school history class in which the majority of students
were new immigrants to the United States. She recounts struggling with the language of the text and rediscovering the novel as an undergraduate at Barnard
College, which she notes Hurston and Ntozake Shange had also attended previously. For Danticat the Haitian encoding in the text is to be found in cultural si-
militude, but she also begins to uncover the possibility that historical events in
Haiti seeped into the text:

> There were so many things that I found familiar in *Their Eyes* . . . : the dead on
> orality in both the narration and dialogue; the communal gathering on open
> porches at dusk; the intimate storytelling (*krik? Krak*); the communal tall-tale
> sessions, both about real people who have erred (*zen*) and fictional folks who
> have hilariously blundered (*Blag*). Her description of the elaborate burial of
> Janie's pet mule reminded me of an incident that she detailed in *Tell My Horse*
> in which Haitian president Antoine Simon ordered an elaborate Catholic fu-
> neral at the national cathedral for his pet goat Simalo, something many Hai-
> tians would laugh at for years. (xv)

Of course, Danticat is speaking here of Matt Bonner's yellow mule, of whom
Hurston writes, "They had him up for conversation every day the Lord sent" (51).
Bonner, unlike President Antoine Simon, is a poor African American male in the
black township Joe Starks has consolidated. Like Matt, the yellow mule is emaci-
ated, underfed, and impoverished. Their destitute state proves to be fodder for
the "porch talk" Hurston is famous for having recorded here as in her other folkloric tales. In an attempt to humiliate Matt the porch men tell emasculating tales
about the mule, such as, "De womenfolks got yo' mule. When Ah come round de
lake 'bout noontime mah wife and some others had 'im flat on de ground usin' his
sides fuh uh wash board" (Hurston, 52). According to Matt the mule is well fed
and taken care of, simply stubborn: "Does feed de ornery varmint! Don't keer
whut Ah do Ah can't git long wid'im. He fights every inch in front uh de plow, and
even lay back his ears tuh kick and bite when Ah go in de stall tuh feed 'im" (53).
As other critics have observed, Matt Bonner's yellow mule is a stand-in for Janie,
herself, and other women of her ilk, "high yella" women seeking a better life for
themselves and resisting patriarchal, as well as racialized, norms that suppress the
trajectory of their lives; when the mule is left hitched to the porch and subsequently

taunted by the porch men, Janie is the only one who refuses to participate: "She snatched her head away from the spectacle and began muttering to herself. 'They oughta be shamed uh theyselves! Teasin' dat poor brute beast lak they is!'" (56). When the mule, spent, finally dies, the carcass is taken off by the townspeople, and a great ceremony takes place; unlike the case of Simon's presidential cere-mony for his pet goat, Hurston's mule continues to be ridiculed. At the same time, Hurston makes use of the incident to impugn Jody Starks's character. For readers the ridicule turns from the mule to Starks: "Out in the swamp they made great ceremony over the mule. They mocked everything human in death. Starks led off with a great eulogy on our departed citizen, our most distinguished citizen and the grief he left behind him, and the people loved the speech. It made him more solid than building the schoolhouse had done. He stood on the distended belly of the mule for a platform and made gestures" (60).

Starks's pomp and insensitivity are remarkable, and they assist the reader in understanding Janie's position, as a "yellow mule," in the marriage. At the same time, by obliquely making use of the Haitian Simon story under a new guise, Hurston comments on the tragic turns of Haitian emancipation, whereby an offici-ating president can rob state coffers to celebrate a pet. That Hurston may have transposed incidents of life from the Haitian landscape to the black South of Florida is suggestive of further "Haitianisms" in the text.

Indeed, though Danticat suggests that, from an immigrant/Kreyòl perspec-tive, the language of the text seemed on first reading impenetrable, something in the lyricism of the language and its lexical difference from other of Hurston's collected (U.S.) folktales offers a different register of black English; it suggests to me that the language of the text, and perhaps even its imaginary, is *kreyolized*. This is to say that although, undoubtedly, the text remains an important reposi-tory of Hurston's black southern folklore, it is simultaneously an encoded text, one that encodes traces of Haitian sayings and sensibilities, transposed by Hur-ston into her imagined black southern landscape. This kreyolization speaks to Hurston's compelling desire to know "the ways of Black folk" and the great means she took, through her travels, to explore cultures of African descent with geo-graphical proximity to the South she knew so well and sought to preserve. Predat-ing late-twentieth-century and early-twenty-first explorations of what has come to be called the "circum-Caribbean," Hurston's *Their Eyes Were Watching God*, along with the anthropological texts she produced around the same period in which she explored both Jamaica and Haiti, contributes to the growing archive on the cross-pollinations of the area that stretches across the Gulf Coast of the United States to the panhandle of south Florida, across the Caribbean ocean to the leeward islands and to the northern tip of the South American continent.

A popular phrase from the novel concerning both geographical and psychic explorations into unknown spaces appears to reflect just such a kreyolism. Janie's narrative is framed by her telling of the story of her three marriages to distinctly different men, who represent different versions of the private sphere for African American women early in the century, to her "kissing friend," Pheoby. When, after having told the heartbreaking story of Janie's loss of the main love of her life, Tea Cake, and of the ensuing trial and acquittal of Janie by an all-white, all-male jury of twelve men for Tea Cake's alleged murder, Pheoby exclaims: "Ah done growed ten feet higher from jus' listenin' tu you, Janie. . . . Nobody better not criticize yuh in mah hearin'" (189).

Janie's response is to express that the opprobrium she has received, and continues to receive, from others, who assume her guilt despite the acquittal, is that they live in ignorance. If the African American audience at the trial, and beyond, can declare, "de nigger women kin kill up all de mens dey wants tuh, but you bet' not kill one uh dem" and thus, conclude, erroneously, that "'uh white man and uh nigger woman is de freest thing on earth" (189), then Janie concludes, in turn, that "dey's parched up from not knowin' things" (192). She adds: "It's uh known fact, Pheoby, you got tuh *go* there tuh *know* there." Janie elaborates on what she means by the latter phrase by expressing that each has to find his or her own way in life and that "they got tuh find out about livin' fuh theyselves" (192).

These phrases seem commonsensical to us today, and Hurston's prefacing of the phrase "you got tuh *go* there tuh *know* there" with the conceit that this is a "known fact" camouflages another fact; that is, the phrase is borrowed from Haitian Kreyol, in which it is said "*fò wal la pou ou konn la*," a phrase that, in common parlance, means that no one can explain to another the vicissitudes of one's life. In other words, life's travails can only be comprehended through lived experience. Though this concept is, in itself, more or less universal, the phrase, utilized as a metaphor to mean that one has to travel into the geography of a particular sensibility or occurrence in order to fully appreciate its terrain, is not. One could argue that this phrase exists in both cultures, but the presence of the phrase in the dialect within the locale in which Hurston wrote the text suggests its transposition. There are a few more key phrases that I would like to explore that make my assertion here less conjectural.

For instance, Hurston peppers her text with evocative phrases that describe the emotional states of her character; some of these are not derived from black English; a number, in fact, are translations of Kreyol proverbs or sayings. The ease with which these phrases fit into the text testify both to Hurston's creative genius and her apprehension of the narrow filaments of expression, whether through dance, ritual, or language, tying together communities originating in part or in whole from Africa.

For instance, early in her story Hurston makes use of a striking phrase to describe Janie's grandmother's state as Nanny explains her reasons for marrying Janie off to an elderly African American man, Logan Killicks. Afraid that her granddaughter will suffer the same fate that two previous generations of women have suffered—that is, rape, abandonment, pregnancy by rape, and alcoholism (in Janie's mother's case)—in the face of her destroyed life, Nanny marries Janie off to a man she perceives to be economically stable and sound of mind. Ignoring the fact that she is simultaneously co-opting Janie's agency and making her subject to a man's will through the marriage, Nanny expounds: "Ah don't want yo' feathers always crumpled by folks throwin' up things in yo' face. And Ah can't die easy thinkin' maybe de menfolks white or black is makin' a spit cup outa you: Have some sympathy fuh me. Put me down easy, Janie, Ah'm a cracked plate" (20). Nanny attempts to force Janie to go along with her plan, and Janie does, by appealing to her own physical fragility, as summarized by the phrase, "Ah'm a cracked plate."

Nanny's entreaty, "Put me down easy, Janie, Ah'm a cracked plate," is, in fact, a quasi-literal translation of two common Haitian proverbs; the first is "*metem atè tou dousman*" [put me down easy],[4] the second "*m'se ze fele*" [I'm a cracked egg]. In the Kreyol either phrase can be used to the same effect, that is, to mean "be careful with me as I am feeling fragile." Used independently, however, the phrases have slightly different meanings. "*Metem atè tou dousman*" can mean "leave me out of the argument" or "please don't involve me," while "*m'se ze fele*" connotes more readily the sentiment of fragility as in "I can't take it anymore." A variation on the latter phrase, "*li se ze fele*," is often used to mean "she or he is vulnerable or she or he gets sick easily."[5] The phrases, though uncommon, can be combined for emphasis: "put me down easy; I'm a cracked egg."

Hurston's creative addition, then, is to combine the two proverbs and her translation of the phrases to amplify her character's psychological state. She also feminizes the meaning of the phrase in pursuing her novel's theme of the emancipation of an African American woman in the early twentieth century. Indeed, this phrase has an interesting corollary in Janie's assertion, broken by her second husband's will, when Hurston writes that "she stood there until something fell off the shelf inside her" (72). The image of women as fragile china that can be broken by a harsh life (as in Nanny's case), by physical abuse (as in the case of Janie's mother), or by emotional abuse (as in Janie's case with Joe) is evocative and, in the context of 1937, is Hurston's means by which to demonstrate that although African American women may be treated as the mules of the world (Hurston, 14), and thus as beasts of burden who can bear the weight of exploitation and denigration, they are, in fact, sentient, sensitive beings whose humanity is also feminine, deserving of care. The domestic imagery points to the inclusion of African American women in the private sphere at the time maintained as the arena of proper white American women. Janie accesses this private sphere, which is associated with white womanhood and virtue, but she is not satisfied with it. Her search for an emancipated life is haunted by Nanny's and her mother's rapes; and in her marriage to Joe, which she once thought liberatory, she experiences Nanny's feeling of being "a cracked plate" or "ze fele," a cracked egg. Hurston's imaginative interpretation of the Kreyol phrases also points to the fact that her own text is actively syncretic, as is the native language of Haitians. In this she performs the pivoting axis proper to cultures of the circum-Caribbean geographical region.

In other instances Hurston's borrowing from Haitian Kreyol is more explicit and more literal, yet Hurston continues to adapt the phrases for her purposes, testifying both to her creativity and the transmutability of African diasporic experience. Take, for example, the Kreyol phrase "m'grangou; ti trip ap vale gwo trip tounen," which literally translates as "I'm hungry; my small intestine has swallowed my large intestine." Another Haitian phrase also voices a similar sentiment with the stomach/intestine entwined: "lestomak mwen ap kòde" [my stomach is tied in knots; my intestines are knotting up]. In the novel Hurston borrows and inverts the phrase when Janie attempts to voice her discontent in her second marriage to Jody Starks: "Ah might take and find somebody dat did trust me and leave yuh." Jody responds: "Shucks! 'Tain't no mo' fools lak me. A whole lot of mens will grin in yo' face, but dey ain't gwine tuh work and feed yuh. You won't git far and you won't be long, when dat big gut reach over and grab dat little one, you'll be too glad to come back here" (30; my emphasis). Interestingly, Hurston inverts the original proverb by imagining that the big intestine will gobble up the small one; physiologically, the image does not quite work; perhaps Hurston simply misunderstood the original phrase. Whether the result of mistranslation, transcodage, or a desire, again, to camouflage the source of a striking image, the phrase is clearly a kreyolism.[6]

Through her linguistic intertextuality Hurston actively participates in what the postcolonial theorist Chantal Zabus has termed "relexification," which Zabus redefines as "the making of a new register of communication out of an alien lexicon" (285). She notes further that "relexification is characterized by the absence of an original" (287). This absence is achieved in Hurston in two ways. First, as I have noted in examples above, she actively camouflages proverbs and sayings taken from a non-English, nonblack English phrasebook, so to speak, through semitranslations, phrase inversion, and the conjoining of like proverbs. Second, this absence is achieved through contemporary failures to read the presence of Haitian influence in African American letters, especially at the threshold of the twentieth century, when travel to and from Haiti by African American men and women of letters took place frequently. The kreyolism evident to a Haitian reader (such as I) or a Haitian Kreyol speaker attuned to the possibility of transliteration across cultures and geographies may not be evident to other audiences, and it is clear that in the time that Hurston wrote, such a readership, in English, would not have existed. Her own accession of Haitian Kreyol, however, was not only very much possible but is evidenced in *Tell My Horse,* the ethnographic and anthropological text she was researching in Haiti at the time that she wrote *Their Eyes Were Watching God.* My very brief sketch, then, of the novel's Haitianisms, what I have otherwise called the text's kreyolization, thus aims to fill this lacuna and to suggest that the text, influenced by a Haitian gaze or overreading, yields its absent referents more readily than might be suspected.[7]

McKay and Hurston wrote their works because they heard the call of their muses: who is to say that they were not called forth from the future? They were well aware that within their imaginary they could claim, without shame, both the traditions of the West and of the African cultures from which they were forcibly divested. They sought also to forge bridges to communities of the African diaspora that lay beyond American borders—McKay in the distant past (Antar), Hurston in her immediate surroundings (Haiti and Jamaica). Their respective peregrinations, reread, suggest a ground for excavating black subjectivities in the twentieth century as articulating a visionary plurality rather than one of fragmentation that has been consistently read into hybrid societies. Under unsuspecting postcolonial eyes their texts perform the service of affirming black subjectivity in a twenty-first century that still dares to question its existence when the two already knew it to be true.

NOTES

1. There are notable differences between the genre of slave narrative emerging in the United States and that composed in the British context; see Moira Ferguson's preface to *The History of Mary Prince.*

2. One has to acknowledge that the quote continues by underscoring the gendered nature of such critiques: "to undercut the educated African witness . . . by appealing direct to the unspoiled woman of the bush who has retained a healthy gratitude for Europe's intervention in Africa"; this also signals the "white men saving brown women from brown men" conceit articulated by Spivak in her signal essay, "Can the Subaltern Speak" (both original and revised versions; see these in Ashcroft et al., *The Post-Colonial Studies Reader*).

3. See Sharp's and Hall's informative and ludic *Black Women for Beginners.*

4. This phrase can also be found in current black English as "putting me down," to mean ending a connection or relationship; it's meaning here, however, resonates with meaning(s) of the standard Kreyol saying.

5. I am indebted to native speaker Adeline L. Chancy for discussions of the Kreyol phrases discussed in this essay and for clarification of their literal and culturally contextual meanings.

6. As I have presented this material at various venues, African American scholars have pointed out to me that this particular phrase has some resonance in southern black English; one scholar who has roots in some part of the Caribbean (though she could not localize her origins) remembered hearing this phrase spoken by relatives in rural Georgia. This suggests to me that Hurston's writing locale may have both generated and recalled to her memory phrases used interchangeably in this period in areas of the Americas between which there was a great deal of exchange during and after enslavement. Also, though some interpretations of this phrase link the image to the sayings analyzed in the previous section, that is, to provide images of Jody's hypermasculinity, the phrase is used here to mean, simply, "hunger." It is this rendering of the phrase's meaning in Hurston's texts that ties it explicitly to Kreyol even if it may have a coterminous existence in the commonspeak of southern African Americans.

7. I am grateful for the corroboration of Harlem Renaissance specialists attending the "Harlem Renaissance Revisited" conference, University of Connecticut-Storrs, March 2008, that the most important of the kreyolisms I have delineated here are not common to current black English.

BIBLIOGRAPHY

Achebe, Chinua. "Colonialist Criticism." In Ashcroft, Griffiths, and Tiffin, *The Postcolonial Studies Reader,* 73–76.
Ashcroft, Bill, Gareth Griffiths, Helen Tiffin, eds. *The Post-colonial Studies Reader.* 2nd ed. London: Routledge, 2006.

Danticat, Edwidge. Foreword to *Their Eyes Were Watching God*. Ed. Henry Louis Gates Jr. New York: HarperPerennial, 2006.

Ferguson, Moira, ed. *The History of Mary Prince*. Michigan: University of Michigan Press, 1998.

Harlow, Barbara. *Resistance Literature*. London: Routledge, 1987.

Holcomb, Gary Edward. *Claude McKay, Code Name Sasha: Queer Black Marxism and the Harlem Renaissance*. Gainesville: University Press of Florida, 2007.

Hurston, Zora Neale. *Their Eyes Were Watching God*. 1937. New York: HarperPerennial, 2006.

Mbembe, Achille. *On the Postcolony*. Berkeley: University of California Press, 2001.

McKay, Claude. *A Long Way from Home*. 1937. New Brunswick, NJ: Rutgers University Press, 2007.

Mudimbe, V. Y. *The Invention of Africa: Gnosis, Philosophy, and the Order of Knowledge*. Bloomington: Indiana University Press, 1988.

Sharp, Saundra, and Beverly Hawkins Hall. *Black Women for Beginners*. London: Writers and Readers Publishing, 1993.

Sree-Ramesh, Koppi, and Kanudula Nirupa Rani. *Literary Identity from Jamaica to Harlem and Beyond*. Jefferson, NC: McFarland, 2006.

Wenzel, Jennifer. "Remembering the Past's Future: Anti-imperialist Nostalgia and Some Versions of the Third World." *Cultural Critique* 62 (winter 2006): 1–32.

Zabus, Chantal. "Relexification." In Ashcroft. Griffiths, and Tiffin, *The Post-colonial Studies Reader*, 285–88.

TEN

The Search for Self in Wallace Thurman's *The Blacker the Berry*

Color, Class, and Community

Martha E. Cook

Wallace Thurman's 1929 novel *The Blacker the Berry: A Novel of Negro Life* was greeted with strong negative reviews. In the *New York Times* for March 17, 1929, an anonymous reviewer bluntly states, "Better novels of negro [*sic*] life have been written before, and written, ironically enough, by white people." The reviewer praises Claude McKay's *Home to Harlem*, just published, and notes that it is by "a West Indian negro"; then he alludes to Carl Van Vechten's "swiftly acquired erudition" regarding, one assumes, black life in Harlem in the 1920s. The reviewer seems to believe that a certain amount of objectivity benefits the novelist yet faults Thurman for lack of "subjectivity" ("Latest Works of Fiction," 6). In the *Crisis* (July 1929) W. E. B. Du Bois praises the importance of Thurman's theme of intraracial prejudice but finds him unable to develop it fully: "The story of Emma Lou calls for genius to develop it. It needs deep psychological knowledge and pulsing sympathy. And above all, the author must believe in black folk, and in the beauty of black as a color of human skin. I may be wrong, but it does not seem to me that this is true of Wallace Thurman" (249–50). A decade later, Sterling A. Brown, writing in the *Journal of Negro Education*, praises Thurman for engaging the subject of intraracial prejudice but finds that he has "little depth in characterizing his heroine" (286). By 1959 Eugene Arden in the *Phylon Quarterly* labels *The Blacker the Berry* "another novel of the Van Vechten type" (30), exhibiting a way other than color prejudice in which values of the majority culture pervade the black community.

The Blacker the Berry was largely overlooked by the critical community for many years, though it is now a critical commonplace that it is the first novel by a black American to treat intraracial prejudice as subject and theme with meaningful complexity. As David Levering Lewis writes in *When Harlem Was in Vogue,* "For the first time, the color prejudice within the race was treated not as a regrettable curiosity or vague mutual aversion of light and dark Afro-Americans, but as the central theme of a novel" (237). Since the civil rights era *The Blacker the Berry* has been primarily marketed as a noncanonical work that has been inaccessible to the reading public—and, of course, to professors of literature whose students might go on to do the critical work it deserves. For example, it is described on the cover of the 1970 Collier paperback as "a lost classic in the annals of American Negro literature" and on the cover of the 1996 Scribner paperback as "A lost classic of Black American literature."

While Thurman has received some critical attention, particularly in regard to his portrayal of male sexuality, *The Blacker the Berry* deserves thoughtful analysis of Thurman's powerful portrayal of his protagonist, Emma Lou Morgan, marked by her dark skin, who searches for self-identity within a community in an America in which all communities are defined by class and race, color, or ethnicity, finally realizing that she can only find identity within herself. Likewise, the role of the character of the white writer Campbell Kitchen, who helps Emma Lou find the way to move beyond a destructive life of self-hatred through articulating a philosophy that enables her to reject self-sacrifice and continue her search for self-reliance, has not received the critical focus it deserves.

Thurman structures his novel by moving Emma Lou through a series of communities. In the powerful first part of the novel, she encounters intraracial color prejudice in her home community of Boise, Idaho, doomed by the legacy of color from her African father never to be part of the "blue vein" circle that defines her class by her color. She goes west to the University of Southern California, where she experiences the same color and class prejudice. Thwarted in her search for self within this community, she then flees east to Harlem. There she believes she will find a place free of color- and related class-bias. As she experiences further discrimination from her race in this community, her own color prejudice and self-hatred become more evident. Late in part 5 Thurman seems to be moving toward a resolution in which Emma Lou will find her self-identity through self-sacrifice within this complex racial community. Instead, Emma Lou moves forward in a search for her inner self that transcends community.

The title of the first part of *The Blacker the Berry* names Emma Lou, leading the reader to assume that she has a strong sense of self-identity. That notion of strength of self is revised in the opening sentence: "More acutely than ever before Emma Lou began to feel that her luscious black complexion was somewhat of a liability." The problem is not so much how she looks as an individual but "that her marked color variation from the other people in her environment was a decided curse" (21). She does not mind "being black"; she minds "being too black." Emma Lou's most immediate community, her family, is concerned to the point of "moaning and grieving over the color of her skin." Apparently from an early age "her skin," wherein her identity lies, has been subjected to "bleachings, scourgings, and powderings," but she is still "black—fast black" (21). At key points in the novel Emma Lou attacks her skin, her self, in a similar manner in attempts to change her identity and thereby find her place in a community. As the second, often ignored, epigraph to the novel, by Countee Cullen, emphasizes, "My color shrouds me in" (quoted from "The Shroud of Color," 26). Still, Emma Lou is determined to escape that deathtrap.

Thurman depicts Emma Lou's home community in Boise, Idaho, as "a semi-white world, totally surrounded by an all-white one" (24). Her family bases its sense of superiority on heritage from its white ancestors in the deep South. Freed because of familial ties to their owners, they migrate to Kansas. Finding there no class distinctions among Negroes, the next generation takes "the best blood of the South" to Boise, where they assert their self-identity by joining "the blue vein circle, so named because all of its members were fair-skinned enough for their blood to be seen pulsing purple through the veins of their wrists" (28). Emma Lou lacks the requisite blue veins because her mother fails to follow the motto of her class, "'Whiter and whiter every generation'" (29). Emma Lou's father's descent from "one of the few families originally from Africa" (30) is not a source of pride and identity in this pre–World War I era.

In the scene of Emma Lou's high school graduation in Boise, Thurman reveals the extent of her negative sense of self. She is "the only Negro pupil in the entire school" (22). She feels that her diploma will not mitigate what she sees as "the tragedy of her life . . . that she was too black." She instead longs for "an efficient bleaching agent, a magic cream." Rather than seeing her color as her positive self-identity, she sees it as something that she longs to remove, in order to assure her a place in this or another community. Emma Lou wants to "remove this un-welcome black mask from her face" and become "more like her fellow men" (23). Thus, Thurman inverts the trope of the mask employed by Dunbar and others as a device by which blacks can control their lives, can survive in a white com-munity. Rather than a mask denoting a conscious effort to play a role, the mask is her identity; it is what she cannot control.

As Emma Lou receives her diploma, the positive images of her identity are subsumed in her sense of alienation, a sense so strong that she feels that she has a negative effect on the white community of Boise: "She had to go get that diploma, so summoning her most insouciant manner, she advanced to the platform center, brought every muscle of her lithe limbs into play, haughtily extended her shiny black arm to receive the proffered diploma" (23–24). Her lively, attractive black body, combined with "her luscious black complexion" (21) and "a thick, curly black mass of hair, rich and easily controlled" (31), is subsumed by her sense that she does not belong here. She "insolently returned to her seat in that foreboding white line, insolently returned once more to splotch its pale purity and to mock it with her dark, outlandish difference" (24). By the narrator's and other objective standards, Emma Lou is attractive, if not beautiful. The powerful illustration by Aaron Douglas for the dust jacket of the 1929 first edition of *The Blacker the Berry* depicts a black woman whose body is long and lithe, and she appears to move that black body with pride. Writing in 1936, Alain Locke praises Douglas's "modern-ized version of African patterns" (68). This artistic style makes Douglas singu-larly appropriate to represent the character of Emma Lou in the cover art for *The Blacker the Berry*, which captures the African beauty and pride that the character herself cannot yet affirm.

That editors and illustrators have read the novel as affirming that image of an attractive dark-skinned woman is reinforced by later paperback covers. Notable is the beautiful silhouette by Mozelle for the 1970 Collier paperback, stark black on a vibrant purple background, an illustration that could be labeled "Black is beautiful," the rallying cry for black pride in the 1960s. Later, a romantic image graces the 1996 Simon and Schuster paperback, a photograph by Buck Holzemer Photography of a svelte woman attired in a white gown that accents her beautiful black body. Yet, contrary to the image created by the narrator, reinforced by the cover art, Emma Lou sees herself, in the requisite white of all the graduates, as a true outcast, an "outland[er]."

So Emma Lou's first flight is from Boise, where she is rejected by both the white and black communities, including most of her family. She despairs that there is no class, no community, that will accept her because of her color, "no place in the world for a girl as black as she anyway" (34). But her sympathetic Uncle Joe encourages her to attend the University of Southern California, believing that there she will find "Negroes of every class, color, and social position" (34), in other words, a place for anyone to assert her or his self-identity. Joe convinces Emma Lou that "only in small cities one encountered stupid color prejudice such as she had encountered among the blue vein circle in her home town" (35). Emma Lou mistakenly believes that she is leaving a "provincial" community (37) for a "'modern'" one (35), where her blackness may even be an asset.

It is easy to assume that Thurman gives to Uncle Joe his own expectations as Thurman himself had transferred from the University of Utah to USC in 1922 (Klotman, 261). The University of Southern California is not, however, a welcoming community for Emma Lou, as it may not have been for Thurman. There is ample evidence that Thurman had dark skin and that it may have marked him, as it does Emma Lou. Regardless of whether Thurman had absorbed class prejudice from his own family, Emma Lou carries the class prejudice of her Boise family to Los Angeles, characterizing the first black person to befriend her, Hazel, as "a typical southern darky" (42). When she meets the sophomore Alma, whom she perceives to be upper class, Emma Lou projects herself into future "contact with really superior people, intelligent, genteel, college-bred, all trying to advance themselves and their race, unconscious of intra-racial schisms caused by difference in skin color." Yet she reveals a preference for Verne, with "her pleasant dark brown face," over Helen, an "anemic-looking yellow girl" (52). Verne, she subsequently learns, is accepted in spite of her color because of her socioeconomic superiority. The only place Emma Lou finds in Los Angeles centers on Grace, a student who has established a community with others like her who have migrated from the Deep South. Emma Lou has traveled west only to end up symbolically in the South of her ancestral past. There the transplanted southern blacks who are of what she considers her "class" (59) still "segregated themselves from their darker skinned brethren" (60) in their new community as they did in their old ones. There is no formal blue-vein circle, but there is a sorority that neither Emma Lou, Hazel, nor Grace is asked to join. Each step on her journey west reinforces Emma Lou's negative sense of self.

Returning to Boise for the summer, Emma Lou once more despairs that "there was no place in the world for a dark girl" (61). A Sunday School Union picnic in "Bedney's Meadow, a green, heavily forested acre of park land, which lay on the outskirts of the city, surrounded on three sides by verdant foothills" (62), brings the entire black community together. There Emma Lou loses her virginity to a man she meets that day. Does she know that her mother met her dark-skinned father "at a church picnic, given in a woodlawn meadow on the outskirts of the city" (30)? Probably not, but Thurman creates an idyllic natural setting, away from the artificial intraracial color prejudice of the city, where a woman can follow her heart—or her sexual desires. Emma Lou thinks she would prefer "that [Weldon's] skin had been colored light brown instead of dark brown" (62), but immediately projects a future of marriage. As Thurman says, she "create[s] her worlds within her own mind" (64–65), as she does when she meets Alma at USC. When Weldon leaves Emma Lou, the narrator reveals to the reader that "it had never occurred to her that the matter of her color had never once entered the mind of Weldon. . . . Emma Lou did not understand that Weldon was just a selfish normal man and not a color-prejudiced one." Yet Emma Lou believes that "there could be no happiness for any woman whose face was as black as hers" (69). Even though she acknowledges that Weldon has never mentioned marriage, she wrongly assumes that he rejects her because of the blackness of her skin rather than his materialistic desire to become a Pullman porter.

Emma Lou returns to Los Angeles and the university; but, realizing that "Los Angeles, too, was a small-town mentally, peopled by mentally small southern Negroes. It was no better than Boise" (69–70), she plans her next flight. She is "determined to go East where life was more cosmopolitan and people were more civilized." At the end of part 1 Thurman tantalizes the reader by stating that "once more Emma Lou fled into an unknown town to escape the haunting chimera of intra-racial color prejudice" (70). This statement characterizes Emma Lou as running from a community that has failed her toward the "unknown." Turning the page, the reader finds that part 2 of the novel is entitled "Harlem."

Part 1 of *The Blacker the Berry* establishes the form for the novel as one of succeeding "geographical flights" (215)—a phrase Thurman uses in the closing pages to describe the pattern of Emma Lou's fictional life. In part 2 the narrator reveals that Emma Lou has seized the opportunity of employment as a maid to a white actress to flee both Boise and Los Angeles. By placing her in the black community in Harlem in the 1920s, Thurman raises the expectations of the reader that Emma Lou has found the community she is seeking, one in which she will find what her Uncle Joe had envisioned for her in Los Angeles. She is not an aspiring writer like her creator; but as he made the journey from Los Angeles to Harlem in 1925 (Klotman, 261), she too seeks a place that is in idea if not reality a haven for black self-identity. In *Harlem: The Making of a Ghetto* Gilbert Osofsky documents both the consolidation of black New Yorkers in the Harlem community, which he terms "a Negro world unto itself" (127), and the migration of blacks, particularly from the South and Midwest. As the Reverend Adam Clayton Powell writes in his 1938 autobiography, "'Harlem became the symbol of liberty and the Promised Land to Negroes everywhere'" (Osofsky, 128). Surely, Emma Lou is aware enough of where she is going to expect a place where her blackness will be a source of positive identity.

In Harlem Emma Lou bobs her hair in the latest style but still laments her blackness, yet the narrator reveals that even she sees her other positive physical traits: "she never faced the mirror without speculating upon how good-looking she might have been had she not been so black" (73). Emma Lou does face barriers in Harlem, mostly of class based on color prejudice, as she seeks appropriate employment and living space that does not confine her. Still she finds hope in the heart of Harlem. She sees Seventh Avenue as "glorious." In images similar to those employed by Claude McKay in *Home to Harlem,* though less concrete, Thurman writes: "Where else could one see so many different types of Negroes? Where else would one view such a heterogeneous ensemble of mellow colors, glorified by the night?" (97). Emma Lou quickly enters into a relationship with a man named John, who is employed in the theater where her employer is performing. John orients her to all aspects of Harlem life, from the YWCA, where he encourages her to seek lodging, to the churches: "Moreover, as they strolled Seventh Avenue, he had attempted to give her all the 'inside dope' on Harlem, had told her of the 'rent parties,' of the 'numbers,' of 'hot' men, of 'sweetbacks,' and other local phenomena" (96).

Yet once more Emma Lou's class prejudice intrudes. She thinks that John "was too pudgy and dark, too obviously an ex-cotton picker from Georgia" (97). In response to remarks of men in the street, Emma Lou cautions, "Be yourself" (98). Too often, however, she will find being herself her greatest challenge. This short section ends with a man casually remarking of her to his companion, "'Man, you know I don't haul no coal'" (98). The contrast of this derogatory remark to the affirmative, albeit sexist, epigraph to the novel, "The blacker the berry / The sweeter the juice," is powerful. Moreover, such encounters distract Emma Lou from trusting her own judgment. She has said to herself the same thing that the white writer Campbell Kitchen will say to her, but only through his encouraging words does she find the strength to seek self-definition not in a community outside but within.

Beginning with part 3, Thurman shifts between his limited omniscient focus on Emma Lou and a new perspective, that of Alva, described as an American mulatto-Filipino. The two characters meet in Small's Paradise cabaret, where Emma Lou goes as a guide for her white employer—who ironically is playing the role of a mulatto in a melodrama. She is puzzled by Alva's seeming to laugh at her after they dance, not knowing that he later tells his roommate Braxton, "'I took pity on her, 'cause she looked so lonesome with those ofays,'" acknowledging, "'She might have been a little dark'" (114). Other encounters openly reinforce her obsession with her dark skin. She turns to the bleaching potions from her childhood and even eats "arsenic wafers" (123). The heavy makeup she uses makes her less attractive, and her sinking self-esteem leads her to pick up a strange man at the movies.

Yet this stranger is a most important plot device; his mention of the Renaissance Casino, another Harlem icon like Small's, leads her to encounter Alva again. Though at first "he could not imagine who this girl with the purple-powdered skin was," and his girlfriend, Geraldine, calls Emma Lou a "'spade'" (131), Emma Lou's flirtation leads Alva to chuckle to Braxton, "'The blacker the berry, the sweeter the juice'" (134), reiterating Thurman's epigraph. Emma Lou and Alva have a sexual relationship, but he mostly segregates her from his friends. While Alva may not totally accept Emma Lou because of her dark skin, their covert relationship stems in large part from the fact that he already has a relationship with Geraldine when he meets Emma Lou.

In part 4 Thurman employs the trope of a Harlem rent party to bring Emma Lou and Alva into contact with a group of characters based on Thurman and his friends and acquaintances in Harlem, who, ironically paralleling her actress employer at Small's, want to experience other aspects of black life. Truman Walter pontificates on the problem of "intra-racial segregation" (144), explaining it in terms of the model of discrimination in white society. He says virtually the same thing Du Bois says in his *Crisis* review of *The Blacker the Berry*. Du Bois attributes the "evil prejudice" of intraracial segregation to "the dominant ideals of a white world" and its influence within "the Negro world" (249). Emma Lou is "disgusted" (147) by Truman, whom she recognizes as a fellow student from USC. She gets so drunk at the rent party that the next morning her landlady asks her to move. In the aftermath of the party, she tries to reconcile the "loving and kind" (156) Alva that she has created with the reality of his accepting her money and his mocking attitude toward marriage. Once more, as with the USC students and Weldon in

Boise, Emma Lou has such a weak sense of herself that she tends to create a false reality.

One of the major critical questions about *The Blacker the Berry* is whether Thurman is portraying himself through Emma Lou, is exploring the question of color and identity through a female character to show how much more difficult life is for a dark-skinned woman, or is exploring his own sexuality through the character of Alva. It is certainly true that Thurman was often identified by the darkness of his skin. Scholars and critics often quote Langston Hughes's descriptions of him from *The Big Sea* as support for their speculation that Thurman's own color was a key element in his self-identity. Hughes states, "He was a strangely brilliant black boy" (182). From the perspective of the twenty-first century it is possible to read Hughes's comments as merely descriptive, but Thurman seems to have believed that his place in the community of Harlem was in large part defined by his blackness—that is, his color, not his race.

As Thurman uses Small's Paradise cabaret and the Renaissance Casino to bring the characters of Emma Lou and Alva together, and the rent party to exacerbate Emma Lou's struggle with self-definition, he employs the iconic Lafayette Theater as a setting to bring the relationship of Emma Lou and Alva to a climax. There Emma Lou's self-identity dominates her experience. She sees every joke about skin color only in relation to herself, accusing Alva of taking her there to "'be insulted'" (175). He finally says, "'You're always beefing about being black. Seems like to me you'd be proud of it.'" When she makes no defense, he concludes: "'It's your kind helps make other people color-prejudiced'" (180). Regardless of his lack of true feeling for Emma Lou, Alva seems to speak the truth. She is obsessed with her skin color to the point of self-hatred. Part 4 of *The Blacker the Berry* ends with Alva's apparent entrapment by Geraldine's announcement that she is having his baby. The disabled baby is little more than a plot device, too; but what could be a trap for Emma Lou as well becomes a powerful symbol of her own strength in seeking her self-identity.

In part 5, "Pyrrhic Victory," the passage of two years finds Emma Lou having moved on, in a way, working as a maid to Clere Sloan, the wife of the white writer Campbell Kitchen, and living at the YWCA. Most critics assume Sloan to be based on Fania Marinoff and Kitchen to be based on Carl Van Vechten. Cleverly, Thurman compares Kitchen's novel of Negro life to Van Vechten's *Nigger Heaven,* both of which give "white people a wrong impression of Negroes" (187), as the narrator indicates. Thurman, however, published an essentially positive review of Van Vechten's controversial novel in the *Messenger* (Thurman, "A Stranger at the Gates"). And Thurman employs the character of Kitchen to inspire Emma Lou's ultimate decision to choose self-reliance over self-sacrifice.

Emma Lou's introspection during this period leaves her open to Kitchen's advice to seek "economic independence" (200) and "salvation within one's self" (216). She actually acknowledges that she has "become more and more resentful of her blackness of skin," that "she had little respect left for herself" (189), and that, indeed, she "hated her own color" (199). While Emma Lou unsuccessfully seeks new relationships with light-skinned blacks who accept her, but with whom she has nothing in common, Alva sinks into alcoholism and illness, and Geraldine abandons him and their child. After a chance encounter with Alva's old roommate, Emma Lou seeks him out when he is at his lowest. She focuses her life on her new position as a teacher in Harlem and on her efforts to rescue Alva and Alva Junior. She no longer seems to be seeking a community in which she can find her identity; in fact, she considers moving to a school that will not have other black teachers. She feels rejected by her peers for her darkness of skin, when, in fact, the rejection is due to her excessive use of makeup.

What seems to be Emma Lou's lowest point comes when she realizes that her Harlem students have labeled her " 'Blacker'n me' " (210), and Alva is introducing her as "Alva Junior's mammy." Having achieved "economic independence," she has still "enslaved" (212) herself—a powerful metaphor. She cannot return to her half-life among her new light-skinned friends: her beau, Benson, is engaged to her friend Gwendolyn. In a re-vision of a journey into the soul, she wanders through the heart of Harlem, finding no refuge on Seventh Avenue and only feeling "too black" (215) on 135th Street. Rather than embark on another physical journey, she acknowledges that she needs "to accept her black skin as being real and unchangeable" (217). She can't go home again; she has fled west to Los Angeles and then east to Harlem, to no avail: "these mere geographical flights had not solved her problems in the past" (215).

In the street Emma Lou has an epiphany: she realizes that she can find herself if she follows Kitchen's advice "that every one must find salvation within one's self" (216). She reaffirms her resolution to leave Alva and Alva Junior and even thinks she might contact John, the first man she met in Harlem, whom she had discriminated against for the same reasons of color and class that some people have discriminated against her. Returning to Alva's room with the determination "to fight against Alva's influence over her" (218), she almost turns away from his door when she hears "raucous masculine laughter." Recalling her resolution, however, "that this was to be her last night there, and that the new day would find her beginning a new life," she walks in and witnesses "the usual and expected sight: Alva, face a death mask, . . . embracing an effeminate boy whom she knew as Bobbie" (219). Thurman leaves the reader with the powerful image of Emma Lou's packing her suitcases, seeming to ignore the cries of a child who needs her, and painfully acknowledging that first she must save herself. She is determined to "be eminently selfish" (217), to follow Kitchen's advice to travel within herself. Rather than sacrificing herself to try to save Alva Junior, or even Alva, Emma Lou seems to have gained the strength to continue her search for self somewhere outside this geographical place. Wherever she journeys, symbolically she will move beyond the confinement by color-consciousness that she finds in Harlem, a community that she and many readers might expect to offer at least an alternative to color- and class-related bias.

Most critical treatments of *The Blacker the Berry* do not emphasize the role of community and the trope of flight in the novel, and hardly anyone has given much attention to Campbell Kitchen's character. Is Thurman being ironic in giving Emma Lou guidance from a white writer who espouses Emersonian self-reliance? Or is he being radical, finding the roots for the answer to Emma's problem in American history and culture? Amritjit Singh is one of the few critics of the novel to comment on the character of Kitchen beyond noting that he is doubtless based on Van Vechten. But Singh does not have much faith in Emma Lou's "new self-awareness" and merely notes that "she finds comfort in the philosophy of Campbell Kitchen" (111). Shirlee Taylor Haizlip, in her brief introduction to the 1996 Simon and Schuster edition of the novel, does not refer to the role of Kitchen, but she asserts her belief that Thurman does give Emma Lou control of her life in the conclusion: "*The Blacker the Berry* . . . is an important story for our times and for the future. One that should be kept alive, told, and retold, in the context of how black self-hate, black rage is created and how black self-love, black empowerment can triumph" (14).

Perhaps Haizlip goes beyond what I have articulated as Thurman's theme of self-reliance, but I do feel strongly that Emma Lou takes control of herself and rejects the notion that her identity lies within any community and that Kitchen's advice plays a key role in her decision. Therefore, I also take issue with several critics' reading of the closing passages of the novel that locate Emma Lou's epiphany in her discovery of Alva's bisexuality. Phyllis R. Klotman articulates this interpretation in *Dictionary of Literary Biography*, labeling her observation of Alva "in a drunken homosexual embrace" as an "epiphanic moment" (269). Several recent articles that focus on homosexuality in the novel follow this line of criticism. For example, Stephen Knadler writes in *Critical Inquiry* in 2002 with reference to *The Blacker the Berry* that "the retreat from Harlem always has as its immediate catalyst the outing of homosexuality" (929). Daniel M. Scott III asserts in *MELUS* in 2004 that Emma Lou "discovers boyfriend Alva's bisexuality at the end of the book—a discovery that hastens her putative change of consciousness at the end of the novel" (329). Later in this article he says "that Thurman reveals to the reader and Emma Lou that Alva is not what he has so far appeared to be," then quotes the passage containing the phrase "the usual and expected sight" of Alva and Bobbie (335).

The reader may not have had any indication of Alva's bisexuality before this passage; but the text of the novel clearly indicates that Emma Lou had knowledge of it prior to this encounter, which does not surprise or shock her. Her own dark night of the soul in the streets of Harlem, with direct reference to Kitchen's Emersonian advice, is the point of her epiphany. Before she sees Alva for the last time, she has gained on her own the strength to leave him. To say that a revelation of Alva's bisexuality, of which Emma Lou is already aware, is the impetus for her discovery of her path to self-knowledge diminishes the impact of Thurman's development of her character and Kitchen's.

Wallace Thurman uses what he labels the "geographical flights" of his protagonist to give form and structure to his novel. As Emma Lou struggles to come to terms with color and class prejudice and her own self-hatred, she seeks a community that will accept and support her. Through her experience and perhaps in large measure owing to the influence of the white character Campbell Kitchen, at the end of the novel she knows that she may need to negotiate geographical spaces—she is, after all, packing her suitcases—but the true salvation she seeks transcends community, which is inevitably defined by class and by race, color, or ethnicity. Against great odds in the battle for self-definition, Thurman allows his character to conclude that her life's journey must continue within herself.

BIBLIOGRAPHY

Arden, Eugene. "The Early Harlem Novel." *Phylon Quarterly* 20, no. 1 (1959): 25–31.
Brown, Sterling A. "The American Race Problem as Reflected in American Literature." *Journal of Negro Education* 8, no. 3 (July 1939): 275–90.
Cullen, Countee. "The Shroud of Color." In *Color*, 26–35. New York: Harper and Bros., 1925.
D[u Bois], W. E. B. Review of *The Blacker the Berry*. *Crisis*, July 1929, 249–50.

Haizlip, Shirlee Taylor. Introduction to *The Blacker the Berry . . .* , by Wallace Thurman, 9–15. New York: Simon and Schuster, 1996.

Hughes, Langston. *Autobiography: The Big Sea.* Ed. with an introduction by Joseph McLaren. Vol. 13 of *The Collected Works of Langston Hughes.* Columbia: University of Missouri Press, 2002.

Klotman, Phyllis R. "Wallace Henry Thurman." *Dictionary of Literary Biography.* Vol. 51, *Afro-American Writers from the Harlem Renaissance to 1940,* ed. Trudier Harris, 260–73. New York: Gale, 1987.

Knadler, Stephen. "Sweetback Style: Wallace Thurman and a Queer Harlem Renaissance." *Modern Fiction Studies* 48, no. 4 (winter 2002): 899–936.

"Latest Works of Fiction: *The Blacker the Berry.*" *New York Times,* March 27, 1929.

Lewis, David Levering. *When Harlem Was in Vogue.* New York: Oxford University Press, 1981.

Locke, Alain. *Negro Art: Past and Present.* Bronze Booklet No. 3. Washington, DC: Associates in Negro Folk Education, 1936.

Osofsky, Gilbert. *Harlem: The Making of a Ghetto: Negro New York, 1890–1930.* New York: Harper and Row, 1966.

Scott, Daniel M., III. "Harlem Shadows: Re-evaluating Wallace Thurman's 'The Blacker the Berry.'" *MELUS* 29, nos. 3/4 (autumn-winter 2004): 323–39.

Singh, Amritjit. *The Novels of the Harlem Renaissance: Twelve Black Writers, 1923–1933.* University Park: Pennsylvania State University Press, 1976.

Thurman, Wallace. *The Blacker the Berry.* 1929. New York: Simon and Schuster, 1996.

———. "A Stranger at the Gates: A Review of *Nigger Heaven,* by Carl Van Vechten." *Messenger,* Sept. 1926. Repr. in *The Collected Writings of Wallace Thurman: A Harlem Renaissance Reader,* ed. Amritjit Singh and Daniel M. Scott III, 191–93. New Brunswick, NJ: Rutgers University Press, 2003.

PART IV: Gender Constructions

Jack Johnson, Paul Robeson, and the Hypermasculine African American *Übermensch*

Paula Marie Seniors

> We are in the midst of a growing menace. The black man is rapidly
> forging to the front ranks in athletics, especially in the field of fisticuffs.
> We are in the midst of a black rise against white supremacy.
>
> —CHARLES A. DANA, ON THE ASCENDANCE
> OF THE BLACK BOXER PETER JACKSON

In 1895 Charles A. Dana likened black superiority in the boxing ring to the loss of white supremacy and predicted the rise of the ultimate representation of black male power, Jack Johnson. In the early twentieth century the prizewinning black boxer changed perceptions of black masculinity forever in the minds of Americans.[1] Boxing has always been a combative and brutal sport, a site where men "prove" their manliness. Before Johnson, whites dominated the sport and used boxing to prove their masculinity and their physical prowess. When Jack Johnson asserted his manliness by defeating white opponents and flaunting his middle-class status, he proved to white and black America that black men were a force to be reckoned with.[2] Johnson challenged the discourse of white male superiority, and he incited fear by unveiling the vulnerability of the white male body. Johnson raised the hopes of the African American community, and his very presence challenged the attempt to subjugate black men by defying the discourse that defined the black male body as unmasculine and weak.[3] Jack Johnson proved that the black male body symbolized a source of supreme power and virility. Johnson's body epitomized the model for black masculinity in much the same way that African American male athletes in the twenty-first century represent the "exemplars for hegemonic masculinity" and doughtiness.[4] This chapter explores how Johnson contested corrosive representations of his personage by utilizing the media to claim black power and to reconfigure African American masculinity into the Hypermasculine African American Übermensch (superman), the ultimate representation of the New Negro. I will also examine how Paul Robeson reinvented and adopted this representation during the Harlem Renaissance by using his body, music, and the films *Song of Freedom* (1936) and *Big Fella* (1937) to reinvent the black male for the twentieth century.

Jack Johnson

Before Jack Johnson and Paul Robeson, Frederick Douglass typified the virility and puissance of the average African male slave body because of his physical resistance to his enslavement. Douglass realized the power of the black male body when in his struggle against slavery and his battle for humanity he fought ferociously and triumphantly against the slave breaker Covey, winning a permanent reprieve from the vicious beatings Covey inflicted. With his domination over Covey in the battle for his dignity, Douglass realized the full potential and potency of his body and his masculine power: "I was nothing before; I was a man now."[5] Because of the physical resistance to African slavery and men like Frederick Douglass, the black male body came to represent a commination to white hegemony. This minacity manifested in the creation of the African American male as an irrepressible sexual threat to white womanhood what James Baldwin referred to as a "walking phallic symbol," a heavy reminder to white men of their insecurities.[6] To control the African American male, white supremacists participated in a campaign of racialized terror and lynching in the name of protecting white womanhood. In 1899 T. Thomas Fortune wrote about a "race war" that occurred in Blossburg, Alabama, when whites accused African American Johnson Shepard of assaulting Mrs. Monroe Jones. This led to a rampage by white supremacists against African Americans, who took up arms to protect themselves from the carnage, which culminated in the murder of four African Americans.[7] In the 1990s the African American newspaper columnist Brent Staples came to the sudden realization that his body presented a menace to whites, given their fearful response when they passed him on his nightly walks. The black male child's body also proved dangerous to whites, as the October 1958 "Kissing Case" of Monroe, North Carolina, illustrates. The police arrested two African American boys—nine-year-old Hanover Thompson and seven-year-old David Simpson—

and charged them with rape, a crime punishable by death, because a young white girl named Sissy Marcus kissed Thompson. Comparably, in the 1990s Patricia Williams wrote of her concern for her three-year-old son, who in trying to play with little white girls in the playground presented such a hazard that one little girl in the sandbox became unhinged, screaming, "Get out of here! Don't come near me!"[8] In all of these cases the black subjects learned that the black male body remains a threat to hegemony and that it must be restricted and subjugated.

One of the strategies used to dominate the black male body included theorizing that it remained inherently different and foreign from the white male body. Several methods emerged to control the black male body, including enslavement, violence, lynching, stereotypes, the black codes, incarceration, and suppression through military training.[9] Controlling the black male body included rendering it impotent to assuage white fears. A jealous and vindictive W. E. B. Du Bois noted that Walter White, the African American executive secretary of the NAACP, gained success in the organization because of his diminutive frame. Du Bois maintained that because White was "small in stature," he made whites comfortable and did not pose a threat to white womanhood or manhood.[10] Jack Johnson's body, however, proved potent and uncontrollable. Many of the theories surrounding the black male body appeared in Johnson's body the incarnation of the Hypermasculine African American Übermensch, prepotent in body and regnant over hegemony, a threat to white male dominion, while at the same time personifying the authoritative ideal for masculinity and power.

Jack Johnson represented the New Negro: he promoted racial superiority, exhibited pride in his African heritage, and physically fought white power and anyone who offended him.[11] Johnson fashioned a public persona as a superconfident erudite sophisticate, a world traveler, a master of many languages, a wealthy connoisseur of fine things (such as fast, expensive cars and luxurious clothing), and a sportsman who graced the cover of *Le sports illustres* and attended the Grand Prix.[12] As part of his public persona Johnson also publicly paraded and courted the forbidden and dangerous—white women. He squired them around the world, married them, and brashly taunted white men and their lynch laws through these associations. These actions added to his celebrity and to the perception that he was one BAD black man who unequivocally refused the consignment of degraded African American male but rather embodied the personage of the Hypermasculine African American Übermensch.

Boxing gave Jack Johnson an avenue to create a distinctive public persona. His boxing career and his successful bouts with white boxers represented the fight between white hegemony and the ascension of black power. In 1908 a bellicose Johnson sought the heavyweight title from the diminutive white boxer Tommy Burns. Burns repeatedly rebuffed Johnson because, like the majority of white boxers of the era, he thought that fighting Johnson would dishonor the white race and tarnish his reputation.[13] White boxers went to great lengths to avoid boxing him; for example, Burns evaded Johnson by trekking across Europe, while the white boxer Jim Jeffries performed in vaudeville, farmed, and summarily snubbed Jack Johnson.[14] The cartoon "The Man They All Dodge" illustrates this. It depicts a well-muscled Johnson in a checkered suit with the caption "Jack Johnson in street togs." His face is drawn beautifully, with expressive eyes gazing off to the right, a bald head, prominent forehead and nose, and smooth lips. He holds a cigar in his right hand and sports a diamond ring on his left. There is nothing stereotypical about this rendering. In the background are black male coonlike images with large eyes and lips. One peeks from behind a door and states, "Mistah Johnson is still waiting for Tommy Burns," while the others play cards with the caption "Mistah Johnson is a player sometimes."[15] They do not detract from Johnson's powerful image but rather advance Johnson as the Hypermasculine African American Übermensch. Omitted are the white boxers who "all dodge" Johnson, which exposes their hypocrisy, while the coonlike images point to the racism of the cartoonist.

Burns finally agreed to fight Jack Johnson in Australia, and on December 26, 1908, Burns lost the match and, many would argue, lost white dominance and masculinity.[16] The cartoon "It Was a Dark Day In Australia" depicts the feeling of emasculation that whites felt when Johnson won the championship. The title contradicts the drawing of Johnson that pictures him as a handsome form in a boxing stance with his chiseled face, smooth bare head, and large muscular arms and legs. Accompanying this larger-than-life image are pictures of the various stages of the fight. Stereotypical renderings of his predecessors, African American boxers Sam Langford (sporting a wide minstrel-like grin) and Joe Gans (smiling more sedately) are strategically placed in front of Johnson's face.[17] These figures lure the viewer in but do not take away from the powerful images of Jack Johnson.

The strategy used by the media to reclaim white preeminence included dethroning Johnson by claiming that he remained unworthy of manhood rights. Wood Cowan described the fight in racist terms—"the big black flattened Tommy for a nine count." Ultimately "[Burns] was no match physically for the big boy from Galveston and Johnson beat him to the canvas in the fourteenth round."[18]

This description exemplifies the tenor of the times and the tone the white press adopted concerning the fight. It also shows how the match came to stand for the struggle to maintain white preponderance in the face of rising black power as embodied by Jack Johnson. Cowan's words also expose the unsuccessful attempts by white racists to wrestle away Johnson's power and put him in his place. By calling Johnson "the big black" and "boy" Cowan suggested that Johnson was animalistic as opposed to humanistic, infantlike as opposed to manlike, an emasculated "boy." Cowan and others failed in enfeebling Johnson given his success in the ring. The photographs and images that showed Johnson's strength and virility, the firsthand accounts of his masculine power, and his self-promotion as the Hypermasculine African American Übermensch all worked to negate the white media's mordant portrayal. Jack Johnson's strategy for combating white supremacy, the media, and his detractors included reaffirming his manliness and presenting himself as confident and articulate: "I never doubted the issue from the beginning. I knew I was too good for Burns. I have forgotten more about fighting than Burns ever knew. I was sure I would win from the start."[19] Johnson proved a worthy opponent on two fronts, the boxing ring and the ring the media created. His win against Burns incensed white supremacists, for Johnson represented black power in its fullest form: intelligent, strong, muscled, impenetrable, jet black and able to crush white hegemony uncompromisingly.

White racists responded to Tommy Burns's loss by calling for the preservation of the white man's honor.[20] White supremacists dragged Jeffries out of retirement, away from his farm, off the vaudeville circuit, and into the ring, where on July 4, 1910, he was annihilated by Johnson, thus further publicizing black power.[21] This win further exposed the white male body and white hegemony as vulnerable and weak and caused lynchings and pandemonium.

To preserve a perception of white puissance and manhood, the news media participated in a campaign to present Johnson as beastlike and minstrelesque. One reporter wrote that Johnson's fist "was like the sweep of a panther's paw; swift, cutting and terrible," while another reported that he was inarticulate, a "wide-eyed, laughing negro," who "flash[ed] his gold plated smile."[22] In 1925 Tex Rickard, the fight promoter and referee, recounted "Mr. Jeffries," said Jack [Johnson], his lips parting in a big grin, "ain't no use in talking. Dis is one time you'se met yo Waterloo! Jes' go an tell em I said so. Yas sir—Waterloo is right!"[23] This dialect exemplifies the tactics used to depose Johnson, by portraying him as an inarticulate minstrel idiot. Jack Johnson employed the media to counter this form of misrepresentation by carefully shaping a public persona as a savant and a master of the English language. On July 5 Johnson avowed, "I won from Mr. Jeffries because I outclassed him in every department of the fighting game. Before I entered the ring I was certain I would be the victor. I never changed my mind at anytime."[24] Johnson cunningly used the word *outclass* as a double entendre and asserted that he outclassed Jeffries, the farm boy, in and out of the ring as a refined cosmopolitan bon vivant, with charisma and a "beautiful" white wife. Ultimately, Johnson incensed racists, for they could not control him; and Johnson taunted their lynch laws by flaunting his white wives. A 1913 photograph offers a glimpse into how Johnson outclassed Jeffries. The photograph shows Johnson in France as the very model of sophistication, dressed elegantly in a black suit, crisp white shirt, bowtie, black hat, binoculars, and walking stick. His white wife is by his side, resplendent in a white-collared black dress, fur shawl, large black hat, and white gloves. Her hand rests delicately on Johnson's arm. The caption reads "Le nois, qui jut tres riche."[25] Johnson exudes pride, masculinity, and wealth in the image, which illustrates how he outclassed Jeffries, the farm boy, as a cosmopolitan, globetrotting citizen of the world.

Johnson cultivated this persona throughout his life, and this drew the admiration of some in the African American community and the ire of others. W. E. B. Du Bois respected Johnson, but Booker T. Washington believed he disgraced the race by marrying white women and living a flamboyant lifestyle. In 1913 Du Bois very cleverly used Johnson's interracial marriages to protect African American womanhood. He argued that Johnson's marriages to white women proved an acceptable model for shielding African American women from the savagery of white men. He maintained that African American women should receive the same safeguards of the law against white men that white women received when they married black men.[26] Du Bois noted that "we know that they [southern white men] would rather uproot the foundations of decent society than to call the consorts of brothers, sons and father their legal wives. We infinitely prefer the methods of Jack Johnson to those of the brother of Governor Mann of Virginia."[27]

Du Bois asserted that African American men must campaign for intermarriage laws not because they want to marry white women but so that "white men shall let our sisters alone." He argued that without intermarriage laws African American women remained vulnerable to "the lust of white men."[28] Du Bois ingeniously used Johnson's marriages to promote the protection of African American women while drolly exposing the degenerate behavior of white southern men toward African American women.

Booker T. Washington believed, however, that Johnson represented the race horribly, given his proclivity for white women, his verbosity concerning his boxing prowess, his lavish lifestyle, and his violation of the Mann Act.[29] Washington never actually admonished Johnson publicly, but rather he used the Tuskegee Machine, a network of supporters, former students, spies, employees, and philanthropists who distributed money and restrained opposition to Washington's agendas. On October 23, 1912, a statement signed by Washington but prepared by Emmett J. Scott and Robert E. Park declared that white men gave Johnson prominence in the United States and that while given a position of puissance Johnson brought "humiliation upon the whole race of which he is a member," and that "the honest, sober element of the Negro people of the United States is as severe in condemnation of the kind of immorality with which Jack Johnson is at present charged as any other portion of the community."[30] Johnson's marriages to white women did not accord with Booker T. Washington's racial uplift ideology, for Johnson not only married and cavorted with white women, but he flaunted them, taunted the lynch laws, and at the same time publically castigated African American women, something that Washington could not abide.[31]

A number of people in the African American community idolized Johnson for his sinew, his kindly demeanor, and his ascendance as the Hypermasculine African American Übermensch, while not giving weight to his choices in women. The African American composers Bob Cole, James Weldon Johnson, and J. Rosamond Johnson admired Jack Johnson's physical skills and tried to emulate his form of African American masculinity and athleticism. While Du Bois's support of Johnson came from his concern for African American women, Cole and the Johnson brothers' admiration of Johnson centered on his athletic prowess, his masculinity, and his Hypermasculine African American Übermensch persona.

Cole and the Johnson brothers befriended Jack Johnson around 1905, and James Weldon Johnson described him as the most interesting person he had ever met, a very likeable, affable, gentle person with his soft spoken "Southern speech and laughter," and a sad face "until he smiled."[32] Jack Johnson's career, physical strength, and expertise remained something that many, including Cole and the Johnson brothers, wanted to emulate. James Weldon Johnson immersed himself in Jack Johnson's masculine power through the "manly art of self-defense."[33] James Weldon Johnson admired Johnson greatly and believed that he embodied African American male power. James Weldon wrote that Jack Johnson symbolized all African American men and their masculinity, and when faced with the myth of Anglo Saxon physical and intellectual superiority, "the black man did not wilt." With this statement James Weldon Johnson fused all African American men with Jack Johnson and put forth that the African American male communally claimed power over white hegemony.[34] James Weldon Johnson noted that Frederick Douglass hung a photograph in his office of the 1886 Australian heavyweight title winner, African boxer from the Virgin Islands Peter Jackson, as an example of an athlete "doing his part to solve the race question," and "solv[ing] the race problem."[35] By offering Frederick Douglass's endorsement of Peter Jackson as a race man, James Weldon Johnson merged Jack Johnson and Peter Jackson together to argue that Jack Johnson also ennobled the race.[36] While Booker T. Washington's and W. E. B. Du Bois's discussion of Jack Johnson revolved around his relationships with white women, James Weldon Johnson followed Frederick Douglass's ideology concerning sports and uplift and linked Jack Johnson with the physical joy of sports, strength, and masculinity as a strategy for apotheosizing African American men.

For a component of the African American community Jack Johnson represented the restoration of the African American male body from slavery and oppression to redemption, potency, and power and a new picture of black masculinity emerged, the Hypermasculine African American Übermensch who would reinvent himself in each historical period in U.S. history.

Paul Robeson

By the 1920s a new Hypermasculine African American Übermensch emerged and fused with the New Negro ideology as educated, talented, physically attractive, and athletic. The athlete, scholar, and performer Paul Robeson embodied this new image of African American puissance with his success from 1915 to 1919 as the first black all-American football player at Rutgers University, his career in professional football with the Akron Pros (1920–21) and the Milwaukee Badgers (1922), and his skills in baseball, basketball, and track. He belonged to the prestigious Phi Beta Kappa fraternity, graduated summa cum laude from Rutgers, earned a law degree from Columbia University, mastered many languages—including several African dialects, Russian, Arabic, and Chinese—and became a renowned actor, singer, and musicologist.[37] Robeson also fought courageously for the rights of African Americans, the working class in the United States and overseas, promoted Pan-Africanism and supported anticolonial movements in Africa. Robeson used his intellect, his athleticism, his political activism, and his body to reinvent the Hypermasculine African American Übermensch as the quintessential intellectual artist, athlete, and political activist. Like Jack Johnson he reconfigured black masculinity through his body by using the tools available to him, photographs, sculptures, and drawings.[38]

Robeson sought to reclaim the black male body from primitivism, jungle imagery, and the perception that the black male body remained impotent and inferior, representations of blackness favored by whites during the Harlem Renaissance. Paul Robeson sought to promote the black male body as virile and powerful. In 1930 Eslanda Goode Robeson, Paul Robeson's wife, maintains that infused within the artistic renderings of Robeson remained an intellectual and athletic spirit, as when Robeson posed for the sculptor Tony Humbly while appearing in the Eugene O'Neill play *The Emperor Jones* in 1924. Goode Robeson writes that the conversations between Robeson and Humbly revolved around the beauty of the human body and the body as prideful as opposed to shameful. Humbly and Robeson participated in informal lessons in art and sports aesthetics as they took frequent trips to exhibits to analyze art and attended baseball games at the Polo Grounds in New York to study the male form in physical action, "the muscular 'winding up' of the pitcher's arms [and] the fine body muscle control shown in the expert fielding." At Humbly's studio, while Robeson posed, intellectuals, writers, and explorers would come to talk about their work, their travels, or Africans in America. Robeson posed, sang, and played records of his favorite black singers, such as Bessie Smith and Ethel Waters, and he shared with the listeners his pride in his "Negro blood and African descent." The atmosphere in the studio remained intellectually stimulating and electrifying and most certainly informed the artists' interpretation of Robeson, as well as Robeson's decision to use his body as the symbol of African American male intellect, athleticism, beauty, and black power.[39] In "Nude Kneeling," a 1926 photograph by Nickolas Muray, Robeson's face is silhouetted but remains recognizable, his gleaming nude body displays strong muscled legs, calves, and arms, conveying black masculinity and supremacy in its most potent form. While Jeffrey C. Stewart maintains that this image of Robeson remains emasculating, masks his sexuality and portrays him as Other, I contend that Robeson's masculinity remains ever present and assaults the eye with its potency, that Robeson conscientiously endeavored to elevate the status of the black male and imbued his pose with erudition and physicality. Robeson's agency remains primary in this image as he restores black manhood, aggrandizes the black male body, and dismisses white attempts to Other him.[40] By 1942 Robeson emerged as a hero for all and the 1942 children's novel *Big Ben,* by Earl Schenck Miers, celebrates Robeson's success as an athlete and scholar as it recounts his college football career, his experience as a law school student, and his early career on the concert stage.[41] The painting of Robeson on the cover of the book draws the viewer in as a result of his penetrating gaze, his strong and noble chin, and his well-formed lips and nose. The image offers us an understanding of the artist and Robeson's efforts to reform black boys and men. Like the cover art of *Big Ben,* a black-and-white painting of Robeson on the cover of *Masses and Mainstream* (1951) successfully communicates his intellect and his power as he proudly sings at the 1949 Peekskill concert. Perchance he is singing in Russian, German, or Chinese, or the pro-union "Joe Hill," and the words leaving his lips are, "Says Joe, 'What they forgot to kill went on to organize.'" Or maybe he is courageously proclaiming in song "Joshua fit the battle of Jericho and the walls came tumbling down," a spiritual with the spirit of battle and triumph.[42] Robeson looks very commanding, standing resolute on the stage in front of the microphone with his head held high. He is dressed in a well-tailored suit, with a tie and a white handkerchief in his chest pocket. His arms remain firmly planted by his side with clenched fists. A human barricade of men and women of every hue face out toward the audience, protecting Robeson and listening intently. A young black boy and a white soldier with a crutch are pictured looking raptly at Robeson, lost in his song, while an older white man carries a placard that reads, "Peace, No War, Ban the bomb."[43] This image of Robeson reflects his political activism, his "Negro Power," and remains representative of the very essence of the Hypermasculine African American Übermensch and the bellicose New Negro, fighting for the rights of African Americans and the oppressed through his revolutionary songs. In 1973 Leopold Mendez, a Mexican artist, created a bust of Robeson in a woodblock print for *Freedomways,* Robeson's academic journal. Mendez envisions Robeson as the definitive symbol of peace, with an effervescent smile and bright eyes. A white dove is pictured in his open palm beneath his collarbone. The dove's wings curve around his head, in effect heralding Paul Robeson as the messenger of peace. The white light of the dove illuminates Robeson and also draws our attention to the broken shackles on each side of his head, representing Robeson's fight against hegemony and subjugation and his ascendance as a man of peace. The caption reads, "Paul Robeson: True Revolutionary." These artistic representations all point to Robeson's masculine power, his role as a political activist, and his iconic heroic world image as a man of peace. All of the representations point to the effort by Robeson and those who captured his image to recognize his heroic accomplishments to reclaim the black male body as powerful, to argue that the black man remained an agent for his own life—the ultimate Hypermasculine African American Übermensch.

As early as 1924 Robeson began singing "black" spirituals and work songs in concerts in the United States and Europe to exalt the genre for the world stage. Robeson adopted the New Negro ideology of promoting black superiority, black power, and black culture to uplift the spiritual and work song. After slavery, and well into the early twentieth century, African Americans rejected the spiritual and work songs as markers of a degraded slave past. Robeson, in effect, argued that the genre remained infused with a liberation theology, a spirit of uprising, and a resistance to slavery and subjugation with songs such as "Go Down Moses," with its insurrectionary "Tell old Pharaoh, Let My People Go! If not, I'll smite your firstborn dead. Let My People Go." Comparably, Robeson sang the work song "Water Boy" because he wanted audiences to "know the strong, gallant convict of the chain-gang, make them feel his thirst, understand his naïve boasting about his strength, feel the brave gaiety and sadness in 'Water Boy.'"[44] Both of these songs are immersed in the Hypermasculine African American Übermensch and the New Negro ideology of fighting back as the songs indicate that the African slaves, their descendants, and Robeson will fight for freedom and their rights.[45] Paul Robeson wanted to elevate "the Black spiritual[s] to their rightful place of respect," and he maintained that these songs belonged on the concert stage. In 1925, while performing in the play *The Emperor Jones* in London, Robeson explained why he wanted to elevate the spiritual. "I want to sing to show the people the beauty of Negro folk songs and works songs. . . . I will concentrate on Negro music, which has never been properly handled."[46] By singing and promoting the spirituals Robeson advocated for black power, beauty, and agency, and he situated himself as a social and political activist, thus reconfiguring the Hypermasculine African American Übermensch for the age of the Harlem Renaissance.

Early in his career Robeson made a conscientious choice to fight for civil and social rights. He contended that the performer could not *just* perform but *must* take action for the social good of the oppressed, be they African Americans, Africans, working-class whites in Europe and America, everyday workers, or victims of war. In the 1930s, while living in Europe, Robeson performed before those fighting oppression in Spain during the Spanish Civil War and in his "Manifesto against Fascism" declared:

Every artist, every scientist must decide, now where he stands he has no alternative. There are no impartial observers. Through the destruction, in certain countries, of man's literary heritage, through the propagation of false ideas of national and racial superiority, the artist, the scientist, the writer is challenged. This struggle invades the former cloistered halls of our universities and all her seats of learning. The battlefront is everywhere. There is no sheltered rear. The artist elects to fight for freedom or slavery. I have made my choice! I had no alternative!

Not through blind faith or through coercion, but conscious of my course, I take my place with you. I stand with you in unalterable support of the lawful government of Spain, duly and regularly chosen by its sons and daughters.[47]

Robeson lived steadfastly by this manifesto, and through song he argued for social and civil rights. During this historical moment he battled U.S. fascism and fascism in Europe and included the Spanish Loyalists song "The Four Insurgent Generals" in his concerts and recordings beginning in 1936:

Los quarto generales
The four insurgent generals,
Mamita mia,
Tis true they betray you,
One Christmas holy evening
Mamita mia
They'll all be hanging
Madrid your tears of sorrow
Mamita mia
We shall avenge them.[48]

Singing the revolutionary and provocative lyrics of "The Four Insurgent Generals" in 1936 and the Negro spirituals foretells his 1946 proposal of "self-defense" for African Americans against American fascists and his 1958 call for "Negro Action" and "Negro Power," which predated the black power movement of the 1960s and 1970s.[49] In 1946, as chairman of the American Crusade against Lynching, Robeson and a delegation of fifteen hundred members met with President Truman and asked him to publicly renounce lynching through a "formal statement" and to recommend a "definite legislative and educational program to end the disgrace of mob violence." Robeson asserted that if the government did not do something, "the Negroes will."[50] The president refused, maintaining that lynching was not a moral issue and became incensed when Mrs. Harper Sibley, the president of the United Council of Church Women, compared fascism against Jewish people in Europe to fascism against African Americans. Like Sibley, Robeson drew the connections with the plight of Nazi concentration camp victims and that of African Americans and had long advocated for both groups through speeches and his musical selections.[51]

Robeson included the Nazi camp prisoners' "Peat Bog Soldiers" in his repertoire singing the song in both English and German to show his support for the victims. His rich, deep bass leads the listener to visualize the dire conditions of the camps, where "guns and barbed wire block our view." The up-tempo rhythm of Robeson's interpretation elucidates the resolve, the rebellious nature of the prisoners: "We are the peat bog soldiers, marching with our spades to the moor." His voice presses forward to declare the prisoners' triumph over intolerable conditions: "but for us there is no complaining, winter will in time be past." But, most significant, Robeson's rendition marches forward with a message of hope: "One day we shall rise rejoicing, Homeland, dear, you're mine at last."[52] Robeson's fight for civil rights extended to the anticolonial movements in Africa and manifested itself in the British movies he made between 1936 and 1937, *Song of Freedom* and *Big Fella*.

During the Harlem Renaissance Paul Robeson appeared in the African American filmmaker Oscar Micheaux's silent film *Body and Soul* (1924), playing both a preacher and a gambler; he also starred in the film *The Emperor Jones* (1933), but it was his disappointment with Hollywood's misrepresentation of the black male body in films such as Zoltan Korda's *Sanders of the River* (1935) that propelled him to gain artistic and editorial control of the films he made. Korda's film was the turning point for Robeson, who had held high hopes for the film but was extremely embarrassed and upset by the finished product, which in the final edited version glorified colonialism and England's imperialistic projects in Africa.[53] In the 1930s Robeson moved to London, where he performed onstage as *Othello* and made the films *Big Fella* and *Song of Freedom*.[54] Robeson had faith in the British system of filmmaking and believed that he could present affirmative representations of Africans in the diaspora. The opening credits of these films carried Robeson's vision, as they announced in large block letters that Paul Robeson was the star, thus heralding the arrival of the Hypermasculine African American Übermensch onto the big screen, quite revolutionary for the time. According to Stephen Bourne when Robeson agreed to star in *Song of Freedom*, he "insisted on a clause in his contract that gave him the right to approve the final editing of the production."[55] Written by Claude Wallace and directed by J. Elder Wills, *Song of Freedom* tells the story of John Zinga (Robeson), an Afro-British man who longs for Africa. Zinga is married to Ruth, played by the African American singer Elisabeth Welsh. The story unfolds as Zinga becomes a famous concert singer, but his longing for Africa becomes more urgent. Zinga eventually discovers that he is the descendant of an African woman, and with this discovery he leaves the concert stage, and he and his wife move to Africa to "help" his people.

This film reflects both Robeson's own discovery of Africa and his efforts to uplift African culture. In 1930, while performing in London, Robeson discovered the beauty of African culture and began to champion Africa, by rejecting "the foreign rulers of that continent [who] insisted that there was no culture worthy of the name in Africa."[56] He and Eslanda Goode Robeson studied African languages at the London School of Oriental Languages, learned of the beauty of African art and music, and remained bemused by European musicians' and artists' discovery of African art: "Those who scorned the African languages as so many 'barbarous dialects' could never know, of course, the richness of those languages and of the great philosophy and epics of poetry that have come down through [the] ages in these ancient tongues."[57]

Robeson joined the West African Student Union and gained an awareness of anticolonial movements in Africa through his friendships with African workers, seamen, and future anticolonial leaders such as Jomo Kenyatta of Kenya and Kwame Nkrumah of Ghana. He and W. E. B. Du Bois founded the Council of African Affairs in 1938 to work toward African liberation from colonialism.[58] With his newfound interest in Africa and its beauty, Robeson worked to dignify Africa and Africans and to reform the image of the African male through the film *Song of Freedom*. According to Mark A. Reid, Robeson worked within the British cinematic framework and successfully negotiated the systematic realities of the industry. Reid maintains that Robeson's films contested colonialism within the British filmmaking framework and challenged Hitler's racist policy and Mussolini's fascist ideals because the films promoted integration and equality by including integrated casts who lived and worked side by side.[59]

Robeson also reinvented the Hypermasculine African American Übermensch as a romantic matinee idol through his promotion of black love and marriage within the movie. *Song of Freedom* includes a fully realized romantic relationship between John and Ruth Zinga. They kiss, and they sing a romantic love song to one another, which worked to break the love-scene taboo that according to James Weldon Johnson dictated that black romance could only be portrayed as buffoonery.[60] This romantic pairing in many ways reflected Robeson's public persona as a loving husband to his wife, Eslanda Cordozo Goode, a "Harlem girl."[61] It also rejects Jack Johnson's vision of romantic love as requiring white women in the discourse. Robeson met Goode, an intellectual and the chief histological chemist at Columbia Presbyterian Hospital in New York City, and they married in 1922.[62] Robeson's inclusion of black romantic love in *Song of Freedom* ushered in a new representative image of the Hypermasculine African American Übermensch that would materialize in *Big Fella* and offer audiences Robeson as a heroic figure.

Robeson's heroic role in *Big Fella* was unprecedented, given the repellent stereotypes of black men that Hollywood typically manufactured. The movie was based on the Afro-Caribbean novelist Claude McKay's *Banjo*.[63] The story takes place in Marseilles and revolves around the adventures of Joe, a dockworker turned detective (played by Robeson), who is hired by the police to find a young white English boy who has vanished, presumed kidnapped from a ship visiting Marseilles. Robeson is again paired with Elizabeth Welsh, who plays Manda, a cabaret singer and his love interest. Joe eventually finds the boy, who, in fact, had run away. Joe tries to return him to his parents, only to be bamboozled by the boy, who insists on staying with Joe; otherwise, he threatens to tell the authorities that Joe kidnapped him. Joe and Manda take care of the boy, and he is eventually returned to his parents, but he insists that Joe come back with them to England. Joe chooses to stay in Marseilles with Manda; thus, the movie ends on a romantic note. This movie completely reconfigures the black male in filmic representations by offering him as a hero, a romantic lead, a New Negro, proud of his African heritage, and it offers far better representations than what existed in the United States at the time. Both Robeson and Welsh are beautifully dressed and speak articulate English. Through these filmic representations Robeson successfully negotiated the British film industry and ascended as the ultimate Hypermasculine African American Übermensch.

The Hypermasculine African American Übermensch would morph over time, with actors such as Sidney Poitier, Harry Belafonte, and Ossie Davis, all of whom idolized Robeson, following his lead of coupling political activism and performance. The Hypermasculine African American Übermensch would metamorphose in the vainglorious and brash Muhammad Ali, who resembled both Jack Johnson and Paul Robeson through his physicality and political activism; he would materialize in the guise of scholar/athlete/activists such as tennis phenom Arthur Ashe and the 1968 black power–infused Olympic track stars John Carlos and Tommie Smith. The Hypermasculine African American Übermensch remains a ubiquitous presence in the twenty-first century, in sports and on the screen, and its ubiquity is attributable in no small part to Jack Johnson and Paul Robeson. Both men worked to change the perceptions surrounding African men in the United States and Europe through the use of their bodies, their intellect, and, for Robeson, political activism. Both men fully embodied the Hypermasculine African American Übermensch and the New Negro and successfully argued that all black men deserve the rights of humanity.

NOTES

Epigraph. Dana, writing in the *New York Sun* in 1895, is quoted in Arthur R. Ashe Jr., *A Hard Road to Glory—Boxing: The African-American Athlete in Boxing* (New York: Amistad, 1993), 11.

1. Gail Bederman, *Manliness & Civilization: A Cultural History of Gender and Race in the United States, 1880–1917* (Chicago: University of Chicago Press, 1995), 3–5, 8–10.

2. Ibid.

3. According to Michael S. Kimmel, in the nineteenth century and much of the twentieth only white men inhabited masculinity while nonwhite men remained inherently unmanly. Kimmel offers the Chicago Columbia Exposition exhibit of the "White City" of 1893 as the site where manhood was clearly defined as white, civilized, and strong, against a backdrop of inferior unmanly races, who despite protests from Frederick Douglass and Ida B. Wells remained excluded from manhood at the exposition. See Michael S. Kimmel, *Manhood in America: A Cultural History* (New York: Oxford University Press, 2006), 67–68.

4. R. W. Connell, *Masculinities* (Berkeley: University of California Press, 2005), 80–81.

5. James Oliver Horton and Lois E. Horton, "Violence, Protest and Identity: Black Manhood in Antebellum America," in *A Question of Manhood*, ed. Darlene Clark Hine and Earnestine Jenkins (Bloomington: Indiana University Press, 1984), 382–98, 383.

6. James Baldwin, *Nobody Knows My Name* (New York: Dial Press, 1961), 217. Patricia Hill Collins argues that rappers in the twenty-first century adopted the notion of the black male body as inherently sexual and rebellious, and this materializes in music videos. Collins contends that African Americans as a whole have bought into the representations in the media that portray them in a negative light, and she suggests that they fight this form of subjugation and learn to love the African American body (Patricia Hill Collins, *Black Sexual Politics* [New York: Routledge, 2004], 160–61, 207, 283).

7. T. Thomas Fortune, "Race War in Alabama, Riot and Bloodshed in the Town of Blossburg," *The Sun*, Wednesday, June 28, 1899. T. Thomas Fortune Scrapbook,

Manuscripts, Archives and Rare Books Division, Schomburg Center for Research in Black Culture.

8. Patricia J. Williams, "Mediations on Masculinity," in *Constructing Masculinity,* ed. Maurice Berger, Brian Wallis, and Simon Watson (New York: Routledge, 1995), 238–49, 238–39; Robert F. Williams, *Negroes with Guns* (New York: Marzani and Munsell, 1962), 58–61.

9. Maurice O. Wallace, *Constructing the Black Masculine* (Durham, NC: Duke University Press, 2002), 103–4. Wallace argues that both General Armstrong and Booker T. Washington participated in a ritual at their respective schools Hampton Institute and Tuskegee, where they regularly watched the black male students participating in military practice.

10. W. E. B. Du Bois, *The Autobiography of W. E. B. Du Bois; A Soliloquy on Viewing My Life from the Last Decade of Its First Century* (New York: International Publishers, 1968), 293. Du Bois omits the fact that Walter White's appearance as a blond-haired, blue-eyed black man also worked to put whites at ease.

11. Nell Painter, *Creating Black Americans* (New York: Oxford University Press, 2005), 189; Davarion Baldwin, *Chicago's New Negroes: Modernity, the Great Migration, and Black Urban Life* (Chapel Hill: University of North Carolina Press, 2007), 5; Paula Marie Seniors, *Beyond Lift Every Voice and Sing: The Culture of Uplift, Identity, and Politics in Black Musical Theater* (Columbus: Ohio State University Press, 2009), 45–47.

12. "Igerje meg, hogy, ezt nem Irja meg . . ." [Promise me this does not require the . . .] (Budapest, 1933). Jack Johnson Scrapbook, box 1. Manuscripts, Archives, and Rare Books Division, Schomburg Center for Research in Black Culture; "Former Champ in Paris." Photo of Johnson and his "beautiful wife," "Former Champ in Paris" (n.d., probably 1933), Jack Johnson Scrapbook, box 3, Manuscripts, Archives, and Rare Books Division, Schomburg Center for Research in Black Culture; photo of Johnson rowing, *Le sports illustres,* France (1933), Jack Johnson Scrapbook SCM90-87, box 3; "Jack Johnson l'ancien champion du monde de boxe arrive ce soir a Paris" (1913), Jack Johnson Scrapbook, box 3, Manuscripts, Archives, and Rare Books Division, Schomburg Center for Research in Black Culture; "Jack Johnson is fined $25 for Speeding," "Auto Speed Costs Jack Johnson $20" (n.d.), Jack Johnson Scrapbook SCM90-87, box 1, Manuscripts, Archives, and Rare Books Division, Schomburg Center for Research in Black Culture; "He is an accomplished linguist, speaking both French and Latin" ("Jack Johnson with the Carnival," by James R. Scott of the Review Staff (n.d. [1940s]), box 2, Manuscripts, Archives, and Rare Books Division, Schomburg Center for Research in Black Culture).

13. Ashe, *A Hard Road to Glory,* 16.

14. "The Man They All Dodge" (n.d.), Jack Johnson Scrapbook, box 3, Schomburg Center for Research in Black Culture.

15. Ibid.

16. "It Was a Dark Day in Australia," *Evening World,* Saturday, Dec. 26, 1908, Jack Johnson Scrapbook, box 3, Manuscripts, Archives, and Rare Books Division, Schomburg Center for Research in Black Culture.

17. African Canadian Sam Langford, who was born in 1886, was known as a superb boxer but, because of racially discriminatory practices, fought only African American boxers. Joe Gans was born in Baltimore, Maryland, and gained notoriety as the first black to win a world title, the lightweight title, which he took from Frank Erne in 1901, and the welterweight title, which he took from Mike Sullivan in 1906 (Ashe, *A Hard Road to Glory,* 12–14).

18. "Them Were the Days Episode No. 2 by Wood Cowan," "Old Timers Scrapbook by Jim McGrath," LA 1942, newspaper clipping, Jack Johnson Scrapbook SCM90-87, box 1, box 2, Manuscripts, Archives, and Rare Books Division, Schomburg Center for Research in Black Culture; "Burns and Johnson Ready for Battle," *New York Times,* Dec. 21, 1908; "Burns Favorite over Negro Fighter," *New York Times,* Dec. 25, 1908.

19. "Johnson's Victory Caused No Surprise: New Champion 'Never Doubted This Issue from the Beginning,'" *New York Times,* Dec. 27, 1908.

20. A Bakersfield businessman offered Jim Jeffries $50,000 to fight Johnson; and Jack Sullivan, the former heavyweight champion who in his heyday refused to fight Afro-Caribbean boxer Peter Jackson, represented some prominent white men who offered $75,000 to Jeffries or any white to fight Johnson. See "Business Man Urges Jeffries," *New York Times,* Jan. 31, 1909; "Sullivan Offers $75,000," *New York Times,* Jan. 21, 1909; "Two More Challenge Johnson," *New York Times,* Dec. 30, 1908.

21. "Jeffries to Sell Ranch: Then He Will Go into Vaudeville—May Fight Again," *New York Times,* Jan. 31, 1909; "Johnson Wins; Police Stop Fight," *New York Times,* Dec. 26, 1908; John L. Sullivan, "Johnson Wins in 15 Rounds; Jeffries Weak," *New York Times,* July 5, 1910; "Life Looks Back, 28 Years Ago to the Johnson-Jeffries Fight in Reno," 1938, Jack Johnson Scrapbook, box 3, Manuscripts, Archives, and Rare Books Division, Schomburg Center for Research in Black Culture.

22. "Johnson Best Defensive Boxer" (n.d.), Jack Johnson Scrapbook, box 3, Manuscripts, Archives, and Rare Books Division, Schomburg Center for Research in Black Culture; "Them Were the Days Episode No. 2 by Wood Cowan," Jack Johnson Scrapbook, box 1, Manuscripts, Archives, and Rare Books Division, Schomburg Center for Research in Black Culture.

23. Tex Rickard, "Tex Rickard Tells How Ring Champions Are Made" (1925, North American Newspaper Alliance), Jack Johnson Scrapbook SCM90-87, box 2, Manuscripts, Archives, and Rare Books Division, Schomburg Center for Research in Black Culture.

24. "I Outclassed Him, Johnson Declares," *New York Times,* July 5, 1910.

25. "Jack Johnson l'ancien champion du monde de boxe arrive ce soir a Paris" (1913), Jack Johnson Scrapbook, box 3, Manuscripts, Archives, and Rare Books Division, Schomburg Center for Research in Black Culture.

26. Henry Lee Moon, *The Emerging Thought of W. E. B. Du Bois: Essays and Editorials from the "Crisis" with an Introduction, Commentaries, and a Personal Memoir by Henry T. Moon* (New York: Simon and Schuster, 1972), 296–97.

27. Ibid.

28. Ibid, 297.

29. The Mann Act of 1910 prohibited transporting women between states for illicit or sexual purposes.

30. On March 23, 1909, Emmett J. Scott asked J. Frank Wheaten, an African American lawyer, to speak to Johnson concerning his boast that he would beat Jim Jeffries. See Louis H. Harlan, Raymond W. Smock, Geraldine McTigue, and Nan E. Woodruff, eds., *The Booker T. Washington Papers,* vol. 10, 1909–11 (Urbana: University of Illinois Press, 1981), 75–76; and Louis H. Harlan and Raymond W. Smock, eds., *The Booker T. Washington Papers,* vol. 12, 1912–14 (Urbana: University of Illinois Press, 1982), 43–44.

31. The *New York Evening Graphic* ran a series of articles written by Jack Johnson, who wrote about a number of subjects, including the Mann Act charge, his love of his white wives, and his open disdain for African American women. He argued that he grew up in a multiracial environment, so it was only natural that he would marry white women. As for the Mann Act charge, he writes that it was "a trumped-up charge, completely without foundation." What is interesting in this article is that Johnson shows great empathy for Belle Schrieber, the woman at the center of the Mann Act charge, and does not hold her accountable for the charges against him. Echoing many a twenty-first-century African American man Johnson asserts that dating African American women proved devastating, and that is why he married white. "My only experiences with girls of my own color were disastrous, one deserting me when I was struggling to become a champion fighter, and the other running away with a friend I had invited to share our home. The first was Mary Austin, a playmate of mine in Galveston, Tex; the second was Clara Kerr, a colored girl from Philadelphia, who ran away with William Bryant, a trainer for Cornelius Vanderbilt racing stable, after I had invited him to live at my home" ("Jack Johnson Revealed in New Light to Harsh Critics" (n.d., probably 1929), *New York Evening Graphic,* Jack Johnson Scrapbook, box 2, Manuscripts, Archives, and Rare Books Division, Schomburg Center for Research in Black Culture).

32. *Along This Way,* in *James Weldon Johnson, Writings* (New York: Library of America, 2004), 360; Seniors, *Beyond Lift Every Voice and Sing,* 45–47. On receiving a speeding ticket, Jack Johnson faced the cheers of youngsters who wanted to shake his hand ("Jack Johnson Is Fined $25 for Speeding" [n.d.], Jack Johnson Scrapbook SCM90-87, box 1, Schomburg Center for Research in Black Culture). "Jack Johnson and his famous golden smile stopped trading on the Stock Exchange today while the bears and bulls of the greatest financial mart ceased in the world of business of juggling quotations for a few minutes to give the former heavy weight champion an ovation" ("Li'l Artha Panics Bears and Bulls on 'Change Visit," Jack Johnson Scrapbook, Schomburg Center for Research in Black Culture).

33. James Weldon Johnson, *Along This Way,* 360–61.

34. James Weldon Johnson, "The Passing of Jack Johnson," 1915, in *James Weldon Johnson, Writings* (New York: Library of America, 2004), 614–16. According to James Weldon Johnson Jack Johnson asserted black power by "not only look[ing] the white man in the eye, but hit[ting] him in the eye," thus piercing the myth of white supreme power over "lesser breeds."

35. Ashe, *A Hard Road to Glory*, 9–12; James Weldon Johnson, "The Passing of Jack Johnson," 615–16; Johnson, *Along This Way*, 360–61. Peter Jackson, a Virgin Islander who was raised in Australia, gained renown as the first African boxer to win a national boxing title. He went on to win the British title from the white boxer Jim Smith in 1889, and in 1891 at the California Athletic Club in San Francisco he fought his most famous match with the white American boxer James Corbett, which culminated in a draw. Arthur Ashe writes that because of the drawing of the color line Corbett and other white boxers refused to box Jackson, which cut short his career. Jackson died in 1901 at the age of forty-one in Australia (Ashe, *A Hard Road to Glory*, 9–12).

36. James Weldon Johnson, "The Passing of Jack Johnson," 615–16; Johnson, *Along This Way*, 360–61.

37. Susan Robeson, *The Whole World in His Hands: A Pictorial Biography of Paul Robeson* (New York: Citadel Press, 1981); Paul Robeson, *Here I Stand* (New York: Beacon, 1988); Paul Robeson Jr., *The Undiscovered Paul Robeson: An Artist's Journey, 1898–1939* (New York: John Wiley and Sons, 2001), 49, 53, 69.

38. Nude photograph of Paul Robeson, Paula Marie Seniors Collection, Mora J. Beauchamp-Byrd, curator, "Body and Soul: Paul Robeson Race and Representation," Robert and Sallie Brown Gallery and Museum, Sonja Haynes Stone Center for Black Culture and History, University of North Carolina, Chapel Hill.

39. Eslanda Goode Robeson, *Paul Robeson, Negro* (New York: Harper and Brothers, 1930), 89–96.

40. Jeffrey Stewart, "The Black Body: Robeson as a Work of Art and Politics," in *Paul Robeson Artist and Citizen* (New Brunswick, NJ: Rutgers University Press, 1998), 152.

41. While the cover image conveys black masculinity and power and presents Robeson and a gentleman scholar, the book contains stereotypical representations of his family and represents them as Mammy and Uncle Tom. See Earl Schenck Miers, *Big Ben, a Novel* (Philadelphia: Westminster Press, 1942).

42. *Paul Robeson: Songs of Free Men*, Sony Classical, 1942.

43. Mora J. Beauchamp-Byrd, curator, "Body and Soul: Paul Robeson Race and Representation," 2007, Robert and Sallie Brown Gallery and Museum, Sonja Haynes Stone Center for Black Culture and History, University of North Carolina, Chapel Hill.

44. Goode Robeson, *Paul Robeson, Negro*, 97.

45. "The Source of the Negro Spirituals," *Jewish Tribune*, July 22, 1927, in Philip S. Foner, ed., *Paul Robeson Speaks: Writings, Speeches, Interviews, 1918–1974* (New York: Brunner/Mazel, 1978), 73–76.

46. Robeson, *Here I Stand*, 56; "Robeson Would Become a Singer; American Negro Actor's Ambition Is to Sing Simple Folk Songs of His Race," *Special Cable to the New York Times*, Sept. 12, 1925; "Will Sing Negro Spirituals: Paul Robeson to Help Entertain for Benefit of Columbus Hill Day Nursery," *New York Times*, March 8, 1925.

47. Quoted in Charles H. Wright, *Robeson: Labor's Forgotten Champion* (Detroit: Balamp Publishing, 1975), 13.

48. "The Four Insurgent Generals," *Paul Robeson: Songs of Free Men*, Sony Classical, 1942.

49. "Group Sees Truman on Lynching Curb," *New York Times*, Sept. 24, 1946; "To Open Crusade against Lynching," *New York Times*, Sept. 23, 1946. Robeson argued that "sixteen million people are a force to be reckoned with. . . . I say that we ourselves have the power to end the terror and to win for ourselves peace and security throughout the land. The recognition of this fact will bring new vigor, boldness and determination in planning our program of action and new militancy in winning its goals" (Robeson, *Here I Stand*, 92).

50. "Truman Balks at Lynch Action," *Chicago Defender*, Sept. 28, 1946; "American Crusade Ends with Anti-lynch Decree," *Chicago Defender*, Sept. 28, 1946; Foner, *Paul Robeson Speaks*, 175, 178. Truman's stand replicates the resistance in the United States and the world in the twenty-first century to calling the attempt to annihilate the Palestinians by the Israeli government genocide or to classify the many atrocities in Africa as genocide.

51. The FBI reported on March 16,1942, from San Antonio that a dinner was given for Paul Robeson by the American Committee to Save Refugees and the United American Spanish Aid Committee to raise funds "which will help pay for the transportation of anti-Axis refugees in French Concentration camps." The FBI believed that the real objective was to transport communists to Latin America and Mexico. See "Communist Activities Paul Robeson, American Committee to Save Refugees United American Spanish Aid Committee," San Antonio, Texas, March 16, 1942, 4–5, Freedom of Information Act, Federal Bureau of Investigation, Part 1A, FBIHQ File 100-12304FBI.

52. "Peat Bog Soldiers," *Paul Robeson: Songs of Free Men*, Sony Classical, 1942.

53. Deborah Willis, "The Image and Paul Robeson," in *Paul Robeson: Artist and Citizen*, ed. Jeffrey C. Stewart (New Brunswick, NJ: Rutgers University Press, 1998), 61–80, 78; Donald Bogle, *Toms, Coons, Mulattoes, Mammies, and Bucks: An Interpretive History of Blacks in American Films* (New York, Continuum, 2004), 95, 99, 100.

54. Thomas Cripps, *Slow Fade to Black: The Negro in American Film, 1900–1942* (New York: Oxford University Press, 1993), 317; Stephen Bourne, *Elisabeth Welsh: Soft Lights and Sweet Music* (Lanham, MD: Scarecrow, 2005), 44–45.

55. Bourne, *Elisabeth Welsh*, 44–46.

56. Robeson, *Here I Stand*, 42.

57. Ibid.

58. Ibid.; see also Paul Robeson Jr., *The Undiscovered Paul Robeson*, 287.

59. Mark A. Reid, "Race, Working-Class Consciousness, and Dreaming in Africa," in *Paul Robeson: Artist and Citizen* (New Brunswick, NJ: Rutgers University Press, 1998), 165–78, 166–67.

60. Johnson, *Along This Way*, 171.

61. Goode Robeson, *Paul Robeson, Negro*; Miers, *Big Ben, a Novel*, 235–38; Martin Summers, *Manliness and Its Discontent: The Black Middle Class and the Transformation of Masculinity* (Chapel Hill: University of North Carolina Press, 2004), 186–87. Summers contends that the Robesons' marriage remained shaky, given Paul Robeson's infidelity, and that the couple separated many times. The discourse surrounding the

marriage in the public eye promoted by both Eslanda Goode Robeson and in the novel *Big Ben* was that of fidelity, loyalty, and Eslanda's (or Laura's, as she was represented in the novel) sacrifice of sharing Robeson with the public and promoting his career over her own.

62. Goode Robeson, *Paul Robeson, Negro*; Paul Robeson Jr., *The Undiscovered Paul Robeson*, 46.

63. Bourne, *Elisabeth Welsh*, 47–48.

TWELVE

Between Black Gay Men

Artistic Collaboration and the Harlem Renaissance in Brother to Brother

Shawn Anthony Christian

> [*Brother to Brother*] strives to make links between [Hughes, Hurston, Nugent, and Thurman] and the lives of young, contemporary African American artists as they begin to emerge and fulfill their full potential. While the film centers on African American artists of the Harlem Renaissance and the present day, I believe the quest for a meaningful identity and an original and truthful artistic voice is a universal theme that resonates on a global level. *Brother to Brother* strives to acknowledge the diversity and complexity within the African American and gay and lesbian communities and to give voice to experiences that have been vastly underrepresented in cinema for far too long. —RODNEY EVANS

Rodney Evans suggests in his "Filmmaker's Statement" that the Harlem Renaissance functions as a usable past. Similar to Isaac Julien's "meditation" on Langston Hughes in *Looking for Langston* (1988), Evans offers *Brother to Brother* as an homage to Richard Bruce Nugent, one of the Harlem Renaissance's more controversial yet marginalized figures. In its depiction of his public and private life as a black male artist during the period, *Brother to Brother* envisions Nugent's social reality through black-and-white imagery, flashbacks, voice-over narration, and the words of black male writers, gay and straight. In these and other ways Evans responds to Ed Guerrero's call to rework filmic images of black males as an absent presence and disrupts practices of representing heterosexuality as *the* referent for black masculinity and black male artistry.[1]

Brother to Brother is the story of Perry Williams (portrayed by Anthony Mackie), a young black artist kicked out of his family home for being gay. Trapped between the worlds of a black community and a gay community, Perry searches for a connection that will enable him to live comfortably between both. He soon meets and befriends Richard Bruce Nugent (portrayed by Roger Robinson), whom he comes to regard as a model for how to name, articulate, and own his experiences as a young, black, gay male artist. The two men embark on a literal and meta-phorical journey to the creative center of the younger, rebellious generation of the Harlem Renaissance. Bruce's memories expose Perry to the legacies and hard-ships of pioneering black authors. By witnessing the pride that Bruce and his friends exude, Perry begins to gain a stronger sense of identity, and his relationship with Bruce helps him articulate and satisfy his desires as a black gay male artist.

Although the Harlem brownstone where Langston Hughes, Zora Neale Hur-ston, Wallace Thurman, Aaron Douglas, and others lived and worked for a period during the renaissance is dilapidated, Perry and Bruce enter it to remember the energizing moment when Bruce and others decide to create a literary and artistic journal that reflects the unfettered expression their generation of black poets, painters, musicians, dramatists, and novelists desires. With a cast of actors whose physical features remind informed viewers of the real Nugent, especially Duane Boutte as Young Bruce, and the other artists who help define the Harlem Renais-sance's younger generation, Evans draws on biography, autobiography, letters, and other artifacts to recreate as a collage the experience of this moment through Bruce's eyes. As Perry and Bruce enter the infamous Niggerati Manor, which the film's present depicts as neglected and forgotten, and broach the stairs, the shot transitions from color to black-and-white flashback. Ragtime music introduces the shot of Young Bruce and Langston Hughes (portrayed by Daniel Sunjata) as-cending the steps outside the brownstone and precedes Robinson's voice-over recount. Once inside Niggerati Manor, we witness Wallace Thurman (portrayed by Ray Ford) pitch his idea to Young Bruce and Hughes:

> WALLY. We actually have this new idea for a journal we been bouncing back and forth.
>
> LANGSTON. Something like *Crisis*.
>
> WALLY. Bite your tongue. No more weepin' and moanin' for respect from white people. Locke and Du Bois have had their say. This is about younger artists. Something with spunk and passion.
>
> YOUNG BRUCE. Sounds like we've all been having the same conversation.
>
> WALLY. We're talking drawing, fiction, poetry, essays anything by young Negroes with something new to say.
>
> YOUNG BRUCE. Well count us in.

In this pivotal flashback, and subsequent collage sequences, Evans reinterprets and values the Harlem Renaissance's signal moment in the group's creation of *Fire!!* Here Evans positions the inhabitants of Niggerati Manor's collaborative work as the zeitgeist, eighth note, and thread that renders their experience a usable past. Such a focus is appropriate given how the period develops as one of intense collaboration.

In addition to *Fire!!*'s existence as the product of collaborative work and its necessity, the literature, art, music, and social activism of the period suggest that collaboration is an important ethic in advancing the Harlem Renaissance. When Alain Locke writes in the seminal *The New Negro* that "there is a growing realization that in social effort the co-operative basis must supplant long-distance philanthropy, and that the only safeguard for mass relations in the future must be provided in the carefully maintained contacts of the enlightened minorities of both race groups" (9), he communicates several ideas that inform the racial uplift and artistic production so characteristic of the period.[2] Although there are several instances of cooperation similar to those that Locke refers to and calls for, such as the Niagara Movement and its subsequent incorporation as the National Association for the Advancement of Colored People (NAACP) in 1909, the production of Eugene O'Neil's *The Emperor Jones*, and the Urban League's celebrated 1924 Civic Club Dinner, in reality, as Locke's focus on the future suggests, such cooperation is more a desired goal than a dominant occurrence of the renaissance. While these and other instances of interracial collaboration produce, what David Levering Lewis aptly describes as a "culture of comity,"[3] Evans tells a compelling story of collaboration and its limitations that emerges from the record of intragroup instances of working together. Focusing on the "new" in "New Negro," Evans redefines the gaps, absences, and acknowledged yet accepted silences that also make up the renaissance's representations of African America as the impetus for collaboration.

Projecting Nugent and others as unnerved, somewhat irreverent, and weathering criticisms and potential isolation together, Evans's depiction capitalizes on the fact that despite reviews of *Fire!!*, which, as Evans recreates them here, are as infamous as the actual fire that destroys a majority of the first issues, and the group's iconoclastic personalities, we remember this "younger generation" for its creativity, rebelliousness, and fervent, if not problematic, belief in the potential of black people's diversity. Evans offers a vision of *Fire!!*'s creators as collaborating artists who are conscious of the opportunity that their historical moment provides and keenly aware of their individual skills and talents. Although we may question the effectiveness of their efforts relative to Locke or W. E. B. Du Bois's perspective, Evans reads and depicts their conviction as viable because it bridges genres, opens up a developing, cultural infrastructure, engages and cultivates audiences, and makes more tangible African American literature's artistic and social functions. *Fire!!*'s ideological impulse fuels the group's collaboration, which Evans depicts through a recovery of Richard Bruce Nugent's visage and art.

Evans's film values Nugent's out status and artistry and reflects the fact that Nugent lived longer than most of his counterparts, including Langston Hughes. He died in relative obscurity, however, despite having newfound celebrity in the last decades of his life because of gay and lesbian pride movements; for example, interview footage of Nugent appears in the documentary *Before Stonewall* (1984). To reimage and imagine the Harlem Renaissance, Evans contemplates Nugent's desire, nostalgia for the collaborations of his earlier life. As I argue in this reading of *Brother to Brother*, rather than engage the Harlem Renaissance as a usable past that offers subjects whose experiences help image and articulate black male, same-sex desire then and, to a degree, now, Evans privileges and envisions a cross-generational, homosocial rather than homoerotic bond.[4]

Drawing from Harlem Renaissance artistic collaborations and the relationships that black male figures' shared experiences as young artists produce, Evans notes that "the structure of the script is built around the gazes of Black men between each other in order to represent us (with all of our nuances and contradictions) as we really are" (Evans). Much of the film's action bears this out. From the opening scenes to the final "portrait" scene, *Brother to Brother* images relationships between black men, artists, gay and straight, young and old, through a series of telling gazes. After the film's opening shot, where we watch, through the window of a subway car, a moving New York City skyline, the camera focuses on a male subject. As the shot's interiority places us in the subway car with him and just before our subject's first gaze, we hear a male's voice: "There are thoughts that have the power to trap me. I write them down to be more honest about them and lessen their potential to do harm. There's a war inside me." We then watch as this black man writes in what appears to be a journal and looks up at another young black man sitting across from him. They exchange glances and suggestive smiles. While they do, the camera turns our gaze to an older black man, whose face registers recognition as he watches these men's exchange. Subsequent scenes reveal that the first black man that we see is the film's protagonist,

Perry, whose introspection establishes the film's language and tone. We learn, too, that our older coviewer is Richard Bruce Nugent. Through his depiction of this fictional relationship, Evans visualizes black gay male desire and subjectivity beyond the sexual. Several of the film's scenes and shots work together and place primacy on Perry's desire for friendship, collaboration, and love.

Just as the establishing shot for the film's present relates Perry's complexity, *Brother to Brother*'s first flashback works to historicize and reinforce black gay male desire. In an early scene Evans uses the subway to figuratively convey temporal movement to a Harlem of the past and literally introduce the film's flashback sequences.[5] While waiting for a train to arrive, the elderly, present-day Bruce turns to look at a younger black man sitting on a bench. The camera follows Bruce's gaze as the shot transitions to black-and-white. When the camera follows the young black man's return look, now in the past, the shot reveals that Boutte's Young Bruce replaces Robinson's Bruce. The following exchange between Young Bruce and the other black man in the flashback communicates Evans's concerns about the gazes between black men:

> YOUNG BRUCE. Excuse me, I was wondering if you might be interested in having your portrait done.
> YOUNG BLACK MAN. What's in it for me?
> YOUNG BRUCE. The pleasure of giving me pleasure for one. And the ability to see the reflection of your beauty through my eyes for two. Isn't that enough?

When Young Bruce defines pleasure as "the ability to the see the reflection of your beauty through my eyes," he communicates the role that art—painting is this case—plays in facilitating the interactions that the black men in *Brother to Brother* have. Perry's relationships with, first, his childhood friend Marcus and then with Bruce turn on these men's shared experiences as artists as much as the relationships turn on their experiences as black men. *Brother to Brother* responds to and extends Eve Kosofsky Sedgwick's assertion about "the potential unbrokenness of a continuum between homosocial and homosexual—a continuum whose visibility, for men, in our society, is radically disrupted."[6] *Brother to Brother* rejects or, more accurately, repairs this "radical disruption" at the level of narrative, especially in its emphasis on continuity across generations, subjectivities, and artistic mediums. In doing so, the film effects an answer to the dynamic that Joseph Beam conceives of in his 1984 essay "Brother to Brother: Words from the Heart":

Dream 84: 15 February 1984

   We have all gathered in the largest classroom I have ever been in. Black men of
all kinds and colors. We sit and talk and listen, telling stories of our lives. All the
things we have ever wanted to say to each other but did not. There is much laughter,
but also many tears. Why has it taken us so long? Our silence has hurt so much.[7]

Evans's *Brother to Brother* makes the point that laughter, hurt, and opportunities to share stories constitute Perry's relationship with other black men. Having
Perry develop his sexual identity through his relationships with other black
men, artists, gay and straight, centers images of black men beyond the often one-
dimensional representations that form a history of such images. As Phillip Brian
Harper notes, "An unwavering focus on the black gay man was rare prior to the
late 1980s. The scenario then was one in which he served as a foil to any number
of figures who, however disaffected from white, bourgeois society, nonetheless
constitute the normative center of the social world presented on screen."[8]

Extending this post-1980s turn to a focus on black gay male characters as protagonists and their environments as central settings, *Brother to Brother* participates in the discourse about black gay male subjectivity that earlier filmmakers
such as Julien and Marlon Riggs forge. The scenes following the initial gazes between the film's black male subjects provide the context for Perry's assertion that
"there's a war inside me," including the one that recounts Perry's return home to
retrieve books, when he encounters (more of) his father's rejection; through the
screen of a patio door, which Evans uses to produce a porous border between both
men and reinforce the father's unwillingness to *see* Perry, his father tells Perry,
"Anything you left in this house does not exist. Now get out of my sight." In a
later flashback scene, Evans shows the rage and physical violence that Perry's
father exhibits once he discovers Perry's intimacy with another male. As the only
instances of Perry's relationship with his father, these two scenes and the film's
account of how Perry values friendships as a reconstituted family underscore
the challenge of negotiating his sexuality in the space of the family. Where Perry's
family comes to symbolize the potential impossibility of developing a relationship with another black man, his interactions with Rashan, an African American
classmate, communicate a similar suggestion about Perry's community of peers.

An important subplot, Perry's "Black Intellectual Thought" class functions as
another register of his struggle. Indeed, Evans presents this struggle as one about
Perry's difficult interactions as a black gay man with other black men. Even the
opportunity to discuss the work of a black gay writer, James Baldwin's *A Fire Next*

Time, does not foster the ease that Perry desires. While seeking not acceptance but the acknowledgment that Baldwin's sexuality matters in a discussion of his ideas about African Americans, Perry confronts another dynamic of silencing and erasure, as Rashan quips in response to Perry's suggestion, "We're talking about activism and political struggle, not what people do with their sex organs." Absent the constraints on his voice and identity in his family home, in class Perry pushes back and utilizes a friend's student film to illustrate the potential impossibility of black men, one gay and the other straight, relating. Following a complex sequence that narrates Perry's relationship with Jim, which I discuss below, the shot cuts to black-and-white footage of a Black Power rally that cuts into a conversation between two black males, one portrays James Baldwin and the other Eldridge Cleaver. Constructed from the "words and thoughts of Eldridge Cleaver and James Baldwin," the camera captures this tense conversation as both men sit across from each other and discuss Baldwin's contributions to the struggles facing black America.[9] Cleaver accuses Baldwin of "let[ting] the white man fuck you in the ass. Now what does that make you? Huh? That makes you the lowest scum on the earth." Following this charge, the breakdown of their potential connection begins and intensifies. The scene concludes with Baldwin's rejoinder: "Who gave you the right to judge?" Throwing the table that separates them, jumping to his feet, and into Baldwin's face, Cleaver aggressively responds, "I'll show you my right mothafucka!" The film then cuts to color footage of a gay and lesbian pride parade.

Rashan is the first to respond to the film with, "Why do we have to watch this?" The exchange that they share over the film and its message ends with Perry's accusation that Rashan's hostile reaction to Baldwin's homosexuality is actually a cover to hide Rashan's own homosexuality. Their teacher intervenes in the exchange but not before Perry and Rashan exchange defiant gazes at one another. Emphasizing the parallels between Baldwin's and Cleaver's relationship and Perry's and Rashan's relationship, and suggesting a history of such tensions, Evans follows with an answer scene to the one in Perry's film where Rashan and a group of other black men attack Perry. In that scene's most graphic moment Rashan burns Perry's face with a lit cigarette and utters, "Here go the fire next time mothafucka," while he does so. Through Perry's father's and Rashan's homophobic and violent responses, Evans provides further explanation for Perry's isolation and desire for love between himself and other black men. These relationships compel Perry to experience such denials and erasure as the loss of any substantive relationships with other black men, especially straight black men.

Evans structures *Brother to Brother* so that Perry's relationships with other men appear as counters to this loss. For example, the scenes that narrate Perry's relationship with Marcus are the first tangible contrasts to the brief but volatile ones between Perry and his father and Perry and Rashan. As the plot develops, we learn that Perry and Marcus are not only childhood friends but support one another's artistic growth; early in the film Perry attends a poetry reading where Marcus recites a new poem, and Marcus, in turn, attends Perry's first exhibition of his work. Although straight, Marcus has and maintains a relationship with Perry and does so in terms of brotherhood. Their exchange after Marcus's reading illustrates this point and demonstrates the role that Marcus plays in Perry's life:

> PERRY. You know what, see this anger you feelin' towards white people? It's the same anger brothers feel toward me for being gay.
>
> MARCUS. What? That's totally different.
>
> PERRY. Oh, it is?
>
> MARCUS. Come on, you know how brothers front. Together they might dis you so nobody else thinks they that way. But you know if you got into any real trouble, you're fam and they got your back.
>
> PERRY. I'm not so sure.

Rather than push Perry on the reasons for his ambivalence, Marcus evokes the history of sports-related incidents from their childhood when Marcus has Perry's "back." While his notions in this exchange about the practice of racial solidarity in the face of homosexuality are problematic and his reference to Perry's athletic abilities as a youth stereotypical, as a contrast to Perry's father's and Rashan's violent denials, Marcus's perspective suggests that there are black straight men who can and do befriend black gay men. The terms of Perry's and Marcus's relationship are historical and less about (Perry's) sexuality.

I do not mean to suggest that what they share erases Perry's life as a black gay man or that Marcus merely tolerates Perry's homosexuality. As his parting words to Perry in this scene reveal, Marcus intends to help Perry find love. As he states, "Everybody in the world ain't out to get you man. But don't worry, Ima find a good brother for you. Got my eye looking out for it." Again, Marcus's concern for Perry as his "brother" and sense of racial solidarity buttress his understanding of and response to Perry's needs as a black gay man. Increasingly, however, Marcus's brotherhood becomes limiting as Perry attempts to work out the "war inside" of him. As later scenes reveal, Marcus's too literal, black-and-white approach to the world, friendship, and art does not account for the contradictions that make up

Perry's experience. Operating with a sense of "right" that their relationship and his heterosexual privilege bestow, after Jim, a white classmate, objectifies Perry, Marcus condemns Perry's relationship with Jim. Marcus then speaks against another black man who condemns Perry's lifestyle on religious grounds and in the name of brotherhood, and he later attempts to broker, ironically, Perry's career with a white male gallery owner.

That Evans structures these events to occur after Marcus's affirmation suggests that Perry's and Marcus's relationship is not a failure but, rather, an incomplete relationship. Even though Evans underscores the script's focus on the gazes of *black* men, Perry's search for this more complete relationship manifests through his gazes at men in general and Jim (portrayed by Alex Burns) in particular. Not only is Jim the sole white student in Perry's class, but he is also the one student who reaches out to Perry. The relationship they develop provides an opportunity for Perry to vent and momentarily forget about his challenges with family and Rashan. For example, in response to Rashan's initial rejection of Perry's efforts to discuss Baldwin's sexuality, as they stand on the campus green after Rashan's and Perry's heated exchange, Jim stresses to Perry that "[he] made [his] point" and encourages Perry to "brush it off man." After a pause, Jim asks if Perry has tickets to a concert by De La Soul.[10] They agree that the concert will be "off tha hook" and solidify their developing friendship.

Jim's willingness to "see" Perry's point of view and to socialize with Perry soon produces an intimacy between them that Perry welcomes. After the concert Perry and Jim return to Perry's dorm room and learn more about one another. Jim appears curious and asks questions about Perry's family and homosexuality:

PERRY. Let's just say that [there are] certain practices I engage in that my
    parents can't understand.
JIM. And you can't talk to them about it?
PERRY. It's clear that they don't want to have anything to do with me. Guess
    you could say I've been cut off.
JIM. That's really fucked up.

In this scene Jim's response to Perry's acknowledgment of his isolation shifts Perry's mood, as it does in the scene of their exchange at the end of their class. After scanning the room for something else to do, Jim notices videocassettes, which Perry notes are porn. While watching two men kiss on Perry's television, Perry and Jim kiss and, as the screen fades to black, we watch them begin their first sexual encounter.

As I noted earlier, Jim's and Perry's relationship suffers because Perry experiences Jim's desire as racialized and objectifying. Their exchange after their second sexual encounter reveals much:

JIM. You make me feel so good.
PERRY. I'm glad. I like making you feel good.
JIM. I love your skin. So smooth. And your lips. You are so fucking beautiful.
And you have the sweetest black ass I have ever seen.

This time in Jim's dorm room, we witness their postsex intimacy, as it turns, for Perry, quickly predictable. While lying next to and caressing Perry, Jim's increasing admiration of Perry's physical blackness registers powerfully on Perry's face. With each of Jim's statements the camera closes in more on Perry's face to ultimately capture his despondent and vacant look in response to Jim's "sweetest black ass" comment. Perry's rapid departure only highlights the recognition of Jim's stereotyping that Perry's eyes reveal. Because of this moment and Jim's later suggestion that Perry coerced him into the entire sexual relationship, Perry tells Jim in a subsequent conversation that "I never meant to put you in an awkward situation, but I've been looking for a boyfriend for a really long time. And I've been intensely lonely a very long time. And I got kicked out of my parents' house recently, which led to a lot of emotional shit. And, I just need someone in my life who's more than a friend. Someone who's willing [pause] to love me. I don't have that, and I thought that you might be that. But I don't think that you are."

Perry's realization is actually the second response that he voices about Jim's desire. The first operates through how Perry intends for Cleaver's criticisms of Baldwin's homosexuality and preference for white men to double as criticisms of Rashan's rejection and Jim's objectifying moment; at the end of his class presentation Perry and Jim stare at one another knowingly. We can argue, too, that Evans intends the dissolution of Perry's relationship with Jim to be, for audiences that know Baldwin's and Nugent's biographies, a commentary on Baldwin's and Nugent's preference for white men. Equally plausible is how Perry's and Jim's relationship renders Perry's experience, albeit fictional, more parallel with his predecessors' experiences. Although *Brother to Brother*'s Bruce never acknowledges his sexual preferences in racial terms, he does describe Jim as, "that cute white boy." It is their connection over Perry's relationship with Jim that conveys the sense that there are more tangible layers to Bruce's and Perry's more personal relationship.

Just before Perry ends his relationship with Jim, Bruce asks Perry about its progress. Perry responds, "It's like one of those things where you're always trying to make someone into something they're not. Anything just to fill the emptiness and to avoid being alone." While Perry delivers these words, the camera offers a close-up of Bruce's face. The recognition this time is one of pain, and instinctively Bruce grabs and hugs Perry as a response. After their embrace, Bruce leaves Perry (because, as they both acknowledge through a moment of camp, "a lady needs a room of her own") and reveals his own desires to "fill the emptiness and to avoid being alone." Bruce announces to one of his black male contemporaries, "I met somebody, somebody who reminds me of what it felt like to fall in love." He continues: "You ever start talking to someone and feel like you've known them forever? Their entire past and future flashes right before your eyes. And your heart starts beating faster cause you know how hard their life is going to be. And it just tears you up inside. I just listened and stared at him. And I wanted to hold him."

As though responding to Perry's declaration to Jim, from both his youth and age, Bruce speaks to and identifies with Perry's struggle. In the final third of *Brother to Brother* we witness how Perry's and Bruce's relationship becomes more central as Perry's relationships with Marcus and Jim become increasingly more difficult for Perry to negotiate. For Perry, Bruce mirrors and affirms his experiences and artistry more completely.

Recognition between these black gay men shapes their initial encounter. Bruce approaches just as Marcus recites the final lines of a new poem while he and Perry chill on the steps of a brownstone. Unsolicited, an approaching Bruce joins in and offers a few lines from "Smoke, Lilies, and Jade." As he does so, the shot moves from both Perry's and Marcus's faces. The close-up of Perry's face registers Perry's identification with Nugent's words, especially the image of the painter that "if colors could be heard, he'd paint most wondrous tunes." Once Perry questions Bruce about his identity, their relationship becomes a visual representation, this time between two black gay men, of the dream that Joseph Beam recounts. While sitting on a park bench, Perry presses Bruce for information and explanation:

> PERRY. I really love ["Smoke, Lilies, and Jade"]. The phrasing, the mood, everything. It's like someone of a different time and place. But it is exactly how I feel.
>
> BRUCE. Well, I hate to break it you, but I'm here and now, flesh and blood right here before your very own eyes.

Conveying the idea that the past is alive, Bruce embraces Perry's curiosity about the Harlem Renaissance and shares his physical and emotional memories of it.

(Young) Bruce is the center of the black-and-white flashbacks that represent *Brother to Brother*'s retrospective of the Harlem Renaissance. His playfulness, sexual openness, and boundary-pushing antics make him a focal point. Evans depicts Young Bruce's contribution as innovative and daring; for example, as the collaborators contemplate the contents of their proposed journal, Young Bruce and Wally "flip a coin" to decide who would write a story for *Fire!!* about "queers [or] whores. The types that [they] were most fond of." In the film's present, Bruce's perspective on how "all these things live inside you until you make your peace with them" enables Perry's own reconnection to the pain of his past. As they sit next to one another in this scene, the shot cuts from close-ups of Bruce and Perry as each one speaks to flashbacks of Perry's abuse at the hands of his father. Expressing a connection to Bruce's experience, Perry notes that,

> It's like when my dad caught [me] with this guy in my room. He was kicking the shit out of me. And he just kept screaming, "Not in my house." Almost like he was trying to convince himself that I was someone else. Like if he just kept pounding on me, this . . . thing would go away. And my mother kept saying, "Where did we go wrong?" Said she felt like killing herself. I thought of the times when the thought of them knowing I was gay was enough to make me want to kill myself. She finally understood how that must have felt.

Bruce affirms for Perry that "no matter how far you run, the connections will always be there. Family is the core stuff, and you got to [try] like hell to let them know who you are. The rest is up to them."

Following Bruce's injunction, the film cuts to another flashback, this time of Bruce's experience with "family." In this scene Evans brings Young Bruce and his collaborators together with an angry mob of African American men and women, described as "proper Negroes," who decry the journal, calling it "smut" and the group of artists "trash." With both groups standing on either side of a burning garbage can and voicing arguments about the "right" way to represent African Americans, the exchange here recalls powerfully the student film chronicling the heated exchange between a fictional Baldwin and Cleaver. As one man throws another copy of *Fire!!* into the burning can—Evans plays here with the line from one review of the journal—and spits on Young Bruce, both groups' stances devolve into a melee of pushing and shouting. As the screaming fades and the shot pulls back, Young Bruce levels, "And don't talk to me about family because we are the family, okay?"

Because Bruce informs Perry of how much Perry reminds him of his friends and collaborators, Wally and Langston in particular, Evans moves their relationship from a focus on Perry's needs to a focus on Bruce's efforts to paint again after a long period away from the art form. Prior to this artistic collaboration we witness an exchange between them that reinforces the homosocial bond that I argue structures the film. Following Bruce's reminiscence of the Harlem Renaissance as a period of play, hard work, and exclusion, Bruce asks Perry to allow him to paint his portrait. When Rashan's attack leaves Perry emotionally and physically unable to sit for him, Bruce goes to find Perry at his dorm. Upset at his absence, lack of communication for at least a week, and unwillingness to report the attack, Bruce exclaims, "It matters 'cause you were supposed to help me, and I was counting on you and you let me down." Bruce forces Perry out of bed to accompany him back to Niggerati Manor.

Once inside, Bruce's transformation of the space into an intimate, candle-lit studio focuses their passion for their shared art. The scene's shots blend to convey the passage of time as the only action we witness is, first, Perry sitting for Bruce and then Bruce for Perry. The results of their labor are two portraits, one of each man. Echoing their stages in life, Perry's is a vibrant blue, and Bruce's is a rust-colored hue. With the portraits positioned side by side, the final shot of them pans out to reify their dialogue, shared talent, and identities. In this moment Evans's film performs a multilayered, double-voiced narration similar to those that Caroline Goeser argues are central to the visual practices of the Harlem Renaissance.[11] Bruce and Perry talk to each other and, through Evans's film, to us. Bruce's art negotiates a long-standing black gay absence just as it marks itself as an emerging, black gay presence. Perry's healing process and remembering of family reveal that the Harlem Renaissance constitutes a viable historical resource for doing both and affirming his identity as a black gay male artist.

With an initial shot of Perry's teacher as he reads the title of Perry's assignment—"Richard Bruce Nugent and the Rebel Spirit of the Harlem Renaissance" (Evans's allusion to informant and writer Thomas Wirth's 2002 *Gay Rebel of the Harlem Renaissance*)—*Brother to Brother* concludes as Perry scatters Bruce's ashes over the sea and his voice-over relates, "His ability to use words and transport me to different realities would forever alter my perception of the world. He taught me how to weave spells and conjure myths, the power of which would not be denied. Through him I learned the complexity of what was inside me was also outside, if I was willing to look deeper. With words and images, I could enjoy the truth of my experience, putting it down and passing it on."

Brother to Brother underscores the forced absence of representations of black male same-sex desire and employs the Harlem Renaissance's suggestions about the presence of such desires as the historic foundation for Evans's effort to redress that absence. Evans's film argues, too, that the absence is still real and that efforts to reveal that presence need to complicate our understanding of that desire further. For Evans, same-sex desire is not solely or primarily sexual. Through Bruce's and Perry's relationship Evans echoes Marlon Riggs's use of the affirmation "black men loving black men is the revolutionary act" (Riggs, *Tongues Untied*).

Evans speaks, as well, to our own nostalgia for the Harlem Renaissance, to our desires for its real culture of comity and use of literature, music, and art to bring people together equitably. In disrupting our romanticized notions and remembrances of the period through depicting the commentary against *Fire!!* and positioning them as similar to Perry's difficult relationships with other black men, Evans asks us to recognize that our nostalgia for the Harlem Renaissance is not unlike his own nostalgia for its collaborative impulse. What we desire is a past that was rarely experienced as we remember it. Indeed, our nostalgia is, as many of us recognize but do not often voice, a commentary on our present. We project an ideal that is not being experienced now into the past that is the Harlem Renaissance. It is the period's pliability for such projections that compel this reading of *Brother to Brother*'s contention that the Harlem Renaissance is a primary site of memory from which to continue imaging and then articulating, among other dynamics, the potential for love between black gay men.

ACKNOWLEDGMENTS

I would like to thank Lauren Rabinovitz, Kent Ono, the participants of the University of Iowa's Center for Ethnic Studies and the Arts' 2007 Junior Faculty Writing Workshop, and my colleague at Wheaton College, Josh Stenger, for their generous feedback on this paper.

NOTES

Epigraph. Rodney Evans, "Filmmaker's Statement," Independent Lens, 2005, www.pbs .org/independentlens/brothertobrother/statement.html (accessed Sept. 21, 2009).

1. See Ed Guerrero, "The Black Man on Our Screens and the Empty Space in Representation," in *Black Male: Representations of Masculinity in Contemporary American Art,* comp. Thelma Golden (New York: Whitney Museum of American Art, 1994), 181–89.

2. Alain Locke, "The New Negro," 1925, in *The New Negro* (New York: Touchstone, 1997), 3–16.

3. David Levering Lewis, *When Harlem Was in Vogue* (New York: Penguin, 1997), xxviii.

4. Here, I refer to Eve Kosofsky Sedgwick's formulation about the structures of male homosocial desire in *Between Men: English Literature and Male Homosocial Desire* (New York: Columbia University Press, 1985).

5. Evans's use of subway trains recalls Spike Lee's similar use of them in *Clockers.* Paula Massood argues that in films such as *Clockers* "the train references the related tropes of mobility and entrapment, two of the most recurrent themes in African American cultural production in the twentieth century and in African American films from this time period" (Paula J. Massood, *Black City Cinema: African American Urban Experiences in Film* [Philadelphia: Temple University Press, 2003], 200).

6. Sedgwick, *Between Men*, 1–2.

7. Joseph Beam, "Brother to Brother: Words from the Heart," in *Fighting Words: Personal Essays by Black Gay Men,* ed. Charles Michael Smith (New York: Avon, 1999), 42–45. After writing and publishing this essay, Beam was compelled to follow up his groundbreaking 1986 anthology *In the Life* with one that borrowed "Brother to Brother" as a title and focused on black gay male solidarity. Beam's untimely death from AIDS complications did not allow him to complete the anthology, which the poet Essex Hemphill and Beam's mother, Ms. Dorothy Beam, published in 1991. Although Evans does not mention Beam, Beam's essay, or the related anthology in his "Filmmaker's Statement," he has noted elsewhere Marlon Riggs and Riggs's film *Tongues Untied* as influences. *Tongues Untied* makes use of much of the poetry collected in the volume *Brother to Brother: New Writings by Black Gay Men* (Boston: Alyson, 1991).

8. Phillip Brian Harper, "Walk-On Parts and Speaking Subjects: Screen Representations of Black Gay Men," in *Black Male: Representations of Masculinity in Contemporary American Art,* ed. Thelma Golden (New York: Whitney Museum of American Art, 1994), 141–48, 142.

9. See "Notes of a Native Son," in Eldridge Cleaver, *Soul on Ice* (New York: McGraw-Hill, 1968).

10. De La Soul is a fusion rap group that formed the same year that Nugent died, 1987.

11. See Caroline Goeser, *Picturing the New Negro: Harlem Renaissance Print Culture and Modern Black Identity* (Lawrence: University Press of Kansas, 2006).

PART V: Politics and the New Negro

THIRTEEN

Perspectives on Interwar Culture

Remapping the New Negro Era

Perry A. Hall

A number of revisionist strains—what some refer to as "the New Harlem Renaissance Studies"—have emerged in recent years regarding discourses around what was traditionally referred to as the "Harlem Renaissance," or "New Negro movement," associated roughly with the interwar period of the early twentieth century, that reflect augmentation and reconsideration along a number of fronts.[1] In addition to reconsidering and adjusting the historical parameters that define the phenomenon, scholars have interrogated settled consensus on the "success" of the movement.[2] Other work has sought to "decenter" the locus of cultural production during this period, pointing to other locales where emerging talents and sensibilities were marshaled and organized, and to examine ways that emerging black musical expression is remembered and represented in connection with this era.[3] Still other work, from American studies scholars, has sought to highlight interconnections among black and nonblack writers and spheres of cultural production, in effect merging the New Harlem Renaissance Studies with the "New Modernist Studies" associated with the same period. This trajectory reverses previous trends where scholarship in either renaissance or modernist studies has traditionally ignored the presence and relevance of personalities, activities, and products associated with the other movement and emphasized or scrutinized cross-racial interrelatedness rather than racial separation.[4]

What emerges from these discourses is the suggestion that a wide range of changes and disruptions took shape during the early decades of the twentieth century, shaping modern life and the mediums through which it was performed and represented, which earlier studies and representations of that historical period had not fully incorporated. The various labels, "the Harlem Renaissance," "the New Negro movement," "the Jazz Age," "the Roaring Twenties," and more infamously, "the Prohibition Era," used to characterize aspects of roughly the same historical ground, suggest a (somewhat fragmented) multiplicity of perspectives, each of which has emphasized certain phenomena while overlooking or not satisfactorily contextualizing others. This fragmentation also reflects the differentiation, in terms of perspective and spheres of activity, that existed and emerged during the period itself, lines of race, class, taste, and other dividers.

For example, in scholarship and memory, the Harlem Renaissance has been conceived largely—until recently, practically exclusively—as a literary movement. This is in part because retrospective essays and articles emerged first among literature scholars, who foregrounded literary products and activity with visual, musical, theatrical, and other arts as ancillary to the literary movement, if at all considered. It is also, however, the result of choices and actions of race leaders of that time, for example the group of civil rights leaders and community notables that David Levering Lewis called "the Six," regarding how to identify, select, represent, and celebrate distinctive elements of an emerging black culture from the broad array of transformations unfolding within that period. In the award dinners, anthologies, and other activities and projects through which they sought to define the meaning of the social and cultural transformations erupting in their midst, they left a legacy of patterns of legitimization and canonization that spoke primarily to their civil rights agenda of cultural elevation.[5] As I have argued elsewhere, this concept privileged literature and high-culture products and gave short shrift to contemporary indigenous black music, at least those forms we now embrace as emblematic of that era. (In accordance with their civil rights agenda, the "new music" that the New Negro model looked to legitimize was so-called "art" music, "literate" forms appropriate for concerts, recitals, and symphonies.)[6]

The perceived failure to significantly advance civil rights through presentation of black artistic capabilities—an agenda cut short, in any case, by the collapse of the economy in the 1930s—is conceptualized as the New Negro movement's failure in Nathan Huggins's *Harlem Renaissance* and David Levering Lewis's *When*

Harlem Was in Vogue, two studies that have laid the foundation for practically all subsequent discourse. As early as 1987 Houston Baker's *Modernism and the Harlem Renaissance* sought to refute that idea and in the process also challenged settled notions of American literary modernism that hitherto had not considered the presence of black writers. His conception pushes the origin of modernism back to "a change in Afro-American nature that occurred on or about September 18, 1895," by making Booker T. Washington the first black modernist.[7] Partially in response to the challenge represented by Baker's work for existing literary canons, American Studies scholars began producing works that sought to reconcile accounts of black literary and expressive activity with that of whites in the so-called modernist period of the 1920s, revising previous accounts in which African American "modernists" are invisible. George Hutchinson's *Harlem Renaissance in Black and White* and Ann Douglas's *Terrible Honesty: Mongrel Manhattan in the 1920s,* for example, are two such works.

Hutchinson focuses on the Harlem Renaissance but situates it within an expanded contextual circle of influence that interacts in inextricable ways with a significant sector of white modernist political and literary circles of the time. Like Baker (but only on this point) he also rejects the conclusion that the interaction among black and white spheres of activity was somehow a "failure." Without changing the literary focus (quite the contrary), Hutchinson wants to challenge many of the premises of earlier influential studies, especially generalized statements about the motives of whites—what he called "insufficiently particularized narratives of the intellectual and institutional mediations between black and white agents."[8] He challenges the view that white writers and patrons were primarily interested in promoting exoticized, primitivist images of black life. He argues quite vehemently that previous accounts unfairly pictured white patrons fundamentally as promoters of exoticism and primitivism, ignoring the variety of motivations that existed among the white agents and institutions involved in the movement. The argument would be more valid if he didn't exaggerate the degree to which previous studies actually reflect the view he challenges, and also—by basically ignoring primitivist patrons like Charlotte Mason—minimizing the degree to which the view is valid.

Though suffering from a few straw arguments, then, Hutchinson does succeed in adding texture and complexity to the surrounding social, and especially literary, context in which the renaissance/movement emerged. Specifically, Hutchinson describes the emergence of a leftist cultural pluralism among white academics, writers, and publishers whose connections to individuals, organizations, and institutions associated with the Harlem Renaissance are both fundamentally important and analytically inextricable. (In response, Lewis complained that in Hutchinson's study "so much broad background is foregrounded that the Renaissance as it actually was is swallowed up by hermeneutics.")[9]

Hutchinson indicates that the "influence" of these offstage white agents and institutions is not satisfactorily accounted for or appreciated in major renaissance texts, citing Huggins and Lewis particularly. For example, he cites William James as a major influence on Du Bois and Alain Locke, but Du Bois's connection to James, who was his Harvard professor, is certainly familiar enough in Du Bois (especially) and renaissance scholarship. He also spends a chapter on the work of the anthropologist Franz Boas. But again, Boas's influence and connection to his students Zora Neal Hurston and Melville J. Herskovits, among others, is not news in scholarly neighborhoods familiar to this writer.

Moreover, the inference he seeks regarding how this influence was structured is unclear. On the one hand, his characterization of how Locke responded to the ideas of mainstream literary critics is plausible—indeed, perhaps quite broadly accurate—as to how such "influence" was constituted: Literary critic "[Van Wyck] Brooks and the *Seven Arts* [magazine] critics probably did not so much 'influence' Locke *in a traditional sense* as confirm positions he had developed or was in the process of developing, while giving him hope for a break in the Anglo-American tradition that would benefit African American letters."[10] In any age, indeed, black intellectuals and leaders look naturally for any formulation in the mainstream edifice of knowledge and truth that will confirm their own convictions and allow a "break" through which paths of escape from proscriptive mainstream constructions of their humanity may be fashioned.

On the other hand, since this is the only instance in which this nuance is voiced, one suspects Hutchinson often means to highlight influence "in the traditional sense." His description does not suggest awareness of the dialectic insight that these emerging and changing views among white intellectuals and artists cannot themselves be considered outside their awareness of, and contacts and relations with blacks struggling to express their equality. In other words, it seems certain that the white agents he seems to valorize had their less-than-perfect views of blacks changed ("influenced") by their encounters and relations with blacks (like Du Bois and Locke) whose bearing and achievements challenged and belied their previous, received notions. Often it has been blacks themselves who must draw attention to the fact that progressive ideas—equality, democracy, cultural legitimacy—apply to them as fellow human beings, not the authors or creators of these ideas. In the grammatically corrected words of my homegirl Aretha Frank-lin, I would ask, "who's zooming whom?" in this scenario?

These issues aside, Hutchinson mainly reifies the centrality of written dis-course in constituting what he fairly consistently refers to as the "Harlem Renais-sance," and which he consistently characterizes as a literary movement. Despite the complexity and breadth he adds to the analysis of textual matters in terms of the renaissance—and although he attends to discourses about various forms of musical expression in relation to the movement—he makes it clear that the uni-verse he analyzes is a literary one: "to divide literature from other modes of cul-tural expression may seem arbitrary from a certain theoretical standpoint . . . but from a practical standpoint it is obvious that what we call 'literature' depends upon unique processes of production, distribution, and reception. Reading a liter-ary text is not only a different type of experience from listening to a blues singer; it is also the final stage in a unique series of productive processes."[11]

Well, what we call music also "depends upon unique processes of production, distribution, and reception." And, while "reading a literary text" *is* "a different type of experience from listening to a blues singer," *both* activities are, as Hutchin-son allows, "modes of cultural expression," and *each,* in truth, represents "the final stage in a unique series of productive processes." At the end of the day, then—although Hutchinson assesses the activities of a particular sector of whites whose motivations and activities he details in an informative way—his, construction of the "Renaissance" as fundamentally a literary movement separates it (and the sepa-ration is indeed arbitrary) from a larger historical conjuncture, involving multi-layered transformations and disruptions.

In a work that more comprehensively links the various "series of productive processes" and "modes of cultural expression" Ann Douglas seeks to include an accounting of the presence and influence of black cultural energies in an expanded account of the 1920s that still focuses more on the white modernists' perspectives and projects. Douglas weaves a panoramic vision, vast in its breadth, of modern-ism's emergence in the aftermath of "The Great War," which was how that emerg-ing generation of modernists referred to World War I. Unlike Hutchinson she goes far beyond literature, to encompass music, technology, architecture, and other dimensions where manifestations of the modernist aesthetic, or "national psyche," to use her terms, took shape. Ruminating on interfacings among these dimensions, she is able to shape unique, if double-edged, statements of conjunc-tural interaction—for example, when she describes the impact of technology on African American musicality and orality: "Radio and records offered black musicians not only a wider hearing but a more accurate one," she states, adding that, by making "possible, for the first time in human history, something like exact representation," they eliminated the "oldest form of censorship, which is sheer inaccuracy."[12] The condition is double-edged because the technology that allows black orality/aurality to spread free of minstrel-distortion and stereotype also opens the door for the kind of exploitation and appropriation that has continued to deprive African Americans of their own cultural capital, a point that she acknowledges only in the most rudimentary terms.

Central to her overall analysis is a "de-patria-cized" Freudian dynamic in which acts of "matricide" freed the new generation from the matriarchal Victorian, genteel tradition of their mothers. Although, as she states, "my black protagonists were not matriphobic to the same degree as my white ones were," images and sensibilities from black cultural sources were often involved as modernist personalities— Ernest Hemmingway, and the poet Hart Crane, for example—overthrew and differentiated themselves from what Douglas theorizes as the previous generation's matriarchal domination.[13] As fascinating as these life/literary studies are, the role of "blackness" in the "mongrelization" she hypothesizes seems to lie more in its refraction through the lives of her "white protagonists" than in the actual presence or agency of black people themselves. Her own words state that "much of the intellectual, economic, and cultural history of the United States I will be discussing in the next few chapters is a history of white Euro-America."[14] Thus, although "black protagonists" are discussed extensively, their overall role in her account of modernity is nearly parallel to a Freudian "unconscious" that fed the individual and national psyches on something like a subliminal level. Again, as her own words state, "the black influence in American popular culture had been dominant; it was denied and minimized not because it was faint or weak but because it was so overwhelmingly strong."[15]

Missing from her account is an adequate, that is to say, more than perfunctory, account of the structures of inequality that relegated black agency to the margins and the subterrain in this unfolding drama of modernity. Speaking in the section alluded to earlier about the way recording technology freed black performers from what she called the "censorship of inaccuracy," she states, "It was an act of abolition almost as important to black Americans—and I say this fully aware of how ceaselessly the media have exploited black talent—as the equally limited but nonetheless crucial Emancipation Proclamation that legally freed them. . . . The blues, like all of African-American musical culture, couldn't have found the market they did without records, radio, and talkies."[16] In this passage and in general Douglas is aware that she must acknowledge structures of discrimination, but it seems clear her real desire is to get past those issues to her more general concerns with the so-called national psyche.

Douglas and Hutchinson (perhaps to a lesser degree) fail to systematically incorporate structural factors that shape and order the cross-racial interactions they examine; and they are both careful to distinguish their perspectives from what they suggest is the "conventionalism" of Marxist approaches. Structures, racial politics, and ideologies more sympathetic to Marxism are emphasized in other recent works, by Barbara Foley, William J. Maxwell, and Anthony Dawahare, that look at cross-racial relations in the interwar period from various new and evolving perspectives. In sifting through the range of reactions and adjustments taking shape in the aftermath of World War I, these narratives describe the advent of the New Negro movement in decidedly more radical terms,[17] connecting the postwar emergence of the idea of a "New Negro"—and thus the roots of the Harlem Renaissance itself—to a wider context of political militancy. A common feature of these narratives is a discursive field, perhaps framed most evocatively by Barbara Foley, that seamlessly ties the emergence of a "New Negro" to a general and concertedly radical wave of political and social ferment that swept the country following the war, when, Foley maintains, "left-wing ideas seeped into almost all the discursive spaces of the day."[18]

A remapped picture can be drawn from these sources, which inject class-based analytical perspective into the discourse that suggests how this period might be linked, in social, cultural, and political terms, with preceding and ensuing historical periods. From the end of Reconstruction until the First World War, waves of immigrants from southern and eastern Europe had entered the expanding American economic sphere on an ascending escalator powered by the phenomenal industrial expansion of that period. The production needs of the war also engendered the Great Migration, adding multitudes of blacks to the multiethnic stream of arrivals coalescing in the industrial manufacturing centers. The manifestation of tensions inherent in this conjuncture, which would fundamentally overdetermine the opportunity structures within which the New Negro would operate, ranged from racism and xenophobia to cultural pluralist radicalism. While consensus accounts of the "Harlem Renaissance" focus on the former in defining the backdrop for creating a narrative, these class-oriented works give considerably more attention to the significance of the latter.

At the heart of these narratives are the contestations of American identity that, like serial earthquakes, shook the grounding on which American culture moved toward modernity after the war. The year 1919 in black historiography is mainly associated with that annum's "Red Summer," when racial violence erupted in more than forty U.S. cities. Those confrontations were themselves indicative of a broader resentment among white industrial workers that blacks were now among their competitors, an attitude that spread widely as migrating blacks appeared, affecting the process of labor organization. The recent war had also unleashed antiethnic sentiment directed at those "foreigners" who, along with their cultures and ideologies, had recently sat down to share the American pie. A xenophobic attitude of "100 percent Americanism" was accompanied by legislative efforts to limit the influx of non-Nordic Europeans, along with cultural and literary efforts to claim and articulate a national culture based on "whiteness" and a revival of the Ku Klux Klan, this time in northern states like Indiana and Michigan. Their targets were not only blacks but Jews, "foreigners," and others perceived as being less than "100 percent American."

For Foley the year 1919 is the "crucible" in which these tensions were forged into the structures of race and class that would ground twentieth-century modernity. These tensions were, in turn, the national manifestation of an international wave of radicalism, influenced both by World War I and the Bolshevik revolution that created the Soviet Union and led to the creation of the Third Communist International in March of 1919 that called for global "sovietization." Unleashed in the wake of these events were "massive class and antiracist struggles" representing a "horizon of revolutionary possibility," felt among various groups at that time, according to Foley. In particular, she writes that "to an extent that many readers in the beginning of the twenty-first century may find difficult to imagine, left-wing ideas enjoyed a mass influence in the period following World War I."[19]

Foley argues that this juncture, when "the political crisis encountered by capitalism in the aftermath of the war was severe enough to engender a discourse of racist anti-radicalism," was also the point when the potential for antiracist radicalism began taking shape that would involve white and black intellectuals and activists in linkages that would help initiate the ensuing New Negro movement on a decidedly militant bent.[20] Thus, an upsurge of labor activism also crested in 1919, a year in which one in seven workers went on strike at some point. A general strike in Seattle resulted in the formation of committees the workers called "soviets" to administer public services. Major job actions also involved coal miners, railroad workers, even policemen, and culminated with the great steel strike of 1919. (The steel company imported thirty thousand to forty thousand blacks to break this strike, according to Foley, and also must have fueled working-class racial tensions.)[21]

Authorities in the United States had already been alarmed enough with labor radicalism during the war to harass, censor, and imprison several black and white left-wing activists and writers, including the Socialist Party leader Eugene Debs, who was imprisoned for sedition, and A. Philip Randolph and Owen Chandler of the socialist *Messenger,* who were tried for violating the Espionage Act.[22] In further reaction to the postwar labor unrest, Attorney General A. Mitchell Palmer created an antiradical unit in the Justice Department with J. Edgar Hoover as the head in August of 1919. The campaign of surveillance, searches, roundups, and jailings culminated in a series of raids on communist headquarters in which thousands were arrested. "The persecution of leftists, both immigrant and native-born, was accompanied by attacks on labor militants; spies were sent into worksites where strike activity was suspected."[23] Deportation proceedings were usually initiated against those who were foreign born.

For David Levering Lewis 1919 is also of signal importance; the opening chapter of his *When Harlem Was in Vogue* begins with a moving depiction of the return of black World War I regiments in February of that year, detailing the victorious march of New York's Fifteenth Regiment up Fifth Avenue to Harlem. Many of the principals of what would become the "Harlem Renaissance," Lewis's opening narration indicates, were among the African American war veterans whose transformed attitudes would help define the "New Negro" on their return from the battlefields. Lewis, however, seems to want to seal this emerging New Negro off from the surrounding ferment that Foley and the other authors insist on including as part of the context. "To the average Afro-American," he speculates improbably, "the 'Red Scare' of 1919 was a white phenomenon that meant little or nothing. . . . He might even have been inclined to favor harsh measures against political malcontents and labor troublemakers. . . . This average Afro-American remained remarkably ignorant of and untouched by the socialisms of the day." Admitting that "hysteria and repression could not be racially segregated," Lewis depicts the violence directed at blacks during the "Red Summer" as the reaction of "white victims of postwar economic hardship" who needed a "scapegoat for their woes." For Afro-Americans, he writes, "that 'Red Summer' was a Gehenna, compared to which the ordeal of anarchists, communists, socialists, immigrants, and white workers was merely scarifying."[24]

Lewis's depiction that socialism was unknown to blacks would seem to be exaggerated. Though Lewis judged that the socialist *Messenger* had a modest impact on the black community (addressing the magazine's position against the war), Attorney General Palmer had decided it was the "most able and most dangerous of all the negro publications." Moreover, some earlier accounts specifically associate the term "New Negro" with *Messenger* editors A. Philip Randolph and Chandler Owens. They were among those advocating a new attitude of defiance and resistance in the face of the violence and repression instead of the accommodating attitudes of "Old Crowd Negroes."[25] The militancy of the context in which these New Negro attitudes emerged is also acknowledged in Lewis's reference to blacks taking up arms against violence directed at them in that "Red Summer": "Washington, D.C., and Chicago had shown how little fear of white men there was among demobilized Afro-American soldiers or peasants who had braved the unknowns of migration. Now, from the lips of virtually every spokesman and the pages of every publication there was suddenly not only a bold new rhetoric— there was a 'New Negro.'"[26] Claude McKay's famous 1919 sonnet "If We Must Die"—articulated in this atmosphere of violence and defiance, and arguably the clarion call of the New Negro movement—was a poetic embodiment of this widely shared sense of boldness and militancy.

Unlike Lewis, Foley and the other class-oriented writers seek to frame this militancy as part of the same field of dynamics that spawned the entire range of radicalism and racist reaction that characterized the postwar period of unrest. While Lewis's and similar accounts focus on the working-class racism that fueled the Red Summer violence, Foley sees this reactionism in context with opposite trends among segments of the labor movement: there was evidence of black-white labor unity in the packinghouse industry in Chicago, where the worst race riot also occurred in 1919.[27] While race hostility was endemic in labor unions, one 1919 incident in Bogalusa, Louisiana, where three white union members were killed defending the life of one black comrade, marked an opposite pole in labor movement ideology and practice. Thus, Foley states, "Whether on the left or the right, those commenting on contemporary events thus encountered, and at times contributed to, a discursive shift that was simultaneously political and epistemological. . . . Was East St. Louis [where the wave of violence against black migrants began in 1917] pointing the way to the future—or was Bogalusa?"[28]

The leftward shift in political discourse affected political debates and associations among African Americans, even moderate ones, as it did other groups. Randolph and Chandler's *Messenger* was joined by the *Crusader,* edited by Cyril Briggs and Richard Moore of the radical African Blood Brotherhood (ABB), in generating socialist discourse among black leaders and intellectuals. Marcus Garvey's Universal Negro Improvement Association (UNIA), while representing contradictory political tendencies, aligned itself with colonial movements at times in its early phases, attracting support and cooperation from Randolph, Briggs, and other radicals. The tone of militancy was also shared in some degree in more moderate quarters of black leadership. Du Bois's famous 1919 *Crisis* editorial "Returning Soldiers" urged, in resoundingly militant terms, that the battle for democracy be brought home. Less well known are the radical strains of Alain Locke's early political ideas, thought to stem from contact with socialists and revolutionaries as a student overseas, and there were several socialist-leaning members of the NAACP board. Even Emmet Scott, a former secretary to Booker T. Washington, was willing to speak at a Marcus Garvey event. James Weldon Johnson showed a similar willingness to connect with radicals by speaking to a conference of the African Blood Brotherhood, as well as hosting interracial parties that "occurred within an explicitly leftist, pro-Soviet ambience."[29] Such associations indicate a shared level of militancy generated around the emergence of the New Negro that would be impossible among these or similar agents in other periods.

I emphasize the militant political surroundings in which the New Negro emerged for Foley (as well as for Maxwell and Dawahare) to contrast that militant image with the elite, high-culture model that evolved as the New Negro movement became the "Harlem Renaissance." This transformation becomes manifest in Alain Locke's selections for the special issue of *Survey Graphic* magazine in 1925, "Harlem: Mecca of the New Negro," and later the same year, the even more historical, expanded anthology *The New Negro,* in which any indication of a radical class analysis is absent. In this context Locke's "appropriation of the term [*New Negro*] for his literary movement" is described as "measured cooptation."[30] Hutchinson's characterization of *The New Negro* as being "the most comprehensive single text of the movement" is somewhat misleading, then, since the anthology is an edited selection that represents a particular view of what the New Negro and the Harlem Renaissance were.[31] Foley refers to it as "less a recognition of the New Negro's arrival as interpreter of black modernity than an attempt—and a politically conservative one at that—to bring a certain version of that modernity into being."[32]

For Maxwell this attempt fails. "The anthology is neither the ordinary moment nor the final truth of the postwar black renaissance, but—among many other things—a polemical attempt to reconfigure this renaissance according to a less radical design." He argues that "the immense rhetorical and institutional success of Locke's wrestling match with his predecessors" obscures the anticapitalist, internationalist sentiments that he claims were influential in the New Negro movement throughout the 1920s.[33] Stressing this premise, Maxwell, along with Dawahare, seeks to revise consensus notions about relations between black activists and writers and the white radical left in general. Acknowledging that labor organizing and leftist thought regarding race were arguably more reactionary than progressive under earlier socialist formations prior to the war, he proposes that the "crucible of 1919" led to a refiguration of racial issues among leftist formations that emerged in the postwar period.

In the context of the labor struggles of 1919 the Socialist Party of America (SPA) lost influence after a split over the issue of pursuing electoral versus direct action strategies; the Communist Party of the United States of America (CPUSA) emerged as the major leftist formation after the constitution of the Third International. The CPUSA's emergence led to a more central concern, in leftist thinking, with race as a factor in creating revolutionary change in America. Consensus narratives have depicted this engagement as largely opportunistic and manipulative, a view that Maxwell and Dawahare challenge, maintaining that it deprives black leftists of agency. Although major inroads in recruiting blacks came in the 1930s, these authors argue that the evolution of the U.S. communist movement's views on race in fact reflected the agency of blacks who were connected to the movement in the 1920s. Thus, against the arguments of Harold Cruse and others, Maxwell, Dawahare, and Foley suggest that the agency of black associates like Claude McKay, according to Foley, a "full-fledged underground party member since the first months of the Communist Party's formation," and the ABB leader Cyril Briggs, whom McKay recruited, were factors in how views, understandings, and policies regarding the race issue in the United States were constructed within the international communist movement.

In this regard Maxwell sets great store by the influence of *The Negroes in America*, a document authored by Claude McKay during his 1922–23 stay in revolutionary Russia. Some think it likely that like the "Black Belt Nation" thesis—which facilitated recruitment gains in the 1930s—evolved within party discourse partly as a fulfillment of the analysis McKay provided. Harry Haywood, official author of the 1928 doctrine, had been a member of the African Blood Brotherhood, as well as an admirer of McKay's famous poem "If We Must Die."[34] Moreover, in this view, the visible involvement of black writers and intellectuals with leftist ideas and formations in the 1930s does not represent a break from the previous period, as some narratives indicate. Leftist influences on cultural production in the 1930s was a continuation, not a disruption, of tendencies present in the previous decade since, from this standpoint, these tendencies always existed, in tension with the culturalist manifestations for which the New Negro movement is now most widely known.

While there may be imperfections in these arguments (the case for cross-race working-class solidarity may be exaggerated; literary interactions were tainted with patronism and residual racism), what becomes clear when the other narratives are incorporated is that the "New Negro" that was canonized for history emerged from a contested range of constructions constituted from a particularly radical moment in history. What Foley calls "the revolutionary crucible of 1919" boiled with the ferment of a range of ideologies, formations, and tendencies, leaning left in the main, all laying claim and contributing to newly evolving forms of African American modernity. In these terms Marcus Garvey was as much a "New Negro" as any who gathered at the famous Fifth Avenue dinner where the anthology *The New Negro* was conceived. Indeed, Lewis observes that in the ferment of 1919 "the UNIA seemed to be on the verge of sweeping aside conservative civil rights organizations," while enjoying the support and cooperation of socialists, Marxists, and radical nationalists like Randolph, Owen, and Briggs.[35] By the early 1920s, however, Garvey had embraced capitalism and undermined his position with radical nationalists by meeting and announcing a racialist accord with the Ku Klux Klan. Meanwhile, the African Blood Brotherhood moved from a culturalist alliance with Garvey's Universal Negro Improvement Association to full membership in the communist movement. Randolph and Owen, who had not joined with the Third International, joined with other, more mainstream, leaders in a campaign of public criticism of Garvey's organization and his leadership, though he (along with Du Bois) avoided signing the letter from black leaders demanding that the U.S. attorney general investigate suspected irregularities.[36]

Thus, one premise suggests, the historically canonized New Negro was an appropriation intended to rescue the community from what it perceived as the chaos of Garvey's Black Zionist crusade. On the other side of the ideological front is the premise that the radicalism of class ideology was perhaps an even greater threat to the civil rights establishment, notwithstanding the earlier radical-leaning associations that some had cultivated. Indeed, those associations themselves may have been a factor. Jeffrey Stewart frankly suggests that Locke may have felt threatened enough by governmental and institutional reactions to the 1919 "Red scare" to prune his philosophies of any radical fringes.[37] In any case by 1925

Locke would state that the New Negro had left the "arid fields of controversy and debate" to take up the "productive fields of creative expression,"[38] on the premise that "the more immediate hope rest[s] in the revaluation by white and black alike of the Negro in terms of his artistic endowments and cultural contributions, past and prospective."[39]

Evaluating this sentiment and a similar statement from elder statesman James Weldon Johnson,[40] Lewis lays out the case for the first premise and points obliquely toward the second in his preface: "In such statements as these and so many more, the Harlem Renaissance reveals itself to be an elitist response on the part of a tiny group of mostly second-generation, college-educated, and generally affluent African-Americans—a response, first, to the increasingly raw racism of the times, second, to the frightening Black Zionism of the Garveyites, and, finally, to the remote, but no less frightening, appeal of Marxism."[41]

The specter of raw racism was real enough, but if Dawahare, Foley, and Maxwell are right, the appeal of Marxism was not as remote as Lewis suggests; and what may have been most frightening was the possibility of how those who embraced such radical ideologies might be repressed in that radical moment. Moreover, these narratives also imply that the silence left by government repression and intimidation is one factor that has obscured the legacy of what one called "the postwar New Negro [who] was, in the eyes of many, an anticapitalist radical who envisioned African American emancipation as inseparable from—if not identical with—the project of a class-conscious, multiracial alliance."[42] These complex and far-reaching issues are not to be resolved in the scope of this essay. To raise them is to suggest areas for future investigation in a remapping project for representing race, class, and cultural production in the interwar period.

NOTES

1. David Chinitz, "The New Harlem Renaissance Studies," *Modernism/Modernity* 13, no. 2 (April 2006): 375–82.

2. See, e.g., Houston A. Baker Jr., *Modernism and the Harlem Renaissance* (Chicago: University of Chicago Press, 1987); and George Hutchinson, *The Harlem Renaissance in Black and White* (Cambridge, MA: Belknap Press of Harvard University Press, 1995), 387.

3. Robert Bone, "Richard Wright and the Chicago Renaissance," *Callaloo* (summer 1986): 446–68.

4. Hutchinson, *The Harlem Renaissance in Black and White*; Ann Douglas, *Terrible Honesty: Mongrel Manhattan in the 1920s* (New York: Farrar, Straus and Giroux, 1995).

5. See David Levering Lewis, *When Harlem Was in Vogue* (New York: Knopf, 1997), esp. chap. 5.

6. See Perry Hall, "Finding Fault in Lines and Sites of African American Cultural Production: Music in the New Negro / Harlem Renaissance Era," paper presented to the 23rd Annual Symposium on African American Culture and Philosophy, "Harlem Renaissance: Aesthetics, Values, and Identity," Purdue University, November 1–3, 2007.

7. Baker, *Modernism and the Harlem Renaissance*, 8.

8. Hutchinson, *The Harlem Renaissance in Black and White*, 3.

9. Lewis, *When Harlem Was in Vogue*, xxviii.

10. Hutchinson, *The Harlem Renaissance in Black and White*, 99 (emphasis added).

11. Ibid., 125.

12. Ann Douglas, *Terrible Honesty*, 425.

13. Ibid., 7.

14. Ibid., 107.

15. Ibid., 353.

16. Ibid., 425.

17. See Barbara Foley, *Spectres of 1919: Class and Nation in the Making of the New Negro* (Urbana: University of Illinois Press, 2003); William J. Maxwell, *New Negro, Old Left: African-American Writing and Communism between the Wars* (New York: Columbia University Press, 1999); Anthony Dawahare, *Nationalism, Marxism, and African American Literature between the Wars: A New Pandora's Box* (Jackson: University Press of Mississippi, 2003).

18. Foley, *Spectres of 1919*, 16.

19. Ibid., 7.

20. Ibid., 164–65.

21. Ibid., 9.

22. Lewis, *When Harlem Was in Vogue*, 17.

23. Foley, *Spectres of 1919*, 12.

24. Lewis, *When Harlem Was in Vogue*, 17–18.

25. Theodore Kornweibel, *No Crystal Stair: Black Life and the "Messenger," 1917–1928* (Westport, CT: Greenwood Press, 1975), 107 (cited in Foley, *Spectres of 1919*, 4).

26. Lewis, *When Harlem Was in Vogue*, 23–24.

27. Foley, *Spectres of 1919*, 14.

28. Ibid., 17.

29. Ibid., 18–22.

30. Henry Louis Gates Jr., "The Trope of a New Negro and the Reconstruction of the Image of the Black," *Representations* 24 (fall 1988): 129–55, 136, 147 (quoted in Foley, *Spectres of 1919*, 4).

31. Hutchinson, *The Harlem Renaissance in Black and White*, 387.

32. Foley, *Spectres of 1919*, 5.

33. Maxwell, *New Negro, Old Left*, 49.

34. Kwame Okoampa-Ahoofe Jr., "Is Black Literature Red-Fleshed?" *New York Amsterdam News*, Aug. 26, 1999.

35. Lewis, *When Harlem Was in Vogue*, 37.

36. Ibid., 40–44.

37. Alain LeRoy Locke and Jeffrey C. Stewart, *Race Contacts and Interracial Relations: Lectures on the Theory and Practice of Race* (Washington, DC: Howard University Press, 1992), xliii (quoted in Foley, *Spectres of 1919*, 35).

38. Quoted in Foley, *Spectres of 1919*, 69.

39. Lewis, *When Harlem Was in Vogue*, xxvii.

40. The elder statesman's oft-cited statement from the introduction to *The Book of Negro Poetry* that "nothing will do more to change the mental attitude and raise his status than a demonstration of the intellectual parity by the Negro through his production of literature or art" (quoted in Lewis, *When Harlem Was in Vogue*, xxvii–xxviii).

41. Lewis, *When Harlem Was in Vogue*, xxviii.

42. Foley, *Spectres of 1919*, 69.

FOURTEEN

"Harlem Globe-Trotters"

Black Sojourners in Stalin's Soviet Union

Maxim Matusevich

An oppressed people can find its freedoms circumscribed in a number of ingenious ways, but restrictions on free travel are among the most obvious and inevitable manifestations of the condition of subjugation.[1] The *helots* of ancient Sparta, Russian serfs under the czars, black slaves of the American South, Chinese peasants under Mao, and citizens of the former Soviet bloc countries— all experienced severe limitations imposed on their ability to travel by repressive states. Consequently, one is hard-pressed to identify a more potent signifier of emancipation than an increased mobility by the underprivileged. Movements of political or artistic liberation often express a yearning for change through the physical, or sometimes imagined, movement by the oppressed across previously impenetrable borders.

One of the great historical achievements of the Harlem Renaissance was in internationalizing the "black soul" through travel. During the early decades of the twentieth century hundreds of African Americans—poets, actors, philosophers, musicians, political activists, young professionals—embarked on long journeys of personal, artistic, and political discovery. The celebrated bard of the Harlem Renaissance Claude McKay, for example, recognized the profound significance of his own trip to the Soviet Union in the early 1920s, or, for that matter, *any* trip by a black person *anywhere*. McKay saw his own globe-trotting, what he called "my tourist rank," as a direct challenge to the system of world capitalism that has privileged with mobility the wealthy and the white. His mission, as the missions by dozens of his black compatriots, was also a propagandist counterweight to those journeys of privilege whereby "every American official abroad, every smug tourist, is a protagonist of dollar culture and a propagandist against the Negro."[2] By aligning himself with the downtrodden he also detected a commonality of fate between the members of the "vulgar and despised classes" in the destination country (Soviet Russia) and the members of his own race. Russia's new travelers ("proletarian agitators, Bolshevist couriers and Jews") might have lacked in European refinement, not a terrible deficiency as far as McKay was concerned, but their newly attained mobility flew in the face of the aristocratic and bourgeois tourists of McKay's colonial youth in the Caribbean.[3] In the case of McKay's "magic pilgrimage" to communist Russia the very term *fellow-traveler* acquires an effective new meaning. Indeed, of all the itineraries available to black travelers of the Harlem Renaissance the one that sent them on "pilgrimages" of the newly founded Soviet Union titillated the most, for it transported them from Jim Crow America straight to the land of purported racial equality.[4]

In the two decades following the 1917 Bolshevik Revolution the new socialist nation developed a dedicated following among an assortment of African American and Afro-Caribbean radicals and intellectuals. Their fascination with Soviet Russia did not always stem from the communist doctrine per se but rather from an experience of having lived in highly racialized Western societies where the individual's skin color predetermined the extent of his or her life options. The emergence of a new type of state in faraway Russia, ostensibly founded on egalitarian principles of class unity and an ideology opposed to Western racism, struck a cord with those African Americans who had grown used to equating their own country with Jim Crow racial segregation and the lynch-mob violence of southern states. As an NAACP official pointedly observed at the time, "The greatest pro-Communist influence among Negroes in the United States is the lyncher, the Ku Klux Klan member, the Black Shirt, the Caucasian Crusader and others who indulge in lynching, disfranchisement, segregation and denial of economic and industrial opportunity [to black people]."[5] Indeed, the very ugliness of American racism supplied the Soviet ideologues with an identity-building device of great propagandist value. In their quest to forge a new multiethnic state the Soviets employed forceful antiracist rhetoric and positioned themselves as the defenders of the exploited nonwhite populations the world over; they, in the words of a *Chicago Defender* correspondent, "buoyed selves in [a] rising tide of color."[6]

But an early alliance between the Soviet Union and the more radicalized and politically attuned sections of the African American community represented more than a natural affinity between the victim of persecution and his or her advocate. There was a symbiotic, mutually beneficial, quality to this relationship, whereby the advocacy for the oppressed helped the Soviets to shape and test their own political and national identity. Consequently, those few Africans and scores of black Americans who in the 1920s and 1930s journeyed to the Soviet land hoping to find true racial equality were serving not only their own needs but also the needs of their hosts.

In the absence of reliable communication links and diplomatic relations between Soviet Russia and the United States, the African American community had to form its opinions of the young socialist state by relying on the accounts and analyses of those few black Americans who either were affiliated with radical political movements *in* America or gained firsthand experience of life in the Soviet Union through travel. As witnessed by the proliferation of lively debates regarding comparative values of American and Soviet ideals in the pages of the black American press, such accounts found an enthusiastic, if rather small, audience among African Americans.[7] Few of the readers harbored deep sympathies for or even understanding of Marxism. After all, not a single African American was involved in the creation of the Communist Party of the United States of America (CPUSA) in 1919.[8] And in the American South, with its parochial conditions, a near absence of industrial proletariat, and a widespread illiteracy among the black population, millions of African Americans were probably sufficiently muzzled by Jim Crowism and too busy eking out their existence to seriously consider a Soviet alternative to their predicament. Yet even the most God-fearing and the least educated could appreciate an uncomplicated fact that there existed a strange new land where "there are no mobs lynching members of another race because their color is different, [no] Ku Klux Klan Kleagles and Imperial Wizards running in night shirts, enforcing the 'laws of God.'"[9] The good news of such a place was delivered to the masses of African Americans by a small number of influential black intellectuals, radicals, and adventurers who sojourned in the Soviet Union during the first two decades of its existence.

In 1922, the year that fifty-one black Americans perished at the hands of lynching mobs[10] while the antilynching Dyer Bill suffered a filibuster in the United States Senate, a young dark-skinned poet named Claude McKay embarked on

what he would later call "my magic pilgrimage" to Russia.[11] Along with Otto Huiswoud, another New York radical of Caribbean extraction, he became one of the
first black Americans to visit Soviet Russia and the first one to introduce Russia to
black America.[12] His impressions of Russia under the new regime were relayed to
the American audiences through a series of articles and a later book, *A Long Way
from Home.* By all accounts the Soviets accorded McKay a royal treatment that
made him dizzy with success. This former Kingston police officer and a railway
porter became the toast of Moscow's political and intellectual elite. During the
fifth anniversary of the October Revolution he stood on the grandstand in the center of the windswept Red Square shoulder-to-shoulder with the crème of the Bolshevik Party, observing the military parade by the victorious Red Army and cheering Soviet Russia's most arresting speaker, Leon Trotsky.[13] Inducted into the
Moscow Soviet community as an honorary member, McKay found himself hob-
nobbing with such communist luminaries as Grigorii Zinoviev, the chairman of
the Communist International (Comintern), and Karl Radek. But it was the mixture of the official adulation with a genuine warm acceptance by the common
Russians in the streets of Moscow and Petrograd that added the "magic" touch to
McKay's journey, turning it into a true "individual triumph" that he clearly saw as
a triumph for his race: "Never in my life did I feel prouder of being an African, a
black, and no mistake about it. . . . From Moscow to Petrograd and from Petrograd
to Moscow I went triumphantly from surprise to surprise, extravagantly fêted on
every side. I was carried along on a crest of sweet excitement. I was like a black icon
in the flesh. . . . Yes, that was exactly what it was. I was like a black icon."[14]

The warm welcome allowed McKay to shed his habitual self-consciousness
and assert himself as a proud representative of his people: "I was welcomed thus
as a symbol, as a member of the great American Negro group—kin to the unhappy black slaves of European Imperialism in Africa—that the workers of Soviet
Russia, rejoicing in their freedom, were greeting through me."[15] For the first time
in his thirty-two years McKay's dark complexion proved to be an asset, a commodity of apparently great political and social value. The Soviets couldn't get enough
of the "Negro comrade" and much preferred him (clearly a point of pride for the
poet) to Otto Huiswoud, a biracial member of the American delegation to the
Fourth Comintern Congress in Moscow. The mulatto, according to McKay, was
"a washout," way "too yellow" for a "typical Negro."[16] Whenever the light-skinned
Huiswoud appeared in public, his Russian hosts, demonstrating a somewhat ap-
palling lack of manners, never failed to inquire about the *chorny* (black), "the real
McCoy," that is McKay himself.

Claude McKay's appeal to the Soviet and Comintern officialdom, as well as to the Soviet street, can be easily explained as reflective of the Bolshevik internationalist and class solidarity paradigms. What had to be more puzzling for McKay and his American readers were the amicable and clearly equal encounters he had with the representatives of the prerevolutionary Russian intelligentsia and the "former" propertied classes. If not "the progression of affectionate enthusiasm" that McKay experienced among the proletarians, his encounters with the prominent Russian intellectuals of the day were marked by mutual respect and cordiality. Often self-conscious and uneasy in the company of white writers, painters, and bohemians of Greenwich Village or Montmartre ("Color-consciousness was the fundamental of my restlessness"),[17] Claude McKay exhibits no trace of color-conscious angst when revisiting the times spent in the company of the literary critic and celebrated children's author Kornei Chukovsky or the great novelist Evgenii Zamyatin. In these sophisticated and cosmopolitan intellectuals, some of them palpably hostile to the Soviets, the usually sensitive McKay detects no racial arrogance, no "vulgar wonderment and bounderish superiority over a Negro's being a poet": "I was a poet, that was all, and their keen questions showed that they were much more interested in the technique of my poetry, my views on and my position regarding the modern literary movements than in the difference of my color."[18]

Again and again McKay presents the color-blind internationalism displayed by his Russian hosts as a national, not ideological, trait. The Bolsheviks, he declares, "had nothing at all to do with it." Indeed, McKay finds as much warmth and hospitality in the company of "bourgeois persons" and former aristocrats as he does among the factory workers and proletarian students. Even the most prejudiced and muddle-headed of the Russians seem to be immune to white-on-black racism. A young woman, who harbors deep resentment of Bolsheviks and Jews, confides her frustrations to McKay because he is "a Negro." Full of prejudice against Jews (whom she equates with communists) and admiration for America, and clearly receptive to racist propaganda, she nevertheless suggests intermarriage as a sure way to bridge America's racial divide. Well, what the hell, she herself would marry a black man if "he had plenty of money and could talk to me intelligently like you."[19]

By his own admission McKay, during his European travels, had grown wary of whites in places like Paris and Berlin and couldn't bring himself to trust them, yet he "had no fear of even the 'whitest' Russians in Russia."[20] The Russians he comes across hold different, and often irreconcilable, political beliefs. But somehow, regardless of their politics and social backgrounds, they readily embrace the black poet, invite him into their homes, and take him into their confidence. Western racism bewilders them. Or so they claim. With clear bemusement McKay paints an affectionate portrait of Kornei Chukovsky, an Anglophile and a great fan of American democracy, who is stupefied by the extent of Anglo-American racism and seems to have genuine difficulty comprehending the phenomenon of racial prejudice and the very idea of racial superiority—so endemic to the cultural traditions he admires. "*I don't feel any difference; we don't understand color prejudice in Russia*," he exclaims naively in the course of his conversation with McKay.[21]

So what are the sources of this tolerance? McKay provides no definitive answer. Marxist-Leninist internationalism is certainly part of the explanation. But, as McKay intimates, the tradition of acceptance of darker races even by the upper crust of Russian society predated the October Revolution of 1917.[22] Some African American observers of Russia were ready to embrace this notion. Was it because Alexander Pushkin, Russia's most beloved poet and the national cultural icon of unsurpassed value, "possessed as much Negro blood as Booker T. Washington?"[23] Or could it be because at the height of transatlantic slave trade General Abràham Hannibal, Pushkin's African progenitor and the godson of Peter the Great, embarked on an illustrious military career in his adopted land?[24] Or maybe because some five years before the adoption of the Emancipation Proclamation Ira Aldridge, the great black American tragedian, found fame on the Russian stage and a celebrity status within Russia's high society?[25] Or was it because of those Russian aristocrats who, in a decidedly un-American fashion, developed a curious habit of falling in love with African American women?[26] Chukovsky, an erudite and diligent student of Russian history and culture, must have been well familiar with the above examples of Russia's unconventional (for the Victorian Age) attitudes toward blackness. It is in this cultural and historical context that we need to place his rendition to McKay of a chance meeting with a black American preacher. The preacher, with whom Chukovsky as a young man in London briefly shared his lodgings, accepted with a puzzling (for the young Chukovsky) equanimity the pariah status accorded to him by other white lodgers. The fact that his Russian neighbor was visibly appalled by the racists impressed him but very little. Russians themselves, the preacher reasoned, were not exactly "white." McKay gives the anecdote some serious consideration. He seems to be tempted to draw a very similar conclusion, predicting, only half-jokingly, the day when "white Americanism" would exclude Russians from the league of "God's white people."[27] The euphoria over being accepted moves McKay to claim Russians as his "own people."[28] He feels close to them and comfortable in their presence; in the streets of Moscow and Petrograd, McKay feels as safe as in Harlem. The only persons that made him afraid in Russia, it turns out, were the very people who had brought him there—the white American communists.[29]

Russia inspired McKay to assert his blackness; he was proud to deliver a formal "Report on the Negro Question" to the Fourth Comintern Congress in Moscow. "I had mobilized my African features and won the masses of the people," he later wrote in his memoir.[30] McKay addressed the audience that had for some time been pondering the connection between the "Negro Question" and the future of an international communist movement. In 1920, just a few weeks before his death, John Reed became the first American communist to bring up the issue at the Second Comintern Congress in Petrograd. Having extended the status of "workers" to the entirety of the black population in the United States, Reed argued that African Americans could only achieve complete equality through interracial class solidarity and social revolution. Any attempts to attain equality within the constraints of an inherently racist bourgeois society would be useless.[31] Vladimir Lenin took some interest in possible propaganda activities among American blacks and included a separate discussion point, "The Negroes in America," in the draft of his *Theses on the National and Colonial Question* distributed among the delegates.[32] But not much would be accomplished until the gathering of the Fourth Comintern Congress, attended by McKay and Huiswoud. Combined, their two presentations to the congress painted a grim picture of race relations in America, especially in the American South, where, according to Huiswoud, blacks survived in conditions reminiscent of "Dante's Inferno."[33] Both Huiswoud and McKay were eager to alert their listeners to a natural connection between the "Negro Question" and the overall aims of world communism. McKay, whose Marxist credentials were rather flimsy, nevertheless couched his argument in terms most familiar to his listeners. If communists failed to adequately address the needs of the oppressed black race, the "international bourgeoisie" might gain a valuable trump card in "their fight against the world revolution." American socialists and communists, complained McKay, had already failed their black compatriots. If anything, within their own ranks they displayed racist attitudes on par with those they habitually decried in their capitalist opponents. Soviet Russia, and Soviet Russia alone, held a special promise for the subject races; it had the wherewithal to guide their fight against the exploiters. "Negroes," McKay predicted, "will also come to Moscow."[34]

"Negroes" did indeed come to Moscow. Between 1922 (the year of McKay's memorable visit) and 1939 (the first year of the Second World War) the Soviet Union received a steady stream of African American visitors, some of whom would remain permanently in the country. Even though their motivations for travel ranged from ideological to personal to opportunistic, most of these "pilgrims" shared expectations of a society free of racial prejudice and oppression. To a large extent these expectations would be realized. In this respect, coming to Russia amounted to an act of personal and collective redemption for many "race travelers" from the United States. Accounts of the first impressions of the land of the Soviets by such travelers are often cast in terms of a religious awakening. Langston Hughes, the celebrated poet and traveler, describes the first emotional encounter with the USSR by a group of young black "pilgrims" crossing the Soviet border in 1932: "In Helsinki, we stayed overnight and the next day we took a train headed for the land . . . where race prejudice was reported taboo, the land of the Soviets. . . . When the train stopped [at the border] for passports to be checked, a few of the young black men and women left the train to touch their hands to Soviet soil, lift the new earth in their palms and kiss it."[35]

Homer Smith, a twenty-two-year-old African American journalist from Minneapolis, traveled to Moscow to find dignity that was denied him in his native land. His motivations bore remarkable similarity to those expressed by his two more famous contemporaries: "I yearned to stand taller than I had ever stood[,] to breathe total freedom in exhilarating gulps, to avoid all the hurts that were increasingly becoming the lot of men (and women) of color in the United States. The solution seemed simple to me: Russia was the only place where I could go and escape color discrimination entirely. Moscow seemed the answer."[36]

And Moscow "seemed the answer" to the great Pan-Africanist W. E. B. Du Bois. Having traveled the length of the Soviet Union in 1926, Du Bois returned to America in a state of amazement at the extent of racial equality he observed and experienced during his trip. "I stand in astonishment and wonder," he wrote in an editorial for the *Crisis*, the NAACP magazine he edited at the time, "at the *revelation* of Russia that has come to me. I may be partially deceived and half-informed. But if what I have seen with my eyes and heard with my ears in Russia is Bolshevism, I am a Bolshevik."[37] Du Bois would preserve these favorable impressions of the Soviet Union for the remainder of his long life, and decades later he still talked about the inspiration he had drawn from his two prewar visits there.[38]

Of the several dozen African Americans who made their appearance in the Soviet Union during the prewar decades, as many as ninety arrived as students of a peculiar educational institution. In 1925 Moscow's Communist University of the Toilers of the East (KUTV) opened its doors to the first contingent of five black American students. Established as an educational arm of the Comintern to train international revolutionary cadres, KUTV aspired to fashion a community of like-minded political activists, well versed in the ABCs of communism and faithful to the general political line set in Moscow.[39] Lovett Fort-Whiteman, a Comintern activist and one of the first radical black Americans to have claimed Moscow as his home, facilitated the recruitment and arrival of the first group of African Americans in the Soviet Union. In the next several years the African American cohort at KUTV (which would eventually allow for the creation of a special *Negro Section*) and at a more prestigious Lenin School would grow to include such prominent black American communists and fellow-travelers as Otto Hall and his brother, Harry Haywood; George Padmore; Oliver Golden; William L. Patterson and his future wife, Louise Thompson; Maude White; and others.[40] It is through their experiences, as well as through the experiences of a smaller number of left-leaning African American celebrities (such as Langston Hughes and Paul Robeson) and of more "opportunistic" arrivals (such as Homer Smith or the mild-mannered engineer Robert Robinson) that black America got a chance to relive vicariously the reality of Stalin's Soviet Union. In the words of Mark Solomon this experience was "a compound of bewilderment, culture shock, pain, and exhilarating empowerment."[41] Whatever later disillusionments, for a time the latter sentiment markedly predominated.

Clear evidence of the fascination with which some African American travelers viewed their Soviet sojourn comes from an unusual source—the consulate records of the U.S. Embassy in Latvia. The United States did not grant diplomatic recognition to the Soviet Union until 1933. In the absence of established diplomatic links Americans used their legation in Riga as a sort of listening post to keep tabs on the developments inside the USSR. Because of its geographic proximity to the Soviet Union the legation paid particular attention to monitoring the visitors' traffic to and from the country. Generally suspicious of the intentions of those who crossed the Soviet border, the legation officers singled out black American tourists for a special interviewing process, which included lengthy questioning sessions and subsequent reporting back to the State Department in Washington. These interviews are as revealing about the racial attitudes in the United States at the time as they are of the impressions that the land of the Soviets had made on visiting African Americans. The race of the interviewee seems to have been an immediate cause for alarm and an indication of possible communist sympathies. In August 1930, explaining his decision to interview Maude White, who was seeking return passage to the United States after a lengthy stay in the Soviet Union (where, unbeknownst to her interlocutor, she had been a

KUTV student), a legation officer reported to his superiors in Washington: "I have an honor to submit herewith passport application, Form no. 176, of Miss Maude Mae White, an American negress [sic] and to report the following information thereto as of possible interest in view of the increasing communist agitation in the United States. . . . Being a negress and having resided in Soviet Russia since December 11, 1927, she was carefully questioned by myself and Mr. Kirley, the passport clerk of this office."[42]

The race of another passport applicant, Norval Harrison Allen, interviewed by the legation just a few weeks earlier, also raised "red flags" in the minds of diligent consular bureaucrats. The title of the special dispatch to the secretary of state, containing the transcript of the questioning session, inadvertently reveals the depth of racial divide in the United States. For the reporting officer the racial categorization of his fellow American Norval Allen, to whom he refers as "a negro and an American" and "an American negro suspected of being a Communist," eclipses Allen's national identity.[43] Harry Haywood recalls in his memoir his own lengthy "debriefing" at the embassy in Riga, where the ambassador himself asked him "all sorts of questions about the Soviet Union." The ambassador's conduct was courteous enough, but behind the mask of politeness Haywood detected hostility directed against him. The purpose of Haywood's visit to the legation (to procure a visa to the United States for his new Russian wife, a white woman) did little to improve his standing with the ambassador, a "Southern gentleman."[44]

Transcripts of these debriefing sessions contain evidence of the atmosphere of mutual antagonism and exasperation that often colored the exchanges between consular officials and African American applicants. For the latter the interview at the legation became a "back-to-reality" experience, a point of transition on their return journey to the racially divided and race-obsessed America. Yet they were returning home less docile and with an enhanced sense of self-worth, less prepared to reassume without questioning the status of second-rate citizens. The humiliation of the grilling at the legation served as an instant reminder of the racial inequality they faced back in the States and stood in stark contrast to the respect and official pampering that had been accorded to them during their stay in the Soviet Union. A natural response to the penetrating questions by the suspicious and often openly hostile officials was to assume an evasive posture. But on occasion evasiveness gave way to a thinly disguised irritation and even anger. Marie Houston, "a negress, born in Nashville," having spent two-and-a-half years in the USSR, taxed her interviewers' patience by giving only the vaguest of answers to their probing questions. Refusing to divulge any particulars of her life in Russia, she claimed that she had "just been visiting" and had lived on her own money.[45] Norval Allen similarly exasperated legation officials by his "evasive and shifty attitude," making them ever more suspicious of his possible communist affiliation.[46]

Other visitors proved far less circumspect regarding their political sympathies and less emotionally restrained. Maude White, in her legation interview, was anything but vague. In fact, she directly challenged the interviewing officers by praising in strong terms the country where "negroes are afforded every possible opportunity for study and may live as social equals to the Russians."[47] She spoke warmly of the Soviets, who, she insisted, always treated her with respect and kindness and were well informed about the United States and "the lynchings there." In the course of her interview White grew progressively agitated and eventually, having lost "all control of herself," startled the humorless bureaucrats by decrying God, refusing to give an oath of allegiance, and (the worst of all sins) declaring her commitment to "social equality." On hearing such apostasy the examining legation clerk summed up his opinion of Miss White in unambiguous and somber terms: "She is a type of American negress that has become embittered by racial discrimination in the United States and is of a communist turn of mind."[48]

It is hard to blame Maude White for her short temper. For many black travelers a return to the States meant an immediate loss of social status and public acceptance that they had enjoyed in the Soviet Union, a rude awakening indeed. William L. Patterson, a prominent communist lawyer of Scottsboro fame, remembered years later the shock of his reentrance into the world of Great Depression America on the completion of his studies in Moscow. He arrived in Pittsburg, where "hundreds of men and women were sleeping in public parks and scrabbling in garbage dumps for food—devoid of hope, jobs, or the prospect of finding help anywhere. Some literally starved to death. For Negroes conditions were even worse—difficult as this is to imagine. They held down the most dangerous, dirtiest and most exhausting jobs. . . . They were always the first to be laid off."[49] Harry Haywood, within several days following his return, ran the gamut of racial discrimination and abuse—yelled at by a customs officer in New York, refused service at a restaurant in Detroit, harassed by white cops in St. Louis.[50] One didn't have to be a young radical to appreciate the power of contrasting experiences. The mystique of the Soviet Union affected not only the Haywood-like firebrands but also a middle-aged Chicago doctor with an established practice and extensive European connections. As his train pulled out of a railway station in Moscow "to return him to the capitalist world," A. Wilberforce Williams cast his last melancholy glance at the Soviet capital. Never before, he admitted, had he experienced "such a complete absence of even any consciousness of race or color prejudice or difference."[51]

So what were the specific elements of this experience that led one African American visitor after another, regardless of economic status and social rank, to take back home the vision of a society free of race chauvinism and brimming with opportunities for people of all colors, a society that "extends to [blacks] the most explicitly cordial welcome"?[52] To answer this question, we have to try to see the Soviet Union of the 1920s and 1930s through the eyes of its black visitors. They arrived in a place hard at work, forging a new identity after almost a full decade of upheaval that included participation in a global war, two social revolutions, and one of the bloodiest civil wars in modern history. Class consciousness and disdain for "bourgeois racism" were cultivated and popularized by new Bolshevik rulers as the essential features of Soviet identity. At least in rhetoric the Soviet leaders articulated the ideals of a multiethnic socialist state.[53] If the empire of the czars had oppressed and exploited its many non-Russian subjects, then the new Soviet state saw it as its special mission to rehabilitate "the accursed ones" and to build the new society based entirely on class solidarity. Racial categories mattered only insofar as they marked the masses of colonial subjects and American blacks for capitalist oppression. For the ideologues of the new regime Western, American-style racism was thus reflective of the general degeneracy of capitalism and as such could not be tolerated. In the eyes of many a Soviet citizen, especially those educated under the Soviet rule, any black visitor to the country represented a natural ally, a victim of the historical injustice the Soviet state had set out to expose and, eventually, correct. To oppose racism and to embrace those most susceptible to capitalist exploitation meant to exercise one's duty as a true communist and a bona fide citizen of the multiethnic Soviet Union. Needless to say, the dark-skinned guests stood to benefit from the atmosphere of racial solidarity prevalent in the country.

African American communists or fellow travelers journeying to Soviet Russia could look forward to an ideological fulfillment in being part of the new socialist experiment. But such travels were also attended by other, more tangible, benefits. Almost every black American arriving in the Soviet Union during the 1920s and 1930s experienced a noticeable enhancement of his or her social status. Just as Claude McKay had found himself miraculously transformed from an obscure Harlem poet, little known outside of his African American community, into a sought-after celebrity of influence, so did other black sojourners enter the ranks of the Soviet elite. African American radicals and students at KUTV, for example, had an unprecedented, for regular Soviet citizens, access to Soviet leadership.

They also had a say in the formulation of the Comintern policies, especially those relevant to colonial and race issues. Otto Hall, one of the first black Americans to attend KUTV, remembered being invited to an interview with Stalin soon after his arrival in Moscow in 1925—quite a coup for the son of a night watchman from Omaha. Having been brought to the Kremlin by Stalin's personal automobile, Hall spent several hours drinking tea and chatting amicably with the soon-to-be "father of all peoples" about race relations in the United States and racial tensions within the American Communist Party. Karl Radek, another Soviet luminary, served as Hall's interpreter.[54] Harry Haywood, Otto's brother and fellow KUTV student, became one of the primary sponsors of the "Black Belt" thesis at the Sixth Comintern Congress in 1928. His proximity to power in the USSR of the late 1920s comes through the pages of his memoir. A dedicated Stalinist until his last day, Haywood speaks with authority about the intraparty struggles in the Soviet Union, of which he apparently had an insider's knowledge. The record of his Moscow friends, colleagues, and opponents reads like a virtual "Who's Who" of the international communist movement.[55] Or take Lovett Fort-Whiteman, another influential African American communist and a longtime Moscow resident. In 1924 Fort-Whiteman, also known to his Comintern comrades as James Jackson, in an irate letter sent from his Lux Hotel suite, chastised the leader of the Comintern, Grigorii Zinoviev, for paying insufficient attention to the "Negro question."[56] In Moscow of the 1920s and 1930s Fort-Whiteman was a true "man about town," sporting colorful outfits *à la Russe*, shaving his head in the latest fashion of Russian communists, contributing articles to the leading Soviet newspapers, going on frequent speaking tours around the country, engrossing himself in a wide variety of internationalist issues (including, for example, the "Hands Off China" movement), and being on familiar terms with the likes of Bukharin, Rykov, Kamenev, Zinoviev, and Kamenev. At the height of Stalinist terror this flamboyant radical from Chicago would pay dearly for some of his past associations.[57] George Padmore, an incredibly prolific would-be Pan-Africanist, fared much better but only because of his timely escape from Moscow and an early break with the Comintern. Yet while in Moscow Padmore enjoyed the high status accorded to a rising Comintern star. He headed the Profintern's Negro Bureau and produced numerous pamphlets and articles for the Soviet press. His expertise was sought on issues ranging from delivering funds to the Comintern affiliates abroad to mediating factional disputes among Chinese communists. In the early 1930s Padmore was elected to the Moscow City Soviet, an elevated position that would often land him on top of Lenin's Mausoleum, right next to Stalin and other Soviet dignitaries, during political demonstrations and military parades in the Red Square.[58] This high honor, however, was not reserved exclusively for the high-flying black revolutionaries. The apolitical Robert Robinson, a fine toolmaker but hardly a politician, also ended up atop Lenin's tomb as an elected member of the Moscow Soviet.[59]

As the Great Depression was deepening in the West, the Soviet Union held yet another powerful attraction for black America. By the late 1920s Soviet front organizations in the United States began to extend lucrative job offers to American technical experts and even common workers. While catering to the needs of Soviet industrial development, the initiative had an unmistakable propaganda value, especially when directed toward the African American community, where unemployment rates were staggering. In 1930 young Robert Robinson was making $140 a month, working as a toolmaker at a Ford plant in Detroit. A Soviet headhunter stunned Robinson by offering him a salary of $250 a month, rent-free living quarters, a maid, thirty-days paid vacation a year, a car, and a free passage to and from Russia. Duly impressed, Robinson signed the contract on the spot: "I thought to myself, 'America is in the grip of a serious depression and I could be laid off any day at Ford. Judging by all the applicants in the outer room, white Americans are lining up for this chance. Why not me too?'"[60]

Homer Smith couldn't find a stable job in his native Minneapolis. Having on a whim sent a letter of inquiry to the Moscow Post Office, he received an almost immediate positive response. Even though any knowledge of the Russian language was demonstratively absent from the list of his qualifications, the largest post office in the Soviet Union offered this twenty-two-year-old journalism major the position of a consultant at a salary higher than he could have hoped to obtain in his own country.[61] Within a year Smith (better known to his African American readers under the pen-name Chatwood Hall) was reputed to hold the "highest government post of any foreigner in the Soviet Union" and was busy reorganizing the postal system in the USSR.[62] And the twenty-one young African Americans who arrived in the Soviet Union in 1932 to participate in the filming of the ill-fated project *Black and White* were probably just as pleased with their four-hundred-rubles-a-month contracts. They also received free meals and reimbursements for their transatlantic passage. Langston Hughes, one of the leaders of the group and the projected writer of the scenario, was given a much higher salary—"about a hundred times a week as much as I had ever made anywhere else." Once the film project fell through, Hughes opted to delay his departure. The poet toured the country for several months, during which time he had plenty of opportunity to practice his literary craft, making "more from writing in Moscow in terms of buying power than I have ever earned within the same period anywhere else."[63] Some dozen graduates of Tuskegee, Hampton, and Wilberforce, whom Hughes visited during his trip to Central Asia, very likely shared the sense of amazed satisfaction expressed by the poet. They had arrived on an experimental cotton farm outside of Tashkent in 1931 under the leadership of Oliver Golden and John Sutton and with blessings from the famous agricultural scientist and educator George Washington Carver.[64] At a salary of around seven hundred dollars a month and ready access to the specialized stores reserved for foreigners, these African American *spetsialisty* (specialists) had plenty of motivation to contribute in substantive ways to the development of cotton production in Soviet Uzbekistan.[65] Professional fulfillment and a prominent status they attained among the upper stratum of the Tashkent professional and political elite (Golden would be elected to the City Soviet) inspired several members of the group to settle permanently in the Soviet Union. The young agricultural experts from Dixie had to be favorably impressed with the importance assigned to their work by Soviet officials. John Sutton, for example, reportedly commanded a team of Russian technicians and had a special department at Moscow's New Fibres Institute put at his disposal. When queried by a correspondent about the sources of his quite spectacular professional success in the USSR, Sutton responded modestly and to the point: "I consider the success of my work not so much a matter of personal capability, but as a result of unlimited opportunities which have been given to me in the Soviet Union."[66]

If modest young technocrats like Robinson and Sutton were dazzled by the dizzying opportunities they found in Soviet Russia, the impact was bound to be greater on African Americans of prominence, whose prestige in Soviet society and the material and emotional rewards such prestige entailed were far greater. Both McKay and Hughes partook of Soviet hospitality, but it was the world-famous singer and actor Paul Robeson who would penetrate the cultural and political stratosphere of the communist nation. Soviet people and the Soviet state would fall in love with the great New Jerseyan, and Robeson certainly returned the sentiment.

Over the years Robeson would develop close personal ties with the USSR. His son, Paul Robeson Jr., attended a high school in Moscow in the late 1930s, and in 1952 Robeson became the recipient of the Stalin Peace Prize. At the height of the Red Scare he famously declared that black Americans would never fight the Soviets, a bold statement that landed him in a lot of trouble.[67] Robeson's genuine popularity among the Soviet people remains unsurpassed. Even the late-Soviet racism made an exception for the black national hero. An African American correspondent in 1980s Leningrad was rudely interrupted by a drunk while attempting to carry a Russian folk tune to cap off a dinner with his friend at a restaurant. "Shut up!" screamed the drunk. "This is not the 1940s and you are no Paul Robeson."[68] Robeson's seventy-fifth anniversary occasioned thousands of congratulatory letters from Soviet citizens. Here is an example of one such letter sent to and read on the air by Radio Moscow. In fact, it's a poem:

> You appeared on stage,
> Head bowed, eyes lowered
> The pianist struck a cord
> And gently your wonderful voice overflowed
> Then the hall and the pit fell silent
> And only your voice was heard.
> And in the spellbound stillness
> It charmed and conjured. . . .
> And everyone wanted to hear again
> Your wonderful voice without ending . . .
> And instead of a fine bouquet,
> To place at your feet our hearts.[69]

The feeling was mutual, and Robeson sustained throughout his life an unwavering support for the land of socialism, which, one might add, led him to turn a blind eye on the Stalinist horrors that claimed the lives of some of his close Jewish friends.[70] Robeson's love for the Soviet Union was real, and its sources were more personal and moral than ideological. For Robeson, as for a number of other black activists of his generation, the USSR remained the place built on peaceful ethnic coexistence and racial equality, the place where (in stark contrast to the United States and other Western countries) "colored folk" could enter modernity and live and toil in dignity on a par with their white fellow countrymen. The awe at this achievement was fundamental to Robeson's attitude to the Soviets and informed his famous heartfelt eulogy for Stalin, composed on the tyrant's death in 1953:

> Here [in the USSR] was a people quite comparable to some of the tribal folk of Asia—quite comparable to the proud Yoruba or Basuto of West and East Africa, but now their lives flowering anew within the socialist way of life twenty years matured under the guidance of Lenin and Stalin. And in this whole area of development of national minorities—of their relation to the Great Russians—Stalin had played and was playing a most decisive role. . . . I was later to travel—to see with my own eyes what could happen to so-called backward

peoples. In the West (in England, in Belgium, France, Portugal, Holland)—the Africans, the Indians (East and West), many of the Asian peoples were considered so backward that centuries, perhaps, would have to pass before these so-called "colonials" could become a part of modern society. . . . But in the Soviet Union, Yakuts, Nenetses, Kirgiz, Tadzhiks—had respect and were helped to advance with unbelievable rapidity in this socialist land. No empty promises, such as colored folk continuously hear in the United States, but deeds.[71]

In his enthusiasm for the Soviet multiethnic project[72] (and undoubtedly as a reflection of the personal fame and prestige he enjoyed in the USSR) Paul Robeson probably contributed more than any other single foreign sympathizer to the efficacy of the Soviet propaganda effort projected onto the developing and nonwhite world. In his public speeches and writings he put forth the image of the Soviet Union, assiduously cultivated by the Soviets themselves, that pointed unambiguously toward a commonality of fate between the first socialist state and the nonwhite colonial and diasporic populations: "All the anger of the reactionaries directed against the Soviet Union is also directed in other forms against the colonial peoples. The latter have learned, thanks to these reactionaries, that there is a natural alliance between the country of socialism and the oppressed people the world over."[73]

Musings like the one above had to be music to Soviet ears. The Soviets enjoyed and cultivated their antiracist image. It was in part correct and genuinely reflective of the official ideology, but, considering the multiethnic composition of the Soviet Union, it also had distinctive internal political utility for the regime. Soviet Marxism purported to lift ethnic minorities above their subservient status *both* in the USSR and abroad. Attacks on racism and racist practices in print and in speech became a staple of Soviet propaganda, as well as an essential part of Soviet cultural production. The iconic revolutionary bard Vladimir Mayakovsky, for example, lambasted American racism and celebrated struggles against racial prejudice in his popular verse "Black and White"—inspired by his 1925 trip to Mexico, Cuba, and the United States. Mayakovsky fully shared the vision of his socialist motherland's being a torch of liberation for the oppressed. "If I were a Negro . . . I would learn Russian just because Lenin spoke it," he solemnly announced in his 1927 poem *Nashemu Yunoshestvu* (To Our Youth). American racism is derided in the famous 1933 children's poem *Mister Twister*, by Samuil Marshak. In the poem "Mr. Twister the Millionaire" arrives in Leningrad from New York as a tourist and experiences a virtual "culture shock" when he realizes that in the Soviet state blacks and whites stay in the same hotels. Needless to say, the capitalist bigot is shaken by this discovery. Having failed to procure "all-white" hotel accommodations, Mr. Twister learns the hard way (that is by sleeping on a chair in the hotel lobby) a lesson in racial tolerance. The message of the poem couldn't be any more straightforward: in the Soviet Union we do not distinguish between black and white, and those who do will never feel comfortable or even welcome here. Posh Moscow hotels, if not readily available to regular Soviet citizens (something that most black American visitors likely didn't realize), were certainly devoid of Jim Crow practices. Maude White, according to her testimony at the Riga legation, stayed for several months at the Hotel Europe in the center of Moscow without having to pay a ruble.[74] The participants in the *Black and White* film project failed to make a movie but had a grand old time dining in style at the October Hotel in Leningrad and, later, staying at Moscow's fashionable Grand Hotel.[75] Paul Robeson, on his first visit to the USSR, in 1935, claimed some poetic justice for his recent humiliating encounter with segregationist practices at a Chicago hotel. On his arrival in Moscow he booked a VIP suite at the Hotel National. The same suite had been previously occupied by the first U.S. ambassador to Moscow.[76]

African Americans journeying to Soviet Russia in the 1930s could look forward to a welcome respite from housing segregation. And many of them were quick to notice the difference.[77] A believer in racial segregation of *any* kind would have obtained little understanding and plenty of hard time from the Soviets. Firsthand accounts by black travelers in the Soviet Union at the time suggest that the kind of misfortune that befell the fictional Mr. Twister could have easily happened in reality. Homer Smith actually experienced a situation so similar to the one described by Marshak that one wonders if the travails of Mr. Twister had not inadvertently added a wrinkle or two to his memory. While on a train from Moscow to Leningrad, Smith found himself in the same compartment with an Anglo-American woman, whose terror over her unexpected proximity to a black man was so great that she asked the conductor for a transfer. Not only was her fickle request denied, but the conductor made a point of expressing his disdain for her racist paranoia. Having received no satisfaction or understanding, the hapless woman fled the compartment and spent what had to be an extremely uncomfortable night sitting on her suitcase in the corridor.[78] Robert Robinson similarly recounts the annoyance expressed by his white compatriots on finding out that while in the Soviet Union they would have to share their hotel and dining accommodations with a black colleague. Their attempts to resist Soviet integrationist practices soundly failed. A physical assault on Robinson by a couple of white American "specialists" would lead to the latter's prosecution and expulsion from the USSR. Following the incident, the workers at the Stalingrad Tractor Plant, where the attack took place, issued a strong-worded resolution, containing a warning to other white Americans employed in the USSR: "We will not allow the ways of bourgeois America in the USSR. The Negro worker is our brother."[79] Likewise, Harry Haywood recalls in his memoir that during the several years he spent in Moscow as a student at KUTV he encountered only one racist incident. On that occasion he and a group of his friends were riding a streetcar when a drunk muttered "Black Devils" in their direction. Having overheard the abuse, Russian passengers seized the drunk ("How dare you, you scum, insult people who are the guests of our country!") and hauled him off to a police station, but not before they had apologized profusely before their exotic-looking "guests."[80] Reading these and similar accounts (and there are quite a few of them available), one gets the distinct impression that the antiracist rhetoric of the government and the lofty internationalism of the Comintern did in fact penetrate the fabric of Soviet society. Not only did the majority of Soviet citizens appear to their black visitors to be immune to Western-style racism, but they also apparently set out to shame and educate by example the occasional American or European racist wading in their midst.[81]

Nowhere is this notion of the Soviet people performing an all-important corrective function and ridding the world of racism rendered more forcefully than in the film *Circus*—the cinematic megahit of the 1930s. *Circus* tells the story of a white American actress with a black child who tours the Soviet Union, the country where she finds much sympathy and understanding. In 1936–37 this feel-good movie took the Soviet Union by storm. Indeed, in the midst of Stalin's terror the Soviets could use some good cheer, and *Circus,* starring the blond and chastely attractive Lyubov' Orlova, offered plenty to cheer about. Orlova played an American circus performer, Marion (Mary) Dixon, on tour in the USSR. The woman, who is conspicuously white, harbors a "dark" secret—her black little son, the fruit of forbidden love back in the States. Predictably, she falls in love with the country of socialism and then in due order with a nice specimen of Soviet manhood whom she fondly addresses by his patronymic Petrovich. Orlova's character seems to have a strange proclivity to go against the grain of bourgeois culture and embrace (often in a very literal sense) things most frowned on in capitalist America—blacks and communists. Mary's German manager, von Kneischitz, represents a highly unflattering portrait of the world of capitalism. Obsessing about money von Kneischitz endlessly haggles over the conditions of the contract. He is materialistic.

He displays little respect for or understanding of the host country and he makes awkward sexual advances toward Mary. He is also an unapologetic racist, sufficiently ignorant of Marxism to fully expect Soviet citizens (who are mostly white, after all) to share his prejudices. When he is rejected by Mary, he takes his revenge on her by exposing what he sees as her shameful past to the audience of Soviet circusgoers, and . . . the whole house comes down with laughter. Thoroughly humiliated, the racist capitalist flees in shame. In one of the celebrated final scenes of the film the audience virtually adopts the dark-skinned boy and passes him around the circus, with different members of the audience, representing the ethnic diversity of the USSR, singing tender lullabies in their respective languages. And very soon the proud mother, with the wholesome Petrovich at her side, marches in a communist parade, surrounded by a joyful crowd and free of any fear of racial prejudice, singing in a delightfully accented Russian, "I don't know any other country where a person can breathe so freely!"

Love indeed was in the air. For the encounter between black America and Soviet Russia spurred not just cinematic but real-life romances. For example, the part of the little mulatto boy in the movie was played by Jimmy Patterson, whose father was a black American expatriate in the USSR. The interracial romance, implicit in the plot of the movie, corresponded with the internationalist values embraced by Soviet society. For many African Americans, their involvement with radical politics and the subsequent sojourns in the USSR held a promise of liberation from the strictures imposed by American racism on interracial romance and sex. Even in the United States, interracial dating and marriages were quite common within radical political circles, especially those linked to the Communist Party. Notably, interracial couples usually consisted of a black man and a white woman, and only rarely the reverse happened. Some of the top Harlem communists (for example, Theodore Bassett, William Fitzgerald, Abner Berry, and James W. Ford) married or routinely dated white (and often Jewish) women.[82] In fact, the propensity of the "Negro party leaders" to seek romantic fulfillment across the color line was such that in the late 1930s a group of women communists from Harlem appealed to "Comrade Stalin and the Executive of the Communist International" with an impassioned plea to intercede on their behalf and correct what they saw as an ongoing "insult to Negro womanhood."[83] A 1935 *New York Amsterdam News* editorial pointedly questioned the sexual politics of American communists, whom the editors accused of using their white female cadres ("the Union Square blondes and brunettes") to ensnare the best of the "Harlem swains."[84]

If even the insulated world of American communism offered such unheard-of romantic opportunities to its faithful, then the country governed by the communist doctrine held an almost unlimited potential for interracial love. Soviet cultural norms and accepted social values became the subject of much mythologizing in the West at the time. The Soviet Union both terrified and fascinated its observers. In the minds of many an ill-informed Westerner, the unprecedented social experiment conducted by the communists in Russia extended into the realm of the senses. The Soviet challenge to capitalism was often perceived in the West as a simultaneous assault on the bastions of Victorian morality. Films like *Circus* only seemed to confirm the persistent titillating rumors of the Soviets' discarding of bourgeois virtues and removing the usual stigma attached to such Western taboos as polygamy, interracial sex, and illegitimacy. In his memoir Langston Hughes recalls a humorous case of a young American woman who, starry-eyed idealist that she was, traveled all the way from Pittsburgh to Moscow to give birth to a child she had conceived out-of-wedlock. By her own admission, she had come to the Soviet Union to have her baby "in a land where illegitimacy didn't matter, where all children were equal, and women were free."[85] And women were certainly free (or so it was frequently reported) to choose partners of whatever skin color. If anything, the Soviet state promoted such mixed marriages as the ultimate expression and realization of its egalitarian principles. The contrast with the situation obtained in the West could not be any starker. An African American observer summed it up quite succinctly: "What the British [and Americans] condemn, the Soviets encourage."[86]

The relative accuracy of the above formulation was borne out by the experiences of the majority of African American visitors (overwhelmingly male) in the USSR. They were clearly in vogue there, and their skin color was no obstacle in establishing romantic attachments with local women, whose "buxom physique . . . present[ed] quite a noticeable contrast to the unshapely forms of women from western countries such as America and England."[87] One can easily dismiss such playful generalizations, yet in an awkward sort of way they probably captured a genuine gratitude of the author for being accepted and desired. Indeed, by all accounts the romantic lives of black sojourners flourished in Soviet Russia. Most of those who resided in the USSR for extended periods, even the austere ideologues— the likes of William Patterson and Harry Haywood—ended up marrying Russian women and/or fathering Russian children.[88] The young Homer Smith, on his arrival in the USSR, noted with amazement that a sort of "reverse discrimination" was occurring at the social functions he attended. Russian girls would happily abandon their Russian suitors to dance with a *negrityanskii tovarisch* (Negro comrade). When informed about the many social and cultural barriers to interracial romance in the States, they would loudly fume over the "decadent bourgeois swine" spawned by capitalism.[89] Russian women, their African American paramours were quick to discover, harbored no bourgeois prejudices—passionately romancing and freely marrying black Americans. We know less about the romantic lives of African American women in Russia, mostly because there were so few of them. It appears, however, that they had to face a brutal competition from local women for the hearts of their male compatriots. In his memoir Langston Hughes gives us a taste of the melodrama surrounding the presence of a group of young black Americans in the early 1930s in Moscow. A heartbroken female member of the group attempted suicide when her "beloved from Harlem" succumbed to the charms of a Russian beauty.[90] Moscow journal entries by Dorothy West (writing under the penname of Mary Christopher) are full of melancholy and vague lamentations—her lover is slipping through her fingers and into the ready proletarian hands of Dorothy's nefarious rival, "Nadya": "I am bitter today. I love you, and I don't want to leave you, but even you could not persuade me to stay. And Nadya, how she will inveigle herself into your very soul during this trip. She knows I am not staying. And the little French girl, well, have her too. And that silly Tania. All your bright birds. Nadya is not my friend. Some day you will see."[91] Even the sexually ambiguous Hughes was not spared the intensity of "Moscow romance," caught up in a mesh set out for him by a married Moscow actress, a young and adventurous woman who is itching to pull off an ultimate Russian coup—to leave an old and established husband for a young and talented poet.[92]

Yes, love was definitely in the air, at least for a while. Yet as with so many other love affairs, the one between black America and Soviet Russia eventually began to wane. By the end of the 1930s the "idea of the Soviet Union" had to a significant extent lost its appeal for the African American community. The reasons for the Soviet Union's diminished popularity among black Americans were complex and rooted in the changing political and economic landscape in the United States, in the increased tensions between American communists and a number of influential black organizations, in the many blunders committed by the Comintern and in its eventual decline, in certain foreign policy decisions by the USSR that antagonized much of black America, and last but not least, in the cultural gap between the two societies as revealed through the specific experiences of a small number of African Americans residing in the USSR.

Jonathan Rosenberg has aptly observed that in their glowing account of the Soviet Union, most African American observers and reformers responded not necessarily to conditions in Russia but rather to conditions in the United States.[93] American racism and the economic strain of the Great Depression induced many African Americans to look longingly toward the beckoning lights of the "Red Mecca." Yet few of them seriously considered the applicability of such exotic things as the dictatorship of the proletariat or a rapid and back-breaking industrialization to their own condition. Such reservations were shared even by the reformers, like W. E. B. Du Bois, who at some point or another found themselves falling under the spell of the Soviet mystique.[94] In this respect the majority of African Americans welcomed heartily Roosevelt's New Deal. The fact that American communists, who were widely seen as the mouthpieces of Soviet communism, vehemently rejected Roosevelt's policies (unfairly labeling them as "fascist") did little to raise the Soviet Union's stakes within the black community.[95]

The famous case of the Scottsboro Boys similarly exposed the tensions between American communists and such major black organizations as the NAACP. In fact, the case, which saw nine African American youths falsely accused of raping two white women on a freight train going through Alabama, turned into an epic turf battle between the communists and the NAACP. The communists succeeded in wrestling the control of the case from the NAACP lawyers, a coup decried in the African American press as serving the interests not of poor American blacks but of a distant communist state in Russia. Toward the end of 1931 Walter White, the leader of the NAACP, saw the signs of an anticommunist backlash generated by the communists' handling of the case. He also questioned the communists' general commitment to improving the lives of black Americans. White suspected that the communists and their Soviet sponsors were not so much interested in saving the innocent "boys'" lives as in turning them into "martyrs" to advance their own cause. "Among Negroes," he opined, "the pendulum swung sharply away from the American Communist program, even among those of intelligence who had looked, if not with sympathy, at least with interest upon the economic and social experiment which is going on in Soviet Russia."[96] By seizing control of the case the communists, wrote the Soviet sympathizer Du Bois, "head them [the poorest and most ignorant blacks] toward inevitable slaughter and jail-slavery." The Soviets' attempt, exercised through their American proxies, to turn the case into a propaganda vehicle was conceited, he argued. It betrayed "a ludicrous misapprehension of local conditions and [illustrated] the error into which long distance interpretation, unsupported by real knowledge, may fall."[97]

An analogous conclusion could be drawn from a bizarre Comintern initiative that envisioned the creation of an independent "Negro Soviet Republic" in the American South. Known as the "Black Belt Thesis," this Comintern fantasy received an official stamp of Soviet approval at the Sixth Comintern Congress in 1928. Even some American communists, generally accustomed to following the Soviet line, found it difficult to accept the idea of African Americans creating a separate nation within the United States. To Otto Hall this "sounded like Jim Crow" in revolutionary disguise. Otto Huiswoud appeared to share the same opinion, and so did Lovett Fort-Whiteman.[98] James Ford, usually an obedient follower of Moscow policies, spoke at the congress, criticizing in no uncertain terms this attempt to promote black nationalism at a time when African Americans hungered for racial equality.[99] For the majority of black Americans striving for integration within the broader American society, the vision of a separate "Negro Republic" in the South smacked of an age-old segregationism. Soviet communists and the Comintern once again demonstrated scant understanding of the workings of American society. They justified their position on the Black Belt by assuming that the majority of African Americans would continue to reside in the American South. Nothing could be further from the truth, especially at the time of the great African American migrations to the industrialized North. The Moscow-concocted theory of the right of self-determination soundly failed to take root within the black community. Even Harry Haywood, one of the original sponsors of the initiative, had to admit that "nearly all non-Communist Negro leaders rejected the Communist theory."[100]

Another example of good intentions gone awry owing to a knowledge gap presents itself in the much-written-about case of the failed film project *Black and White*. In 1932, twenty-two African Americans journeyed to Soviet Russia to take part in making a propaganda film about racial (and class) oppression in the American South. The Soviet officialdom seemed to have a better idea than black Americans themselves of what life was like for black people in the former Confederate states. When, on their arrival in Moscow, the American visitors were presented with a script of the film, they did not know whether "to cry or to laugh." Langston Hughes, who was among the would-be actors, remembered years later: "I was crying because the writer meant well, but knew so little about his subject and the result was a pathetic hodgepodge of good intentions and faulty facts. . . . The writer's concern for racial freedom and decency had tripped so completely on the stumps of ignorance that his work had fallen as flat as did Don Quixote's valor when good intentions led that slightly demented knight to do battle with he-knew-what-not."[101] Despite their professed antiracism the Soviet sponsors of the project obviously shared some of the entrenched Western stereotypes of the blacks as they expected every member of the hapless troupe to be able to sing and dance in the picture. According to Hughes, Soviet officials were flabbergasted to find out that very few of their guests (most of whom were young intellectuals and knew very little about acting) could actually carry a tune.[102] Eventually the project was shelved, and the visitors were given a choice of either going back home or staying in the land of socialism.

It was misunderstandings like this one that tempered the spirits of the early African American enthusiasts of the Soviet Union, many of whom would grow disillusioned with the rigidity of the Soviet dogma and with Moscow's conspicuous inability to recognize the importance of race as a vehicle of political discourse. George Padmore, for example, would eventually break with Stalinism on these grounds. Having come to doubt the sincerity of Soviet commitments to black liberation, he would ditch his dizzyingly successful political career in the USSR to pursue Pan-African aspirations.[103] The evolution of the Soviet foreign policy throughout the 1930s left much doubt, indeed, regarding the sincerity of Moscow's anticolonial and antiracist rhetoric. Increasingly, the Soviet Union was seen by its early supporters and champions in the colonial and African American world as just another powerful state (and a "white" state at that), whose foreign-policy decisions reflected not the interests of the "oppressed and downtrodden" but those of one particular nation—the Soviet Union itself. The *Black and White* fiasco, a number of informed observers suggested, was the result of a pressure exerted by the U.S. State Department on Soviet authorities. Supposedly, the Soviets got cold feet vis-à-vis the project once they realized that the making of an explicitly "anti-American" film might jeopardize the establishment of diplomatic relations between the two countries.[104] Another explanation attributed the failure to an undue influence on the Soviet government by a Colonel Hugh L. Cooper, "an American engineer with large contracts in Russia."[105] There is little doubt that the persistent allegations of the Soviets' shipping oil and other strategic supplies to Italy during Mussolini's 1935 invasion of Ethiopia further tarnished the image of the Soviet Union among African Americans.[106] And then came the "Great Betrayal" of the Nazi-Soviet Pact of 1939. Considering the Nazis' well-publicized views on race, the Soviet apologists among African American communists were hard-pressed to rationalize the Soviet foreign-policy about-face to their fellow black Americans. Largely to no avail. According to one source, in 1939 "over fifteen hundred Negroes" left the Communist Party in the state of New York.[107] A bitter editorial in the *Crisis* conveys a sense of profound disillusionment with a once noble cause:

> These September actions have unmasked the Soviets. The Kremlin has staged the *great betrayal* and ranged itself alongside Hitler, not only on the battlefield, but at the conference table where treaties and pledges are but scraps of paper. . . . Needless to say, the followers of the Soviet in foreign countries have been left high and dry by the turn of events. Hundreds of thousands, if not millions, have been disillusioned. Minority groups, such as the Negro in America who had been looking to Soviet Russia to furnish the example by which minority problems might be worked out equitably are likewise in confusion.[108]

By shedding any pretenses that its foreign policy reflected interests other than its own, the Soviet Union lost much of its clout with black America. And so did the American Communist Party, whose support for the maddening fluctuations of the Soviet political line affected its credibility within the African American community. Disgust with the cynicism of Soviet foreign policy and frustration over the American communists' readiness to justify its most incongruous twists and turns permeated the debates at the Third National Negro Congress. A. Phillip Randolph, congress president, openly accused the Soviets of "imperialistic expansion of power over weaker peoples regardless of color." It seemed clear to Randolph and his many supporters at the congress that American communists carried out the decisions by a foreign state whose policy "may not be in the interests of the Negro people." The Soviets held no answers for the African American community. Quite to the contrary, by their reckless and self-serving policies they only "added to the handicap of being 'black' the handicap of being 'red.'"[109]

The Nazi-Soviet collusion carried less drama for those black Americans who permanently resided in the Soviet Union. Available memoirs indicate that there existed an inverse correlation between the degree of infatuation with the country of equal opportunities and the length of stay there. Emma Harris, the proverbial "Mammy of Moscow," having lived in the Soviet Union longer than any other black American of her generation, had the least respect for the regime, daydreaming, by her own admission, of poisoning Stalin.[110] Both Homer Smith and Robert Robinson lost their affection for the Soviet state as their sojourn in Russia extended into perpetuity. As the 1930s unfolded and as they integrated more and more into the Soviet society, the two began to comprehend the horrors of Stalin's state lurking just below the surface of its internationalist rhetoric. They had solid reasons to be wary and afraid. Return to the States often proved to be problematic owing to a double jeopardy of the State Department's distaste for and the Soviet authorities' suspicion of American residents in the country. The purges swept off the streets of Moscow the affable Lovett Fort-Whiteman soon after he had failed to renew his U.S. passport. His death of "heart failure" in a remote Gulag camp became only recently revealed by the findings in the newly opened Russian archives.[111] Other "pilgrims'" life stories may have lacked the tragic pitch of Fort-Whiteman's odyssey (even though Smith alleges in his memoir that there were other African American prisoners in the Gulag) but were still quite cheerless. John Sutton returned to the States in 1938, but his colleague Oliver Golden died young in Tashkent, leaving behind his Jewish American wife and their little daughter, Lily.[112] Gary Johnson, a one-time KUTV student with a well-established reputation for troublemaking, ran afoul of the Comintern and Soviet authorities and ended up in exile in the southern city of Krasnodar. He would die in obscurity in 1967.[113] The actors Robert Ross and Wayland Rudd fared better by being able to practice their craft, but both had limited visibility on the Russian stage and screen, typecast for "Negro" parts and delivering an occasional lecture on "Negro" life in America.[114] With the notable exception of the great Paul Robeson, who never permanently settled in the land for which he harbored such deep passion, African Americans in Russia overall fell significantly short of their early euphoric expectations of prosperity and high achievement in the "promised land" of socialism. Yet the legacy of that early romance between black America and Soviet Russia would continue to exist for decades as a residue of goodwill toward the USSR among many African Americans. And it would certainly continue in the official Soviet rhetoric and in the later vain attempts by the decaying Soviet Union to salvage the crumbling multiethnic and internationalist identity of its early days.

ACKNOWLEDGMENTS

Parts of this work have also appeared in Maxim Matusevich, "Journeys of Hope: Two Generations of African Diaspora in the Soviet Union," *African Diaspora* 1 (2008): 53–85. I would like to thank the Kennan Institute of the Woodrow Wilson Center for International Scholars and the W. E. B. Du Bois Center for African and African American Research at Harvard University for providing me with the much-needed support for this project.

NOTES

1. See Orlando Paterson, *Slavery and Social Death* (Cambridge, MA: Harvard University Press, 1985).

2. Claude McKay, "Soviet Russia and the Negro," *Crisis*, Dec. 1923 (pt. 1), 61–65, 63.

3. Claude McKay, "A Moscow Lady: A Study in Prejudice," *Crisis*, Sept. 1924, 225–28, 227.

4. See Allison Blakely, *Russia and the Negro: Blacks in Russian History and Thought* (Washington, DC: Howard University Press, 1986).

5. "Lynchings Food for Soviets," *Chicago Defender*, Oct. 4, 1930.

6. "Russians Buoy Selves in Rising Tide of Color," *Chicago Defender*, Dec. 30, 1922.

7. For a useful overview of the treatment of the early Soviet Union by the African American press see Henry Williams, *Black Response to the American Left, 1917–1929* (Princeton, NJ: Princeton University Press, 1973).

8. John L. Garder, "African Americans in the Soviet Union in the 1920s and 1930s: The Development of Transcontinental Protest," *Western Journal of Black Studies* 23, no. 3 (1999): 190–200, 192.

9. Robert W. Dunn, "What I Did Not See in Russia," *Labor Herald* (Official Organ of the Trade Union Educational League) 2, no. 6 (Aug. 1923): 14–15.

10. "Lynchings for 1922," *Union*, Jan. 13, 1923.

11. Claude McKay, *A Long Way from Home* (New York: Lee Furman, 1937), 151.

12. Kate A. Baldwin, *Beyond the Color Line and the Iron Curtain: Reading Encounters between Black and Red, 1922–1963* (Durham, NC: Duke University Press, 2002), 37.

13. Charles Recht, "An American in Moscow on November 7," *Soviet Russia Pictorial*, March 1923, 48.

14. McKay, *A Long Way from Home*, 168.

15. McKay, "Soviet Russia and the Negro," *Crisis*, Dec. 1923, 61–65, 61.

16. McKay, *A Long Way from Home*, 173.

17. Ibid., 245.

18. Claude McKay, "Soviet Russia and the Negro," *Crisis*, Jan. 1924 (pt. 2), 114–18, 116.

19. McKay, "A Moscow Lady," 225–28.

20. McKay, *A Long Way from Home*, 169.

21. McKay, "Soviet Russia and the Negro," *Crisis*, Jan. 1924, 114–18, 118.

22. For the most complete account of the history of African and African American presence in prerevolutionary Russia see Blakely, *Russia and the Negro*.

23. "Russia's Greatest Poet," *Crisis*, Feb. 1937, 58.

24. See Frances M. Somers Cocks, "The African Origins of Alexander Pushkin," in *Africa in Russia, Russia in Africa: Three Centuries of Encounters*, ed. Maxim Matusevich (Trenton, NJ: Africa World Press, 2006), 13–35.

25. Sergius Kara-Mourza, "Ira Aldridge in Russia," *Crisis*, Sept. 1933, 201–2.

26. Having spent several months on the social circuit of Petrograd and Moscow, McKay was very likely familiar with the story of Coretti Arle-Titz, a black opera

singer from New York, who had arrived in the "land of Pushkin" before the revolution. Her first marriage to a Russian noble fell apart but "not so much on account of the bride's color for color prejudice is not strong in Russia." She would later marry a prominent Soviet musician and piano professor at the Moscow Conservatory, Boris Titz. See "Russians Hear Soprano Voice of Dark Singer," *Chicago Defender*, April 18, 1925; and Chatwood Hall, "A Black Woman in Red Russia," *Crisis*, July 1937, 203–4. Or there was an example of the famous Moscow socialite Emma Harris, also known as the "Mammy of Moscow." Emma's past remains somewhat murky, but it appears she had lived the high life before 1917 as a mistress of one of the grand dukes. Having lost everything (including a mansion complete with Russian servants) in the revolution, she nevertheless preserved her optimism and showed a lot of resilience in coping with the harsh realities of Soviet life. In the period before the Second World War she would turn herself into something of an unofficial guardian to a small colony of Moscow's black residents. See "The Mammy of Moscow," in Langston Hughes, *I Wonder as I Wander: An Autobiographical Journey* (New York: Hill and Wang, 1994), 82–86. Also see "Emma: Mammy of Moscow," in Homer Smith, *Black Man in Red Russia: A Memoir* (Chicago: Johnson Publishing, 1964), 34–39.

27. McKay, "Soviet Russia and the Negro," *Crisis*, Jan. 1924, 114–18, 117–18.

28. The alleged affinity between Russian and African American cultural traditions, between their respective spiritualities (e.g., the idea of the "soul"), has lately attracted some serious scholarly attention. Dale Peterson, for example, has suggested a sort of intellectual kinship between Russian and African American literatures. The two, he argues, share a history of subjugation to and the subsequent resentment of "narrow Western standards of civility and literacy" (Dale E. Peterson, *Up from Bondage: The Literatures of Russian and African American Soul* [Durham, NC: Duke University Press, 2000], 6).

29. McKay, *A Long Way from Home*, 169.

30. Ibid., 173. For a detailed account of McKay's report to the Congress, as well as its interpretation, see Baldwin, *Beyond the Color Line and the Iron Curtain*, 37–42; and William J. Maxwell, *New Negro, Old Left* (New York: Columbia University Press, 1999), 72–76.

31. RGASPI (Russian State Archive of Social and Political History), "Second Comintern Congress. Minutes of the 4th Meeting," vol. 489, leaf 1 (1920).

32. Theodore Draper, *American Communism and Soviet Russia: The Formative Period* (New York: Viking, 1960), 320–21.

33. Huiswoud's presentation at the Fourth Comintern Congress, as quoted in Draper, *American Communism and Soviet Russia*, 327.

34. Claude McKay, "Report on the Negro Question: Speech to the 4th Congress of the Comintern, Nov. 1922," *International Press Correspondence*, vol. 3 (Jan. 5, 1923), 16–17.

35. Hughes, *I Wonder as I Wander*, 73.

36. Smith, *Black Man in Red Russia*, vii.

37. W. E. B. Du Bois, "Editorial," *Crisis*, Nov. 1926, 8.

38. W. E. B. Du Bois, *The Autobiography of W. E. B. Du Bois: A Soliloquy on Viewing My Life from the Last Decade of Its First Century* (London: Oxford University Press, 2007), 16–25.

39. See Woodford McClellan, "Africans and Black Americans in the Comintern Schools, 1925–1934," *International Journal of African Historical Studies* 26, no. 2 (1993): 371–90. By the same author see also "Black *Hajj* to 'Red Mecca': Africans and Afro-Americans at KUTV, 1925–1938," in *Africa in Russia, Russia in Africa: Three Centuries of Encounters*, ed. Maxim Matusevich (Trenton, NJ: Africa World Press, 2006), 61–84.

40. A number of former KUTV students left memoirs in which they describe in some detail the life of black American radicals in Moscow. See, e.g., Harry Haywood, *Black Bolshevik: Autobiography of an Afro-American Communist* (Chicago: Liberator Press, 1978); and William L. Patterson, *The Man Who Cried Genocide: An Autobiography* (New York: International Publishers, 1971).

41. Mark Solomon, *The Cry Was Unity: Communists and African Americans, 1917–36* (Jackson: University Press of Mississippi, 1998), 90.

42. National Archives II (hereafter NA II), "Passport Application of Miss Maude May White," RG 84, *Records of Foreign Service Posts: Correspondence of American Consulate, Riga, Latvia*, vol. 104/3, file nos. 630-886.7 (Aug. 5, 1930).

43. NA II, "Strictly Confidential Dispatch to the Secretary of State," RG 84, *Records of Foreign Service Posts: Correspondence of American Consulate, Riga, Latvia*, vol. 108, dispatch no. 7096, enclosure no. 1 (July 10, 1930).

44 Haywood, *Black Bolshevik*, 387–88.

45. NA II, "American citizens who entered the Soviet Union or departed therefrom via Latvian frontier in the period from February 21 to April 14, 1930," RG 84, *Records of Foreign Service Posts: Correspondence of American Consulate, Riga, Latvia*, vol. 108, dispatch no. 6949, enclosure no. 2, list no. 7 (1930).

46. NA II, "Strictly Confidential Dispatch to the Secretary of State," RG 84, *Records of Foreign Service Posts: Correspondence of American Consulate, Riga, Latvia*, vol. 108, dispatch no. 7096, enclosure no. 1 (July 10, 1930).

47. NA II, "Passport Application of Miss Maude May White," RG 84, *Records of Foreign Service Posts: Correspondence of American Consulate, Riga, Latvia*, vol. 104/3, file nos. 630-886.7 (Aug. 5, 1930).

48. Ibid.

49. Patterson, *The Man Who Cried Genocide*, 119.

50. Haywood, *Black Bolshevik*, 342–49.

51. Chatwood Hall, "Dr. A. Wilberforce Williams, Noted American Physician, Makes Tour of the Soviet Union," *Chicago Defender*, Oct. 3, 1936.

52. Henry Lee Moon, "A Negro Looks at Russia," *Chicago Defender*, March 3, 1934; also see Chatwood Hall, "N.Y. School Teacher in Red Russia," *Chicago Defender*, Oct. 24, 1936.

53. For an in-depth exploration of early Soviet attempts to create a multinational state see Terry Martin, *The Affirmative Action Empire: Nations and Nationalism in the Soviet Union, 1923–1939* (Ithaca, NY: Cornell University Press, 2001).

54. Account by Otto Hall as recorded in Draper, *American Communism and Soviet Russia*, 333–34.

55. See Haywood, *Black Bolshevik*, 148–341.

56. Russian State Archive of Political and Social History (RGASPI), 495/155/37/42–43.

57. Homer Smith has a chapter in his memoir devoted to the tragic fate of Lovett Fort-Whiteman. See Homer Smith, *Black Man in Red Russia*, 77–83. Also see "Situation of Negroes in the United States of North America," *Izvestia*, June 24, 1924. The American legation in Riga recognized Fort-Whiteman's political clout by regularly reporting on his activities in Russia. See NA II, "Soviet Communist Agitation against the Western Powers, with Respect to the Civil War in China," RG 84, *Records of Foreign Service Posts: Correspondence of American Consulate, Riga, Latvia*, vol. 043, American Foreign Service Report no. 449 (Oct. 2, 1924). Also see enclosure no. 2 to the same report.

58. For more on Padmore see Solomon, *The Cry Was Unity*, 177–83. I also recommend Padmore's fascinating autobiography tracing his political evolution from communism to Pan-Africanism: George Padmore, *Pan-Africanism or Communism?* (New York: Roy Publishers, 1956).

59. See Robert Robinson, *Black on Red: My 44 Years Inside the Soviet Union* (Washington, DC: Acropolis Books, 1988), 95–105.

60. Ibid., 29.

61. Smith, *Black Man in Red Russia*, 2.

62. Tyra J. Edwards, "Another American Youth Making Good in Moscow," *Chicago Defender*, Dec. 29, 1934.

63. Jack El-Hai, "Black and White and Red," *American Heritage Magazine*, May/June 1991 (available online at americanheritage.com); Langston Hughes, *I Wonder as I Wander*, 75, 196.

64. Allison Blakely, "African Imprints on Russia: An Historical Overview," in *Africa in Russia, Russia in Africa: Three Centuries of Encounters*, ed. Maxim Matusevich (Trenton, NJ: Africa World Press, 2006), 47–49.

65. Garder, "African Americans in the Soviet Union in the 1920s and 1930s," 196.

66. Homer Smith, "A Column from Moscow," *Chicago Defender*, Oct. 27, 1934.

67. "Robeson Blasted for Paris Speech," *Chicago Defender*, April 30, 1949. Also see Robert Alan, "Paul Robeson—the Lost Shepherd," *Crisis*, Nov. 1951, 569–73.

68. Gary Lee, "Black among the Reds: A View from the Back of the Soviet Bus—My Four Years on the Racial Firing Line," *Washington Post*, April 21, 1991.

69. "Tvoi Chudnyi Golos" [Your Wonderful Voice], Letters to Paul Robeson on the Occasion of His 75th Birthday, Manuscript Division, Moorland-Spingarn Research Center, Howard University, Washington, DC, quoted in Blakely, *Russia and the Negro*, 154–55.

70. For an exhaustive analysis of Robeson's ties to the Soviet Union see Jeffrey C. Stewart, ed., *Paul Robeson: Artist and Citizen* (New Brunswick, NJ: Rutgers University Press, 1998).

71. "To You Beloved Comrade," in *Paul Robeson Speaks: Writings, Speeches, Interviews, 1918–1974*, ed. Philip S. Foner (New York: Brunner/Mazel, 1978), 347–49.

72. Black observers of and visitors to the Soviet Union were particularly intrigued (as Paul Robeson was) by the emancipation of the nonwhite ethnicities in Central Asia. The Uzbeks, the Tadjiks, and others evoked powerful feelings of racial solidarity in visiting Afro-Americans. Their lifestyles (cotton farming) and recent history (second- and third-class status in the prerevolutionary colonial society) mirrored to an extent the black experience in the American South. It was for this reason that the Republic of Uzbekistan became a destination of choice for African Americans journeying in the USSR, attracting not only idle travelers but also those willing to contribute to the agricultural development of Soviet Central Asia. Matt Crawford, one of the members of Hughes's *Black and White* group, wrote home to his wife that Central Asia was crucial to "believing in Russia": "There is an exact parallel between the condition that these people were under during the Czarist regime and the position of Negroes in the States now" (quoted in Arnold Rampersad, *The Life of Langston Hughes*, vol. 1, *1902–1941* [London: Oxford University Press, 2002], 256). John Sutton, who had first-hand experience of living and working in Soviet Central Asia, was of the same opinion. Three decades later he would thus encourage his younger African American friend to visit the Soviet Union: "But, Elton, if you have the opportunity to visit the USSR by all means go! And if you can manage to get to Uzbekistan, go there too. You will find the Uzbeks so like our own people. After all, they, too, are among the colored peoples of the world" (Elton C. Fax, *Through Black Eyes: Journeys of a Black Artist to East Africa and Russia* [New York: Dodd, Mead, 1974], 134).

73. Paul Robeson, *The Negro People and the Soviet Union* (New York: New Century Publishers, 1950), 8.

74. NA II, "Passport Application of Miss Maude May White," RG 84, *Records of Foreign Service Posts: Correspondence of American Consulate, Riga, Latvia*, vol. 104/3, file nos. 630-886.7 (Aug. 5, 1930).

75. Faith Berry, *Langston Hughes: Before and Beyond Harlem* (Westport, CT: Lawrence Hill, 1983), 158.

76. Chatwood Hall, "Soviets' New Hotel Unsullied by Jim Crow Existing in U.S.," *Chicago Defender*, Feb. 15, 1936.

77. See "Jim Crow Unknown in Soviet Russia," *Chicago Defender*, April 2, 1938; also see Chatwood Hall, "Moscow Has No Housing Segregation," *Chicago Defender*, April 23, 1938.

78. Smith, *Black Man in Red Russia*, 56–57; also see Chatwood Hall, "American Woman in Russia Raises Jim Crow Issue," *Chicago Defender*, Sept. 19, 1936.

79. Quoted in Walter Duranty, "Americans Essay Color Bar in Soviet," *New York Times*, Aug. 10, 1930. For a detailed account of the Stalingrad incident see Robinson, *Black on Red*, 65–73.

80. Haywood, *Black Bolshevik*, 170–171.

81. A. L. Foster, leader of the Chicago Urban League, toured the USSR in 1936 and found the country and its people to be the eponym of racial equality: "It is the

Communists alone, who offer colored people just what they say they are fighting for— political, social, cultural and economic equality" (quoted in Solomon, *The Cry Was Unity*, 173).

82. Mark Naison, *Communists in Harlem during the Depression* (Urbana: University of Illinois Press, 1983), 136–37.

83. Claude McKay, *Harlem: Negro Metropolis* (New York: Dutton, 1940), 234.

84 "Editorial," *New York Amsterdam News*, Feb. 9, 1935.

85. Hughes, *I Wonder as I Wander*, 205.

86. L. Morgan Emmerson, "What England Thinks of Its Black Population," *Chicago Defender*, Feb. 11, 1939.

87. Chatwood Hall, "A Column from Moscow," *Chicago Defender*, April 28, 1934.

88. See the memoirs by Langston Hughes, Homer Smith, William L. Patterson, and Harry Haywood. For important insights into the lives of the African American colony in Stalin's USSR see the memoirs by Yelena Khanga (*Soul to Soul: A Black Russian American Family, 1865–1992* [New York: Norton, 1994]) and her mother, Lily Golden (*My Long Journey Home* [Chicago: Third World Press, 2003]). Woodford McClellan mined the RGASPI archive in Moscow for information on the public and personal lives of black American expatriates in Moscow. See McClellan, "Black *Hajj* to 'Red Mecca.'"

89. Smith, *Black Man in Red Russia*, 56–62.

90. Hughes, *I Wonder as I Wander*, 88.

91. Mary Christopher, "Russian Correspondence," *Challenge* 1, no. 2 (Sept. 1934): 14–20.

92. Hughes, *I Wonder as I Wander*, 201–4, 223–26.

93. Jonathan Rosenberg, *How Far the Promised Land? World Affairs and the American Civil Rights Movement from the First World War to Vietnam* (Princeton, NJ: Princeton University Press, 2006), 88.

94. Ibid.

95. See Harry Haywood, "The Road to Negro Liberation: Report to the Eighth Convention of the Communist Party of the USA, Cleveland, April 2–8, 1934," in *American Communism and Black Americans: A Documentary History, 1930–1934*, ed. Philip S. Foner and Herbert Shapiro (Philadelphia: Temple University Press, 1991), 125–45. Also see William A. Nolan, *Communism versus the Negro* (Chicago: Henry Regner, 1951), 100.

96. Walter White, "The Negro and the Communists," in *American Communism and Black Americans: A Documentary History, 1930–1934*, ed. Philip S. Foner and Herbert Shapiro (Philadelphia: Temple University Press, 1991), 274–88.

97. W. E. B. Du Bois, "Postscript," *Crisis*, Sept. 1931, 13–21.

98. Draper, *American Communism and Soviet Russia*, 334.

99. *International Press Correspondence*, no. 74 (Oct. 25, 1928): 1346.

100. Quoted in Draper, *American Communism and Soviet Russia*, 354.

101. Hughes, *I Wonder as I Wander*, 76.

102. Ibid., 80.

103. See Padmore, *Pan-Africanism or Communism?*

104. Smith, *Black Man in Red Russia*, 29.

105. "Deny Story That Politics Halted 'Black-White,'" *Chicago Defender,* Oct. 15, 1932.

106. Solomon, *The Cry Was Unity,* 271. Also see Blakely, *Russia and the Negro,* 113.

107. Quoted in Wilson Record, *The Negro and the Communist Party* (New York: Simon and Schuster, 1971), 62; also in Blakely, *Russia and the Negro,* 112.

108. "Editorial: The Great Betrayal," *Crisis,* Oct. 1939, 305.

109. "Negro Conference Split on Red Issue," *New York Times,* April 28, 1940.

110. Smith, *Black Man in Red Russia,* 34–40. Harry Haywood, himself a convinced Stalinist, corroborates in part Smith's portrayal of Emma Harris as antagonistic to the regime (Haywood, *Black Bolshevik,* 166–67). Langston Hughes also spent some time in the company of the extravagant woman and also noted her distaste for the Soviets in his memoir *I Wonder as I Wonder.*

111. "Document 65: Death certificate for Lovett Fort-Whiteman, 13 January 1939," in Harvey Klehr, John Earl Haynes, and Kyrill M. Anderson, *The Soviet World of American Communism* (New Haven, CT: Yale University Press, 1998), 225.

112. See Golden, *My Long Journey Home;* and Khanga, *Soul to Soul.*

113. McClellan, "Black *Hajj* to 'Red Mecca.'"

114. Blakely, *Russia and the Negro,* 101, 144–47.

Afterword

Jeffrey O. G. Ogbar

As the fourteen essays in this volume demonstrate, the Harlem Renaissance was a far-reaching discursive moment of artistic and political expression. It created a new and intriguing disruption in the arenas of art and politics for bold articulations of hope, as well as defiant displays of blackness. Individuals formed collective voices of resistance to the pervasive and widely accepted practice of racial subjugation. These resistive voices were sometimes guided by an inveterate faith that the United States could be pushed, prodded, inspired, or coerced to do the right thing. Democracy, access to education, civil rights, and dignity were not privileges to be exclusively enjoyed by whites, they insisted. Others, however, were not so driven to make explicitly defiant art. But, can the sophistication, creativity, work ethic, grace, and brilliance of Duke Ellington's music be seen as anything other than inherently resistive to the prevailing hostile stereotypes of the slow-witted, lazy, crude, and infantile Negro? Yet others, not convinced that white supremacy could be dismantled or that racial reconciliation was possible, chose more overt expressions of affirming black humanity. And although these generally nationalist voices have not been traditionally given much attention in examinations of the Harlem Renaissance, the inflections of nationalism are pervasive. In fact, they provide texture to the spirit of the New Negro. The thrust of black nationalist racial pride, celebration of and identification with ancient African civilizations, institution building, and copious attention to subverting humiliating racial etiquette can be found throughout the art and expressions of the period. Therefore, even as many remained hopeful that the country could be reformed, they constructed a resistive discourse that carved out a racially affirming space that had never been as conspicuous in America. And though these expressions were not confined to Harlem, it was this community that had loomed large as a racialized locus of incredible activity and creative attention regarding black people worldwide.

As we have seen here, Harlem during the 1920s became the de facto capital of black America. In addition to the concentration of major black literati, musicians, and intellectuals, it was headquarters for some of the largest—and competing— black political organizations of the era.[1] Harlem was a veritable city of its own, where being a "minority" had different implications than in any other party of New York City. And where black people were either rendered invisible or an undifferentiated mass in white popular culture, the black community was anything but. Much like the UNIA and NAACP, the wider community of architects of the Harlem Renaissance reflected the diversity of experience, perspective, and ambition of a people and a country.

But beyond the wide range of artistic creativity, the Harlem Renaissance developed a standard for bold and audacious styles of art that have remained salient in the style of African American political and artistic expression. The subsequent generations of African American writers, playwrights, musicians, and political activists have all explicitly celebrated and recognized the legacies of Hughes, Hurston, Robeson, Fauset, Ellington, and Garvey. Indeed, they are venerated as part of a pantheon of style, substance, aspiration, defiance, and hope. These figures shaped the subsequent flow of discourse, ideas, rhetoric, and symbolism found most notably in the Black Arts movement of the 1960s and 1970s. From the UNIA's nationalist tricolor flag to the special attention of celebrating what it means to be black and American—while not assiduously trying to prove either case—one finds the legacy of the Harlem Renaissance firmly situated in the creativity of modern African American art and politics.

It may be argued that the seeds of the modern civil rights movement and Black Power movement can be found in the high-water mark of creative black expression in the 1920s. In general, artists and intellectuals rejected the idea that they (1) wal-low in terrible conditions, accommodating a superstructure of racial subjugation in the hope that things will improve owing to their "good behavior" or (2) seek freedom by leaving the United States for Africa or elsewhere. Moreover—and perhaps most important—they sought to realize freedom in the United States, while also celebrating the cultural differences that brought attention to their blackness. It was, indeed, an implicit rejection of a "melting pot" agenda that sought absolute assimilation and integration, though it insisted on unfettered access and inclusion into the fabric of the country. It was, in many respects, a precursor to the axiological thrust of the Black Power movement: freedom for black people in the United States and copious celebration of racial pride and self-determination.

In terms of the very development of African American Studies as an academic discipline, this historic phenomenon remains as significant as the civil rights and Black Power eras in terms of importance. Its contributions to African American Studies are found in the interdisciplinary construction of the field. From music to literature to dramatic arts, gender, social protest, and politics, even to urban studies, there is little not affected by the Harlem Renaissance.

Though traversing new ground, these essays have continued to broaden our understanding of the Harlem Renaissance without coming close to an exhaustive study. The historical moment is much too dynamic, broad, and deep to be reduced to a single volume or even to many such volumes. Additionally, as the legacy of the Harlem Renaissance continues to manifest itself in various creative endeavors, it will continue to offer fertile ground for historical exploration.

NOTE

1. The NAACP's headquarters in Manhattan were a few miles south of Harlem. Many of its notable black staff, like James Weldon Johnson, W. E. B. Du Bois, Jessie Fauset, and others, however, lived and socialized in Harlem, becoming iconic figures for the Harlem Renaissance.

CONTRIBUTORS

Mónica González Caldeiro obtained her *Diploma de estudios avanzados* [Diploma of Advanced Studies] in American Studies at the University of Santiago of Compostela. She teaches Spanish at various institutions; she also teaches poetry at creative writing workshops.

Myriam J. A. Chancy is a professor of English at the University of Cincinnati. Her first novel, *Spirit of Haiti* (London: Mango, 2003), was a finalist in the Best First Book Category, Canada/Caribbean region, of the Commonwealth Prize 2004. She is also the author of *Framing Silence: Revolutionary Novels by Haitian Women* (New Brunswick, NJ: Rutgers University Press, 1997); *Searching for Safe Spaces: Afro-Caribbean Women Writers in Exile* (Philadelphia: Temple University Press, 1997 [*Choice* Outstanding Academic Title award, 1998]); *The Scorpion's Claw: A Novel* (Leeds: Peepal Tree Press, 2005); and *The Loneliness of Angels: A Novel* (Leeds: Peepal Tree Press, 2009). Her work as editor of *Meridians* (2002–4) earned her the CELJ Phoenix Award for Editorial Achievement (2004).

Shawn Anthony Christian is an assistant professor of English and African American Studies at Wheaton College. He is completing a manuscript entitled " 'The New Negro Is Reading': Black Writers on the Harlem Renaissance's Other Literary Audience."

Martha E. Cook is Professor Emerita of English at Longwood University in Virginia. She is the author of a number of articles and conference papers on modernism and the Jazz Age in literature. In 1995 she published a critical article to accompany the reprinted text of a short story by Ellen Glasgow entitled "Ideals," which she located after it had been lost to scholars and critics since its magazine publication in 1926.

Jacob S. Dorman is an assistant professor in the Department of History and the American Studies Program at the University of Kansas. Oxford University Press will soon publish his first book, *Chosen People*, about the formation of black

Israelite religions, as well as relations between New York's Ashkenazi and African American Jews. His second book focuses on African American Muslims and American orientalist discourses from slavery to spiritualism and minstrelsy to freemasonry.

Claire Oberon Garcia is a professor of English and American Cultural Studies at Colorado College, where she teaches courses on modernism, gender, and race. Originally a Jamesian scholar, she is a contributor to the forthcoming book *From Bourgeois to Boujie* (Detroit: Wayne State University Press, 2010) and has published work on class and race issues in the classroom.

Perry A. Hall is an associate professor of African and African American Studies at the University of North Carolina, Chapel Hill. He is the author of *In the Vineyard: Working in African American Studies* (Knoxville: University of Tennessee Press, 1999); and "African American Studies: Discourses and Paradigms," in *African American Studies,* edited by Jeanette R. Davidson (Edinburgh University Press, forthcoming).

Jacqueline C. Jones is an associate professor of English at Francis Marion University. She is completing a book entitled "Unmasking the New Negro: Harold Jackman and the Harlem Renaissance." She is the author of two entries ("Cullen–Du Bois Wedding" and "Jackman, Harold") in the *Encyclopedia of the Harlem Renaissance,* edited by Cary Wintz and Paul Finkelman (New York: Routledge, 2004); and her article "The Unknown Patron: Harold Jackman and the Harlem Renaissance Archives" was published in the *Langston Hughes Review* 19 (fall 2004): 55–64.

Maxim Matusevich is an associate professor of world history at Seton Hall University, where he directs the Program in Russian and East European Studies. He is author of *No Easy Row for a Russian Hoe: Ideology and Pragmatism in Nigerian-Soviet Relations, 1960–1991* (Trenton, NJ: Africa World Press, 2003); and editor of *Africa in Russia, Russia in Africa: Three Centuries of Encounters* (Trenton, NJ: Africa World Press, 2007). Since 2007 he has served as Sheila Biddle Ford Foundation Fellow at the W. E. B. Du Bois Institute for African and African American Research at Harvard University.

McKinley Melton is a doctoral candidate in the W. E. B. Du Bois Department of Afro-American Studies at the University of Massachusetts, Amherst. His research interests include twentieth-century literatures of Africa and the

African diaspora and religious and spiritual traditions throughout diasporic communities.

Jeffrey O. G. Ogbar is an associate dean for the humanities in the College of Liberal Arts and Sciences and a professor of history at the University of Connecticut. He is author of *Black Power: Radical Politics and African American Identity* (Baltimore: Johns Hopkins University Press, 2004), which was the recipient of a 2005 *Choice* Outstanding Academic Title award; and *Hip-Hop Revolution: The Culture and Politics of Rap* (Lawrence: University Press of Kansas, 2007), winner of the 2008 W. E. B. Du Bois Book Prize from the North East Black Studies Alliance.

Aija Poikāne-Daumke is a lecturer at the University of Latvia and the author of *African Diasporas: Afro-German Literature in the Context of the African American Experience* (Berlin: Lit Verlag, 2007).

Ousmane Kirumu Power-Greene is an assistant professor of history at Clark University, where he teaches courses on African American social and political movements.

Frank A. Salamone is a professor and chair of the Sociology and Anthropology Department of Iona College. He is the author of *The Culture of Jazz: Jazz as Critical Culture* (Lanham, MD: University Press of America, 2008); *Italians in Rochester, New York, 1900–1940* (Lewiston, NY: Edwin Mellen Press, 2001); *Italians in Rochester, New York, 1940–1960* (Lewiston, NY: Edwin Mellen Press, 2008); *The Hausa of Nigeria* (Lanham, MD: University Press of America, 2009); and other books.

Paula Marie Seniors is an assistant professor of Africana Studies and sociology at Virginia Tech. She is the author of *Beyond Lift Every Voice and Sing: The Culture of Uplift, Identity, and Politics in Black Musical Theater* (Columbus: Ohio State University Press, 2009), which won the 2009 Letitia Woods Brown Memorial Book Prize for junior faculty, given by the Association of Black Women Historians.

INDEX